LOCKE'S PHIL

Locke's Philosophy

Content and Context

Edited by
G. A. J. ROGERS

CLARENDON PRESS · OXFORD
1994

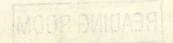

Oxford University Press, Walton Street, Oxford OX2 6DP

Oxford New York
Athens Auckland Bangkok Bogota Bombay
Buenos Aires Calcutta Cape Town Dar es Salaam
Delhi Florence Hong Kong Istanbul Karachi
Kuala Lumpur Madras Madrid Melbourne
Mexico City Nairobi Paris Singapore
Taipei Tokyo Toronto

and associated companies in
Berlin Ibadan

Oxford is a trade mark of Oxford University Press

Published in the United States by
Oxford University Press Inc., New York

© the several contributors 1994

First published 1994
First issued as paperback 1996

British Library Cataloguing in Publication Data
Data available

Library of Congress Cataloging in Publication Data
Locke's philosophy : content and context / edited by G. A. J. Rogers.
Papers presented at the Clarendon Locke Conference, held at Christ
Church, Oxford, Sept. 1990.
Includes bibliographical references and index.
Contents: Locke at Oxford / John Milton — The foundations of
knowledge and the logic of substance / M.R. Ayers — The real
Molyneux question and the basis of Locke's answer / Martha Brandt
Bolton — Locke on the freedom of the will / Vere Chappell — Locke
on meaning and signification / Michael Losonsky — Solidity and
elasticity in the seventeenth century / Peter Alexander —
Rediscovering America / James Tully — The politics of Christianity
/ Ian Harris — John Locke and the Greek intellectual tradition /
Paschalis M. Kitromilides — John Locke and the Polish enlightenment
/ Janina Rosicka.
1. Locke, John, 1632-1704—Congresses. I. Rogers, G. A. J.
(Graham Alan John), 1938- .
B1297.L65   1994   192—dc20   94-9678
ISBN 0-19-824076-7
ISBN 0-19-823684-0 (Pbk)

Printed in Great Britain on acid-free paper by
Bookcraft (Bath) Ltd, Midsomer Norton, Avon

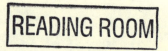

For Peter Laslett
and John W. Yolton

Preface

The chapters in this book were in earlier forms all given as papers at a conference held at Christ Church, Oxford in September 1990 and initiated by the Board of the Clarendon Edition of the Works of John Locke. The conference marked both the 300th anniversary of the publication of Locke's major works and also the new Clarendon Edition, several volumes of which had by then been published. The volumes of the Clarendon Edition to date mark a high point in Locke publication with the establishment over a number of years of texts produced to the highest scholarship that will eventually provide a firm and comprehensive basis for Locke studies into the foreseeable future.

The Clarendon Locke Conference brought together a large number of scholars from around the world whose interest in Locke reflected the many facets of his thought. But it is not surprising that the main focus was on the *Essay concerning Human Understanding* and the *Two Treatises of Government* and the present selection, of about one-third of those given at Oxford, in part reflect that. What the conference demonstrated and what it is hoped this volume will show is that Locke remains rewarding not only as a seminal influence on our history but also as a source for relevant insights into our modern predicament.

The chapters also reflect the buoyant state of Locke studies. This is in part the consequence of the availability of the rich sources of Locke's large manuscript collection now in the Bodleian Library, which provide us with such a full understanding of his philosophy, his person, and his times. Locke scholars and historians of the seventeenth century more generally are greatly indebted to a number of people who have made that source possible. One such is Paul Mellon, whose generosity in donating the bulk of Locke's library and many of his manuscripts to the Bodleian Library has added enormously to the value of the original purchase of the Lovelace Collection in 1947. Others to whom we are all indebted include the first General Editor of the Clarendon Edition, Peter Nidditch, who set a standard difficult to follow with his edition of the *Essay concerning Human Understanding*, and the first Chairman, Robert Shackleton. I would also like in this context to mention Esmund de Beer, who is remembered not only for his monumental edition of the *Correspondence* but also for his generous help to all Locke scholars, and particularly for his help to younger colleagues just tipping their toes in Lockean waters.

I would also like to pay tribute to the two scholars to whom this volume is dedicated, Peter Laslett and John Yolton. Peter Laslett's account of the recovery of Locke's library was one of the highlights of the conference and something that I very much hope will achieve a permanent record elsewhere. But that story is only a small part of his commitment over many years and in many ways to Locke scholarship, which all of us familiar with Locke studies know to have been of the highest order and many-dimensional. Similarly, John Yolton has given enormously to Locke studies for over forty years, not least as General Editor and Chairman of the Editorial Board until 1992, but also, like Peter Laslett, as teacher and friend. Through their example, generosity of spirit, knowledge, and efforts the world of Locke scholarship has been immeasurably strengthened.

There are many others who deserve mention in this Preface. The original conference, held in Locke's Oxford college, was the ideal setting in which to consider his philosophy, and my thanks are due to the authorities at Christ Church, particularly the Librarian, the Assistant Librarian, Mr John Wing, and, most especially, to Mr Hugh Rice, who took every care to ensure the excellence of our environment. A feature of the conference was the participation of Mr David Summerscales, Headmaster of Locke's old school, Westminster, and scholars from the school, which added greatly to the occasion. I would also like particularly to thank my wife, Jo, who not only fulfilled the not easy task of conference secretary perfectly but also prepared this volume's Index.

The production of this volume, as with the production of the Clarendon Locke Edition, owes much to Angela Blackburn and Frances Morphy at Oxford University Press. That it has taken rather longer to emerge than it should is the fault of neither.

G. A. J. R.

Keele
November 1993

In my Preface of 1993 I failed to identify all those institutions who had supported the Locke conference of 1990 financially. May I here and now make amends. The following bodies all contributed grants without which the meeting could not have taken place: the British Academy; Christ Church; the Clarendon Locke Board; the sub-Faculty of Philosophy, University of Oxford; the Mind Association; Thoemmes Antiquarian Books; and Waterfields Bookshop. I and the conference participants are most grateful to them.

G. A. J. R.

Keele
March 1996

Contents

Notes on Contributors

PETER ALEXANDER is Professor of Philosophy Emeritus at the University of Bristol.

MICHAEL AYERS is a Fellow of Wadham College, Oxford.

MARTHA BRANDT BOLTON is Professor of Philosophy at Rutgers University.

VERE CHAPPELL is Professor of Philosophy at the University of Massachusetts at Amherst.

IAN HARRIS is Lecturer in Politics, University of Leicester.

PASCHALIS KITROMILIDES is Professor of Political Science at the University of Athens.

MICHAEL LOSONSKY is Professor of Philosophy at Colorado State University.

J. R. MILTON is Lecturer in Philosophy at King's College, London.

G. A. J. ROGERS is Reader in Philosophy, Keele University.

JANINA ROSICKA is Associate Professor of Philosophy at Jagiellonian University, Cracow.

JAMES TULLY is Professor of Philosophy at McGill University.

List of Abbreviations

Aaron	R. I. Aaron, *John Locke*, 3rd edn. (Oxford, 1971).
Aaron and Gibb	John Locke, *An Early Draft of Locke's 'Essay', together with Excerpts from his Journals*, ed. R. I. Aaron and Jocylyn Gibb (Oxford, 1936).
BL	British Library
Bodl.	Bodleian Library
Correspondence	John Locke, *The Correspondence of John Locke*, ed. E. S. de Beer, 9 vols. (Oxford, 1976–93). Reference is either by letter number or by volume and page.
Cranston	Maurice Cranston, *John Locke: A Biography* (London, 1957).
Drafts, i	John Locke, *Drafts for the 'Essay concerning Human Understanding' and Other Philosophical Writings*, i Drafts A and B, ed. Peter H. Nidditch and G. A. J. Rogers (Oxford, 1990).
Education	John Locke, *Some Thoughts concerning Education*, ed. John W. and Jean S. Yolton (Oxford, 1989).
Epistola	John Locke, *Epistola de Tolerantia. A Letter on Toleration*, ed. Raymond Klibansky, trans. J. W. Gough (Oxford, 1968).
Essay	John Locke, *An Essay concerning Human Understanding*, ed. Peter H. Nidditch (Oxford, 1975). Reference either by book, chapter, and section number (e.g. II. vi. 4), or by page and line number (e.g. 47 (16)).
Fox Bourne	H. R. Fox Bourne, *The Life of John Locke*, 2 vols. (London, 1876, repr. Bristol, 1991).
Harrison and Laslett	John Harrison and Peter Laslett, *The Library of John Locke* (Oxford, 1965).
Laslett	John Locke, *Two Treatises of Government*, ed. Peter Laslett (Cambridge, 1964).
Law of Nature	John Locke, *Essays on the Law of Nature*, ed. W. von Leyden (Oxford, 1954; repr. 1988).
Money	John Locke, *Locke on Money*, ed. Patrick Hyde Kelly, 2 vols. (Oxford, 1991).
Paraphrase	John Locke, *A Paraphrase and Notes on the Epistles of St Paul*, ed. Arthur W. Wainwright, 2 vols. (Oxford, 1987).
PRO	Public Record Office

Two Tracts   John Locke, *Two Tracts on Government*, ed. Philip Abrams (Cambridge, 1967).

Works   John Locke, *The Works of John Locke*, 10 vols. (London, 1823).

Introduction

G. A. J. ROGERS

John Locke remains, after over 300 years, a central figure in philosophy and a key thinker for an understanding of the culture and categories of modern society. This collection underlines ways in which his thought continues to be rewarding and takes us further in appreciating why he has been such an influential figure. A feature of recent Locke scholarship, reflected in this volume, is the connection between Locke's political theory, his religious beliefs, and his epistemology and metaphysics. The first part of this Introduction is offered as a contribution to further appreciation of that unity in his thought through an account of aspects of the context in which Locke wrote his major works. This is followed in Section II by a summary of the chapters that constitute this volume.

The theme that I offer in Section I is that, despite their diverse subject-matter, there is an intellectual unity in Locke's work not always appreciated by his commentators. To understand that unity we need to take account of the composition of his works, and the overlap in their content and objectives, including the contribution that Locke, as an intellectual, saw himself as making to the wider fabric of society. They were objectives that take us to the grounding principles of the modern liberal democratic state.

I

If philosophers are gauged by their publications then the year 1689 marked the beginning of Locke's intellectual achievements. It also marked their zenith. For when Locke arrived back in England in February, at the age of 57, he had still to publish a book, or indeed anything of any consequence. But by then he had completed the manuscripts of the works on which his reputation rests. Before the year ended three of them were in print.

The first to appear was the *Epistola de Tolerantia*, produced in Holland under the supervision of Locke's close friend Phillipus van Limborch. Limborch sent three copies to Locke on 6 May.[1] This was followed in early autumn by *Two Treatises of Government*, which was licensed on 23 August, and published by Awnsham Churchill, with whom Locke was to remain associated for the rest of his life, and, indeed, well beyond.[2] The third was the *Essay concerning Human Understanding*, which was in the bookshops of London and Oxford in December.[3] Interestingly, it was published not by Churchill but by Thomas Basset. Of these only the third revealed its author's name and, as Locke was able to preserve some kind of anonymity until his death, it was largely on the *Essay* that his intellectual reputation rested for the remainder of his life.[4]

Locke's biography is already well recorded but it is worth recalling those features which bear most centrally on his writing. His major works were the product of his activity between early 1671 and 1689, a period of eighteen years beginning when he was 39 and subsequent to his move from Oxford to London in 1667 to join Shaftesbury's household. Prior to this, as J. R. Milton's chapter in this volume shows, his interests, though wide, had focused most centrally on the study of medicine and iatrochemistry. Although he was never to abandon his medical interests (and some of his most important work was done in those early years in London as he worked with Thomas Sydenham) his knowledge and involvement with politics in various dimensions were enormously strengthened through his connection with Shaftesbury. To this was added that very special event in his biography, the gathering with a group of friends in the winter of 1670–1 to explore questions of 'morality and revealed religion',[5] themselves topics with, in the 1670s especially, major political implications. It is even possible, as Richard Ashcraft has argued,[6] that the epistemological questions raised in Samuel Parker's *A Discourse of*

---

[1] Cf. Limborch's letter to Locke of that date, *Correspondence*, iii, no. 1134.

[2] For the date of the licence, see Laslett, 121.

[3] Cf. *Essay*, p. xv.

[4] Of course some close friends, such as Limborch, knew him to be the author of the *Epistola*. His authorship of *Two Treatises* was a matter of even greater concern, even though as early as Aug. 1690 William Molyneux was told in London that Locke was the author of both works; *Correspondence*, iv, no. 1530.

[5] From a note in James Tyrrell's copy of the *Essay* in the British Library.

[6] Richard Ashcraft, *Revolutionary Politics and Locke's 'Two Treatises of Government'* (Princeton, NJ, 1986), see esp. in this connection pp. 104–12.

Ecclesiastical Politie of 1670 were a stimulus to Locke and his friends towards exploration of just those issues at the discussion that winter. Certainly what I have called the 'Argument from Ignorance'[7] in favour of religious toleration, itself presupposed an epistemology of the kind that Locke was to develop in the *Essay concerning Human Understanding*. Locke's notes on Parker's book bring out very well the epistemic weaknesses of Parker's case for the imposition of religious orthodoxy and invite the kind of discussion that was to lead to Locke's production of the early drafts of the *Essay*.[8]

If these considerations have any plausibility then we immediately see that Locke's political philosophy was from early days closely aligned to questions of epistemology. It was just such questions that were to be his deep, if sporadic, concern from then on, and it is some of the common intellectual themes running through Locke's major works and their connections with the writings of his books that this section of the Introduction will explore.

Although Locke was the author of five or six major works it was undoubtedly the *Essay concerning Human Understanding* of which he was most proud, the beloved *De Intellectu* that he had carried since its conception in the winter of 1671 and which he was carefully to nurse through subsequent editions for the remainder of his life. His natural modesty barely conceals his pleasure at its publication. His first acknowledged offspring, born to an ageing parent, had had a long and difficult gestation. Locke was duly looking for praise at his achievement, and at this early stage had no clear anticipation of the problems that parenthood would bring.

The Composition of Locke's Philosophy

Locke's account of the origin of the *Essay* is familiar enough. Five or six friends, he tells us, gathered together to discourse on 'a subject very remote from this'.[9] From James Tyrrell's comment we know this other subject to have been that of 'morality and revealed religion'.[10] The friends

---

[7] In 'Locke and the Latitude-Men: Ignorance as a Ground of Toleration', in Richard Kroll, Richard Ashcraft, and Perez Zagorin (eds.), *Philosophy, Science, and Religion in England 1640–1700* (Cambridge, 1992), 230–52.

[8] On this whole matter, see further my Introduction to *Drafts*, ii (Oxford, forthcoming). Locke's notes on Parker are substantially reprinted in Cranston, 131–3.

[9] 'Epistle to the Reader', in *Essay*, 7.

[10] Tyrrell was one of the group, and the comment is written by him in his copy of the *Essay*, now in the British Library.

soon found themselves in difficulties and Locke offered to draft some
thoughts on 'what Objects our Understandings were, or were not fitted to
deal with'. After those early discussions the subject continued to hold his
interest and those of his friends. The writing, having 'begun by Chance,
was continued by Intreaty; written by incoherent parcels, and after long
intervals of neglect . . . [until] at last, in a retirement, where an Attend-
ance on my Health gave me leisure, it was brought into that order, thou
now seest it'.[11]

There are three early drafts of the *Essay* extant, Drafts A and B of
1671, and Draft C of 1685. Between them, together with the entries in
Locke's journals and other manuscript sources, they allow a detailed
reconstruction of the path from that early meeting to the printed work.
The two early drafts reveal that much of Locke's argument, often in
unfinished form, was in place by the summer of 1671. But the manuscript
seems largely to have languished until he once again gave it full attention
in his years of exile in Holland following his retreat there in 1683. When
he returned in February 1689 he had with him a version which was very
close to that of the first edition, though no doubt still requiring final
polishing and the addition of the Dedication and the Epistle to the Reader.

The Motivation for the Essay

There are many reasons why Locke wrote the *Essay* which went beyond
the purposes of those early drafts, and these reasons increased in number
with the length of the manuscript. Some of them are obvious: genuine
engagement with the intellectual issues; the desire to make his mark; a
belief that he had something important to impart; a concern to rectify the
mistaken views of others. But these very general categories do not in
themselves take us very far. Can we be more specific? I suggest that we
can be. There is an important moral basis for Locke's work which until
recently has not been fully or properly appreciated.[12] It is one that gives

---

[11] Epistle, in *Essay*, 7.

[12] Others have also seen something along the same lines as I shall urge here. Neal Wood,
in his *The Politics of Locke's Philosophy: A Social Study of 'An Essay concerning Human
Understanding'* (Berkeley, Calif., 1983), anticipates some of my claims, though not always in
the same detail. (See also my review of Wood's work in *Philosophical Books*, 27 (1986), 18–
21.) Richard Ashcraft argues strongly for intellectual overlap between the issues raised by
Locke's politics and his epistemology (see esp. *Revolutionary Politics*, chs. 2 and 3), as does,
in a somewhat different style, Ruth Grant, *John Locke's Liberalism* (Chicago, 1987). See
also John Dunn, 'The Claim to Freedom of Conscience: Freedom of Speech, Freedom of
Thought, Freedom of Worship?', in Ole Peter Grell, Jonathan I. Israel, and Nicholas
Tyacke (eds.), *From Persecution to Toleration: The Glorious Revolution and Religion in
England* (Oxford, 1991), 171–93.

a coherence and strength to Locke's writings which has often been overlooked by his readers. To see something of that inner unity we need to follow Locke's and the *Essay*'s development in the context of his wider concerns.

We begin with that early meeting in Locke's London chambers in Exeter House in the Strand.[13] We have already seen that the enquiry was closely related to matters of religion and morals, which in the great debates of Restoration England, and particularly in the household of Shaftesbury, could not be separated from the great religious and political issues of the day. Some of this had already found expression four years before, in 1667, in his first extant essay in favour of religious toleration— a manuscript perhaps drafted either for or in conjunction with Shaftesbury as a position paper in the current political debate. The argument that Locke provides, though respectable enough, touches, but never reaches far into, the epistemic issues that, I am suggesting, provide the backcloth against which the first drafts of the *Essay* were penned. The 1667 essay contains two elements to feature centrally in his later epistemology. With reference to central matters of doctrine, 'pure speculative opinions, as the belief of the Trinity, purgatory, transubstantiation, antipodes, Christ's personal reign on earth, etc.', Locke makes the political point that these are matters on which there is an absolute universal right to toleration, because, as they are merely speculative, they do not impinge on the life of one's neighbour or threaten the state. He then goes on to make two more overtly epistemic ones. The first is that a person should not give power to others over that which he himself has no control. This is the case with belief, with which one 'cannot apprehend things, otherwise than they appear to it, than the eye see other colours in the rainbow than it doth, whether those colours be really there or no'.[14] It is the last sentence which identifies a central philosophical claim of Locke, namely the compulsion of belief.[15] The further epistemic issue, the Argument from Ignorance, is also acknowledged. In considering how far 'practical principles, or opinions' should be tolerated Locke emphasizes our lack of knowledge as a relevant factor. He writes:

For all these opinions, except such of them as are apparently destructive to human society, being things either of indifferency or doubt, and neither the

[13] For it was almost certainly there that the meeting took place although there is only circumstantial evidence to support it. The only likely alternative is Locke's rooms in Christ Church, but there is no evidence that he was in Oxford at the time.

[14] Fox Bourne, i. 176.

[15] For a recent discussion of this feature of Locke's thought, see Michael Ayers, *Locke*, 2 vols. (London, 1991), i. 104–12.

magistrate nor subject being on either side infalible, he [i.e. the magistrate] ought no further to consider them then as the making laws and interposing his authority in such opinions may conduce to the welfare and safety of his people.[16]

I put this point down as a marker to which we shall return.

Locke's epistemic enquiries were overtaken by other interests and commitments, some of which led, by the end of the decade or the early 1680s, directly into the drafting of what was eventually to be *Two Treatises of Government*.[17] Peter Laslett is surely right that the manuscript of this work is to be identified with the papers with the cover name *De Morbo Gallico*. And if so, then when Locke fled to Holland in 1683, for 'flight' seems more and more the appropriate category in which to place Locke's departure, he had with him a manuscript of *De Intellectu* but not, it would appear of *Two Treatises*. He had, it would seem, largely completed it before he left English shores, and it was too sensitive a document for him to carry.[18] He was, however, engaged in thought and in writing about related matters. As we have it from Le Clerc, Locke's *Epistola* on toleration was written in Amsterdam between the first days of November and the second half of December in 1685.[19] Although others have suggested slightly different dates and places, all agree it was in Holland soon after the revocation of the Edict of Nantes on 18 October 1685. That Locke should have written this work and the final version of the *Essay* at the same period of his life and in Holland are perhaps not as unconnected as is sometimes supposed. But that is to anticipate. Let us, then, return to the *Essay*.

We may start with the question what precisely Locke wrote of the *Essay* in those five years in Holland? As we shall see, there are major problems with regard to the transformations which the *Essay* received in that time. To begin with, and fairly crucially, we wish to know what

---

[16] *An Essay concerning Toleration*. There are several manuscript versions of this essay. I quote from the one first published in Fox Bourne, i. 178.

[17] Peter Laslett dates their composition as 1679–80 (Laslett, Introduction, esp. p. 59). Ashcraft in his *Revolutionary Politics* has a different and later dating (1680–2) to which Laslett responds in his 1988 edition of *Two Treatises* (pp. 123–6). Nothing in my argument turns on which is correct, though I assume that *Two Treatises* was written between 1679 and Locke's departure for Holland in 1683.

[18] On the probable composition of *Two Treatises*, see Laslett, Introduction, 62–5. See also Ashcraft, *Revolutionary Politics*, 388. Locke appears to have wished to regain the manuscript from Clarke, who had a version in mid-February 1687 (see Ashcraft, *Revolutionary Politics*, 536). That the correct title of Locke's work is as here given is substantiated by Laslett (note opposite his title-page and his p. 154).

[19] On the dating of the writing of *Epistola de Tolerantia*, see Mario Montuori, *John Locke on Toleration and the Unity of God* (Amsterdam, 1983), p. xv.

exactly was its state on its arrival on Dutch soil. We want to know how, if at all, Locke's contact with Dutch thinkers modified the shape which it took. Did his reading whilst in Holland impinge on his argument? How far did the political events of those years find an imprint in the finished text? Should we, perhaps, read the *Essay* as being itself in some substantial part a political tract, closely associated with the events before and after Locke's voluntary exile in Holland? Is there, in any sense, a link between the way the *Essay* is and the way Holland was in the period of Locke's stay there? These and other big questions await an answer. Nor are they to be set aside as merely of antiquarian interest, for they are likely to reveal something of Locke's objectives in writing his great work and to help shape our understanding of it and of his other writings, just as Laslett's discovery that Locke had written much of the *Two Treatises* by 1681, well before the revolution of 1688, so that the latter gave concrete expression to a view already formed, has reshaped readings of that work.[20]

Locke's Style

Before turning to detailed examination of Locke's letters, journals, drafts, and so on, we should notice a certain feature of Locke's intellectual style. It is reflected in the role that he so often gave himself in his enquiries and it is captured by him in famous words at the beginning of the *Essay* when he depicts himself as the underlabourer, clearing the ground a little for the great master-builders Boyle, Sydenham, Huygens, and Newton.[21] I suspect that there is something deep in Locke's psyche which made him prefer the role of the assistant to that of the leader. Consider the cases. In Oxford, when he began serious scientific research it was as the assistant of Robert Boyle. His own original contributions in his researches in human blood are totally ignored in the contemporary discussions and have only come to light as a result of careful scholarly enquiry. Yet now we know that Locke was a contributor of high rank, and, surprisingly to those who know only of his views on science from a reading of the *Essay*, a man whose strength lay not in his careful experiments but in his imaginative speculation.[22]

Locke, we all know, was a physician, and was to gain a reputation as

---

[20] See Laslett, Introduction, 45–66. [21] *Essay*, Epistle to the Reader, 9–10.
[22] On this, see Robert Frank, *Harvey and the Oxford Physiologists* (Berkeley, Calif., 1980), ch. 7 and p. 219.

a very good one. But he rarely claimed any distinction for himself.[23] He worked as Sydenham's assistant, as he had done for Boyle, happy to engage in that capacity and eager to learn all he could from his distinguished teacher. Yet the quality of his contribution was so high that we now cannot always be sure which of their writings was written by whom.[24] Both Boyle and Sydenham went out of their way to acknowledge Locke's contributions.[25]

In politics, too, Locke was happy to play the self-effacing role behind the physically small but politically massive form of Shaftesbury. Partly because of the latter's enormous influence it is easy to underestimate Locke's contribution. Following Shaftesbury's death, Locke continued to play a very active role in politics in both Holland and England but, once again, never seeking attention. The shadowy figure, in some respects only now, in the later twentieth century, becoming visible, may well have made contributions at which we can now only guess. Did he, for example, as one tradition has it, really play a part in drafting the Act of Toleration?[26] With his position as an adviser to the rising politician John Somers, who in some ways was to fill the gap in Locke's life left by the death of Shaftesbury, there is certainly evidence of Locke fulfilling a political role of some importance, but which is only hinted at in his correspondence.[27]

Locke's relationships with others on his return to England continued to exhibit this self-effacing character, even though, with the publication of the *Essay* in December 1689, he might have begun to see himself as a major intellectual figure in his own right. One such, and one of the most important in Locke's later life, was that with Newton. Locke could never have obtained to Newton's mastery of mathematical physics, but it was typical of him that he should produce, possibly with Newton's help, a school text, *The Elements of Natural Philosophy*, which remained popular well into the eighteenth century.[28]

---

[23] There is a hint in a letter to Lord Pembroke that Locke thought his work as a physician had perhaps been undervalued, but the letter, which is discussed below, was written in such special circumstances that there is doubt about how the passage should be understood. See *Correspondence*, ii. 663.

[24] The fragment *De Arte Medica* has often been regarded as by Locke as the manuscript is in Locke's hand, but Kenneth Dewhurst attributed it to Sydenham on the basis of contemporary evidence; see *Dr Thomas Sydenham (1624–1689): His Life and Original Writings* (London, 1966), 73.

[25] For these, see Sydenham's remarks about Locke's medical skills in his Dedication to *Observationes Medicae* (1676) and Boyle's *Memoirs of the Natural History of the Humane Blood* (London, 1683), which is dedicated to 'the very Ingenious and Learned Doctor J. L.'.

[26] See Lord King, *The Life and Letters of John Locke* (London, 1884), 176.

[27] On this, see further Cranston, 324–6.

[28] On this topic, see James L. Axtell, 'Locke, Newton, and the Elements of Natural Philosophy', *Paedagogica Europaea*, 1 (1965), 235–45.

One reason for dwelling on these aspects of Locke's personality is to underline difficulties in tracing his intellectual and other paths and doing them justice. His natural and attractive inclination to undersell himself leads his biographers and others to do so as well, especially when, as they so often do, the sources pull in differing directions. We shall come to some examples shortly. We might take these traits to reflect some inner failing: a lack of confidence, perhaps. But this would be a mistake. For Locke exhibits no such lack of confidence in his philosophical writings. A decent modesty perhaps, at least most of the time, but nothing which smacks of diffidence. He knew he was good at philosophical enquiry and need concede to nobody. The same may also be true of theology, but there were other reasons for caution on that front, as there were on the political.

The Writing of the Essay

With these preliminary remarks concluded let us now return to the writing of the *Essay*. We have the two extant 1671 drafts, and much could be said on them. But I shall forgo that tempting path and turn to its subsequent history. More precisely, and to give us a point from which we may look both backward and forward, I shall ask what exactly was the state of the *Essay* when Locke arrived in Holland in September 1683? As we have seen, we have no drafts from this period. Furthermore, the evidence we have about the state of the *Essay* in 1683 is conflicting. It is not possible to consider all of it here, but some relevant facts are these. Locke's friend and confidante James Tyrrell, with whom Locke often stayed in his country house at Oakley, a few miles from Oxford, reported to Locke on the reception of the *Essay* in Oxford shortly after its publication. There are some in Oxford who claim, Tyrrell reports, that Locke had 'taken all that was good in it from divers moderne French Authours'. In defence of Locke, Tyrrell says that he replied to this charge that as long as he, Tyrrell, had enjoyed Locke's conversation in England, '*which was when the maine body of the booke was written*: to my knowledge you utterly refused to reade any bookes upon that subject: that you might not take any other mens notions'.[29] Tyrrell, it will be remembered, was one of that group that had been present at the meeting which Locke tells us gave rise to the *Essay*, but almost certainly he is referring not to 1671, when that meeting occurred, but to 1681 and 1682, when Locke was back in Oxford, and we can see from his journal entries that he was much engaged in

---

[29] *Correspondence*, 18 March 1690, iv. 36, my italics.

philosophical enquiries of the kind that were to feature in the *Essay*.[30] So, on Tyrrell's understanding, Locke had substantially written the *Essay* in England before going to Holland. Unfortunately we have only a fragment of Locke's reply to that letter from Tyrrell so we do not know whether Locke accepted Tyrrell's account.[31]

There is further ambiguous evidence about the date of the composition of the *Essay*. Robert Ferguson, the arch-plotter in the Netherlands for the overthrow of James II, attended Shaftesbury at his deathbed in Amsterdam. On the night before he died, 20 January 1683, Ferguson raised the issue of religious belief. As Shaftesbury's biographer tells us, 'if Ferguson is to be believed, Shaftesbury declared himself to be a professed Arian, saying that he believed Jesus Christ to be the first creature that God made, and that by him He (God) made the world, rejecting the doctrine of satisfaction by Jesus Christ's death'. Another version of the conversation, also derived from Ferguson, has it that the Earl 'talked all over Arianism and Socinianism, which notions he confessed he imbibed from Mr. Locke and his tenth chapter of "Human Understanding"'.[32] Although I cannot accept the conclusion drawn by one distinguished Locke scholar that this shows that by 1682 Locke had 'carried forward his preparatory work on the *Essay* to such an extent that it already included the substance of his views concerning God's existence as we find them in the tenth chapter of Book IV of the final version of 1690',[33] there can be little doubt that the main lines of Locke's position had been the subject of conversation between Shaftesbury and Locke. To what extent these existed on paper, beyond the journal entries on God and religion made in 1681 and 1682, must for the present at least remain a matter of conjecture.[34]

Some further evidence, again far from conclusive, also relates to the Shaftesbury household. Among the Shaftesbury Papers is a document

---

[30] See e.g. the extracts from the journals in Aaron and Gibb, 77–125.

[31] It is worth noting one misunderstanding about the composition of the *Essay* that appears in the literature. Aaron, to whose pioneering work on Locke's manuscripts all Locke scholars are indebted, wrote a brief and very useful, but not definitive, account of the history of the writing of the *Essay* (Aaron, 50–5). In it he mistakenly presumes that a reference to a book in a letter of Locke's to Toinaird in June 1679 refers to the *Essay*. Locke writes, in French, that he thinks too well of his book to let it go out of his hands. The 'book' was in fact a collection of papers written by Toinaird which he had sent at different times to Locke and which the latter had had bound together. It exists still and may be found in the Bodleian Library (see Harrison and Laslett, entry no. 2934 and p. 39 n.). So Aaron's belief that there was something like a finished book by June 1679 cannot on that evidence be sustained.

[32] Quoted in K. H. D. Haley, *The First Earl of Shaftesbury* (Oxford, 1968), 732.

[33] W. von Leyden, in his Introduction to *Law of Nature*, 67.

[34] See Aaron and Gibb, 116–25.

with no date but endorsed 'F.C.', which may possibly be Shaftesbury's second wife, Frances Cooper. The document is presumably written after Shaftesbury's death. Referring to Locke the author writes: 'My Lord imparted to him from time to time all the secretest affairs then in agitation and by my Lord's frequent discourse of state affairs, religion, toleration and trade, Mr. Locke came to have wonderful knowledge of these things . . . He writ his book concerning Human Understanding whilst he lived with my Lord.'[35] These few words do not establish much. But they do indicate that Locke was known to be writing a book—the *Essay*—prior to 1683, and presumably it was known that he had made considerable progress with it. Perhaps the manuscript and his concern for its safety was a matter of comment, even humorous comment, in the Shaftesbury household, for Locke's concern, even over-concern, for his papers is a prominent feature of his personality.

Further evidence about the state of Locke's manuscript is given by Tyrrell. Locke had sent him soon after his arrival in Holland a version of the *Essay*. Months before this, in June and July 1683, Locke had visited him as he was making preparations to leave the country in the wake of the Rye House Plot. A spy for the government sent an official report on Locke's behaviour whilst in Oxford which included the following observation: 'it is taken notice of in Oxford that from Mr. Locke's chamber in Christ Church, that was a great confidant if not secretary, to the late Earl of Shaftesbury, in a clandestine way several baskets of papers are carried to Mr. James Tyrrell's house at Oakley . . . or to Mr. Pawling's, the mercer's, house in Oxford'.[36] It might be thought that it was in one of those baskets that the manuscript of the *Essay* was transported, though from what follows we shall see this was not the case. And the fact that Locke did not leave it or a copy behind suggests that at this stage either he had no copy to leave or that he did not think that what he had was sufficiently well ordered to impose it on even a close colleague.

Tyrrell wrote to Locke in the following February with some comments. 'I shall now tell you further concerning your papers,' he wrote, 'which I have now read over with all the care I could a second time, and like them better then at the first, which I take to be one maine signe when I am not fed with empty notions instead of things and I have made bold since it is your foul copy to note it on the blanck pages whene I doubt anything; or where I think I can illustrate any thing you have sayd by a

---

[35] From a document in the Shaftesbury Papers (PRO 30/24, xlvii, 28, 3), and quoted in Laslett, 26.   [36] Quoted from Cranston, 228.

fitter example . . .'.[37] Clearly what he had was some substantial document, a less satisfactory ('foul') copy of Locke's own version. And what emerges is that they have been the fruit of Locke's labours over the winter months, since, that is, his arrival in Holland the previous September, for Tyrrell remarks, 'so that if your thinking has bin your hunting, and hawking this winter, I may safely say, it has bin mine to read what you have thought on and put together with so much Judgment'.[38] From this I believe we may securely infer that Locke had written up the draft of the *Essay* by early January, early enough for it to be then copied, and the copy (or the original amended version, the 'foul copy') sent to Tyrrell in time for him to have given it serious attention before about the third week in February.

How close this version was to that which Locke was to bring back from Holland we have no way of knowing. We do not even know if it contained all four books. But there is one comment by Tyrrell which suggests it was quite a long work, and we should in any case expect that, if we remember that Draft B of 1671 is of the order of 60,000 words. Tyrrell says, comparing it with two other works, the *De Mente Humana Libri Quatuor* of J.-B. Du Hamel, and Hobbes's *Human Nature*, both of which he had lately read, that he finds 'as much difference, as between a Short Epitomee, and an exact work'.[39] It looks as though, even by this stage, we have something rather like the first edition of the *Essay*.

So it would appear that we have at least part of the answer to one of our problems. When Locke arrived in Holland he had a manuscript of the *Essay*, but it was far from finished. However, over the first winter of his stay he produced another version which was probably something like the final version, much more so, at any rate, than Draft B had been. We will now turn to another account of these things, one supplied by Locke himself, but, for reasons that we shall soon come to, this account must be treated with caution.

The Politics of Philosophy

On the first day of the New Year 1685, as it was in Holland, Locke wrote a long letter to Edward Clarke. We shall begin with a quotation from it, and then pause to begin to consider its import.

Sir

I have been very unfortunate and other people very malitious to raise Suspitions upon me without any ground but their owne misinterpretations of my most

---

[37] *Correspondence*, ii. 610.   [38] Ibid. 611.   [39] Ibid.

innocent actions. For I am more and more confirmed in my opinion that my being much in my chamber alone the last winter and busy there for the most part about my enquiry concerneing *Humane Understanding* . . . has been the occasion of my misfortune.[40]

Locke explains that he had brought his papers to Holland so that in peace and quiet he could get on with writing the book which he had promised friends, and he underlines many times how he has spent most of the time 'in the absence of my friends and almost all company' innocently writing the *Essay*. The misfortune to which Locke is confident this has led is his expulsion on 15 November, on the orders of Charles II, from his position at Christ Church. This was without doubt a major blow to him, for, as he says, it was the only real home he had, and his plans were made against the presumption of that stability. More ominously, it was public identification as someone unacceptable to the political establishment.

Locke's long letter to Clarke was not the first he had written on the matter. Three weeks before, on first hearing of the expulsion, he had written at equal length to Thomas Herbert, Earl of Pembroke, seeking support for his reinstatement and proclaiming his innocence of any involvement in matters political. Once again, he claims that, far from being involved in any kind of politicking, he had largely shunned the coffeehouses:

My time was most spent alone, at home by my fires side, where I confesse I writ a good deale, I thinke I may say, more then ever I did in soe much time, in my life, but no libells, unlesse perhaps it may be a libell against all mankinde to give some account of the weaknesse and shortnesse of humane understanding, for upon that my old theme de Intellectu humano (on which your Lordship knows I have been a good while a hammering), has my head been beating, and my pen scribleing all the time I have been here except what I have spent in travelling about to see the country.[41]

We shall return to some of these remarks shortly. But the first thing that we must note is that neither letter can be accepted at its face value. In his discussion of the letter to Pembroke Richard Ashcraft has argued well that it contains both half-truths and worse.[42] Locke kept company with at least some of the leading radicals who had been implicated in the Rye House Plot and were now plotting Argyll's and later Monmouth's Rebellion. He may have had a major part in moving monies between Holland and England to finance the radical plans: it appears, in short, that Locke

---

[40] Ibid. 671.   [41] Ibid. 665.
[42] Ashcraft, *Revolutionary Politics*, 435. See also Cranston, 248–9.

was deeply implicated in the plots of the English exiles, which were, in the end, to give substantial support to the success of William's invasion in 1688.

These few remarks are only a gesture at the story, which, in particular, Ashcraft has told us. But granted its general plausibility, if not of every detail of his reconstruction, then we must also rethink Locke's letter to Clarke.[43] For, if Locke was the radical Ashcraft believes him to have been, then so was Clarke, and Clarke therefore knew that the letter he received from Locke was disingenuous. Why, then, did Locke write it? One possible answer is that he wished Clarke to show it to others, perhaps in particular to Pembroke, as further evidence of Locke's blameless activities. The solitary scholar in his ivory tower. It was, in short, written to strengthen Locke's standing with those who might bring pressure to bear to have Locke reinstated at Christ Church and to remove suspicion from him in Holland.

But what then are the implications for the composition of the *Essay*? How far was what Locke said true? We have already seen that by February 1684 he had dispatched one version to Tyrrell. We know also from his Journal that by 30 November, eight days before he wrote to Pembroke, he had a copy of a version of Book II of the *Essay*, and at the end of the letter he offers to send Pembroke 'a part of what I have been doeing here',[44] presumably the same Book II which is now in tolerable order. There can be little doubt that he had indeed been hard at work on it for much of the time. Through the course of 1685 we can trace its progress through his letters and journals. By May, when Locke heard from Clarke that Pembroke wished to see it, it had grown to 'at least three quires of paper'.[45] And Draft C, dated 1685, gives material testimony to that claim. Through 1686 Locke sends to Clarke to pass on to Pembroke successive books of the *Essay*, with the fourth and last being dispatched on the last day of the year.[46]

A Return to Locke's Motives

The picture of Locke as the philosopher, the intellectual remote from the political forces of the real world, if it ever had any merit, has surely been at least badly dented by Ashcraft's book. We do not, however, have to

---

[43] For important qualifications on Ashcraft's thesis, see Gordon J. Schochet, 'Radical Politics and Ashcraft's Treatise on Locke', *Journal of the History of Ideas*, 50 (1989), 491–510.   [44] *Correspondence*, ii. 666.
[45] Ibid. 721.   [46] Ibid. iii. 88–9.

follow him in all his conclusions in order to construct a new picture of Locke's motivations in settling down in Holland to produce his masterpiece. In his letter to Pembroke to which we have already made much reference Locke claims that since he had received so little from Shaftesbury he certainly had no reason to support his cause once he was dead.[47] Locke could only have brought himself to write such words when he felt extremely vulnerable. For an examination of his life reveals, at least from his early years in London right through to his death in 1704, a loyalty to a range of intellectual ideas which he attempted to transform into practice which were identical with those to which Shaftesbury too, at least in his better moments, had subscribed. As one great, and, one might add, non-English, historian has expressed it:

He [Shaftesbury] started from the conception of tolerance, as Locke had done: Locke's principles are those of Shaftesbury; their friendship rested, like all true friendships in men of mature years, upon a community of ideas. However much the phases vary in which Shaftesbury appears, through all there runs . . . one single principle, logically pursued . . . He may be regarded as the principal founder of that great party which, in opposition to the prerogative and to uniformity, has inscribed upon its banner political freedom and religious tolerance.[48]

This ideal did not die with Shaftesbury. On the contrary, it was this ideal, no doubt along with others, that found expression in Locke's *Essay* and was part of his motive for writing it.

To this it might be objected that epistemology is one thing and politics another. But it is very doubtful that Locke would have seen it in that way. We must not forget that discussions of toleration were seen almost totally within a religious context, and the epistemology of the *Essay* has a wide variety of religious applications, as anybody familiar with its reception will know full well: it was precisely the supposed threat to religious orthodoxies that sparked off most of its critics. When, in the letter to Pembroke from which we have already quoted, Locke speaks of his enquiry as being about 'the weaknesse and shortnesse of humane understanding' he was, I believe, referring to a major theme of the work which he saw as having wide social implications. For if we have no right to our claims to certainty in central areas of enquiry, then we have no right to condemn others for their differing beliefs, unless their beliefs could, within our narrow confines, be demonstrated to be false. Locke, of course,

---

[47] Ibid. ii. 662–3.
[48] Leopold von Ranke, *History of England*, trans. Sir Oliver Lodge (London, 1875), iv. 166–7, as quoted in Haley, *The First Earl of Shaftesbury*, 741.

did not doubt but that certain matters could be demonstrated. We could indeed come to know the moral laws of nature, at least to some degree. But much had to be left open. Thus it is that the fourth book of the *Essay* has disappointed many readers who hoped there to find large chunks of knowledge, but instead found that Locke holds that much of what men have traditionally taken to be knowledge was something less, merely matters of belief, more or less probable.

The moral fervour which I am suggesting underlies the *Essay* is not much to the fore. But it can be detected. One such passage occurs at the end of Book I when Locke launches a strong attack on those who make claims to authority based on innate ideas. The passage appears in identical words in the 1685 Draft C. But it finds its first expression in Draft B of 1671, testifying to it as an enduring theme in Locke's work. Though long, it is none the less worth quoting in full:

When men have found some general Propositions that could not be doubted of, as soon as understood, it was, I know, *a short and easy way to conclude them innate.* This being once received, it eased the lazy from the pains of search, and stopped the enquiry of the doubtful, concerning all that was once stiled innate: And it was of no small advantage to those who affected to be Masters and Teachers to make this the Principle of *Principles*, that Principles must not be questioned: For having once established this Tenet, That there are innate Principles, it put their Followers upon a necessity of receiving some Doctrines as such, which was to take them off from the use of their own Reason and Judgement, and put them upon believing and taking them upon trust, without farther examination: In which posture of blind Credulity, they might be more easily governed by, and made useful to some sort of Men, who had the skill and office to principle and guide them.[49]

We are not at all surprised to learn that the man who wrote this in a work which was by his own word overtly non-political should in the same year have composed a major work on religious toleration, originally addressed to one of his distinguished Dutch hosts, Philippus van Limborch.[50]

There are many other passages in Draft B, Draft C, and the first edition of the *Essay* which reveal Locke's deep concern for religious toleration and his hostility to intellectual positions which could be used against it. Book I, chapter iii is particularly rich in such remarks, and many of these are anticipated in Draft B.[51] Thus he writes: ' 'Tis easy to foresee, that if different Men of different Sects should go about to give us

---

[49] *Essay*, I. iv. 24, 101–2. The corresponding passage in Draft B, sect. 13, which may be found in *Drafts*, 122–3.

[50] This has been the standard view on the origin of the *Epistola*, though it has recently been challenged by Montuori, *John Locke on Toleration*, esp. pp. xxv–xxvii.

[51] See e.g. *Essay*, I. iii. 8, 11, 14, 20, 21, 24, 26.

a List of those innate practical Principles, they would set down only such as suited their distinct Hypotheses, and were fit to support the Doctrines of their particular Schools or Churches: A plain evidence, that there are no such innate Truths.'[52] In the *Essay* and in Draft B Locke offers us explanation of the otherwise amazing fact that different men are prepared even to die for contrary principles, which, Locke says, can be understood once we realize that from a very early age the principle has been taught the child as if it were an undeniable truth, even though it really had no higher source 'than the Superstition of a Nurse, or the Authority of an old Woman'.[53] These are words of a man who is sure of the fundamental relevance of an epistemological tenet—the rejection of innate ideas as a source of knowledge—to morality and religion, and, through them, to politics.

It is of interest to note at this point that although Draft B does contain many such remarks hostile to innate ideas and to unjustified claims to certainty in matters of morals and religion they are not nearly so prevalent in Draft A. But we should not, for that reason, ignore the ones that are there. Thus, the passage quoted above is anticipated in Draft A with:

There is noe thing more ordinary then that children should receive into their mindes propositions (espetialy about matters of religion) from their parents nurses or those about them. which being insinuated into their unwary as well as unbiased understandings & fastend there by degrees are at last (equally whether true or false) rivited there by long custom & education beyond all possibility of being puld out again . . . men . . . looke on them as . . . set up in their mindes immediately by god him self to be the great & unerring deciders of truth & falshood . . .[54]

Draft A is written in the same Commonplace Book that also contains the early essay on toleration in which, as we have seen, there are links between epistemic and political issues. But it is worth noticing that even in the 1660 *First Tract on Government*, although it differs from the later political writings in opposing toleration in matters indifferent, nevertheless underlines the danger of unjustified presumption in matters of religion: 'if men would suffer one another to go to heaven every one his own way, and not out of a fond conceit of themselves pretend to greater knowledge and care of another's soul and eternal concernments than he himself'.[55] In other words, Locke from an early stage was well aware of the epistemic difficulties in many matters of religion and morals.

---

[52] Ibid. I. iii. 14.   [53] Ibid. I. iii. 22. Cf. Draft B, sect. 9, in *Drafts*, 115.
[54] Draft A, sect. 42, in *Drafts*, 70.
[55] *Two Tracts*, 161. For similar sentiments, see also Locke's letter to Henry Stubbe of Sept.? 1659, *Correspondence*, i, no. 75, and Locke to Boyle, Dec. 1665, ibid., esp. p. 228.

This 'epistemology of toleration', as I shall venture to call it, had wide and deep implications not only for politics and religion but also for what we today call the natural sciences—too wide and deep to be considered here in any detail. But the general position is clear. Just because our powers to comprehend the truth are so limited we must refrain from making unwarranted claims to certainty for our theories and hypotheses about the natural world. We cannot even comprehend the nature of the 'bodies that are about us', let alone 'the whole nature of the Universe'. And 'as to a perfect *Science* of natural Bodies, (not to mention spiritual Beings,) we are, I think, so far from being capable of any such thing, that I conclude it lost labour to seek after it'.[56]

This rejection of the certainty of natural science was also a rejection of the a priori route to knowledge of nature, which Locke had detected in Descartes and some of his followers and which he (with Newton) whole-heartedly wished to resist. But the rejection of certainty in science was never a rejection of its *usefulness*. The study of nature can bring great utilitarian rewards for mankind. It was rather that 'we should not be too forwardly possessed with the Opinion, or Expectation of Knowledge, where it is not to be had; or by ways, that will not attain it: That we should not take doubtful Systems, for complete Sciences; nor unintelligible Notions, for scientifical Demonstrations'.[57] The great enemy in natural science, as in theology, and indeed of all truth in general, was the sin of enthusiasm: the 'assuming an Authority of Dictating to others'.[58] It was for Locke the most heinous of intellectual sins.

The Essay *and Holland*

Lastly in this section, why was it in Holland that Locke composed the final version of his great work? Did it offer some special feature which provided a catalyst to stimulate Locke's writing? Of course much of the answer must be that he completed it there because he was just at the point in his life that he could bring his thoughts together. But there may also be another factors. We have already noticed the way in which Locke liked the role of assistant, to Boyle, Sydenham, Shaftesbury, and such. Yet he overcame his diffidence when he returned from Holland and rapidly published all his most important works.

One of the reasons for this that I would like, rather tentatively, to

---

[56] *Essay*, IV. iii. 29.   [57] Ibid. IV. xii. 12.
[58] 'Of Enthusiasm', ibid. IV. xix. 2.

suggest is that Locke had become overwhelmingly convinced that a society that practised toleration in religious and intellectual matters, including medicine and the natural sciences, within the wider framework of certainties that the mind could fix was the most desirable kind of society that mankind could hope to achieve. He had probably reached this conclusion well before leaving England in 1683. Much of it was already firmly in place before Shaftesbury's death, and goes back at least to the meetings in 1671 which gave rise to the early drafts of the *Essay*. But when he arrived in Holland, his world badly damaged by the death of Shaftesbury and the political failures of the English reformers, he discovered a country in which many of the goals he sought, intellectual, political, medical, social, seemed already to be in place. We must not overstate the liberal nature of Dutch society in the 1680s, but in important respects it contrasted favourably with its English counterpart of the same period.

As the topic is so large I can only gesture at the evidence to substantiate these claims, and the following examples could be expanded with ease. Thus, to take the matter of medical practice, a matter of considerable importance to Locke, he discovered that the method that he and Sydenham had striven to introduce was already widely followed.[59] On other matters, his journals reveal that in the universities he found the method of examination much superior to that of Oxford. They also reveal his admiration for and intrigue with the Dutch achievements in constructing dams and building on waterlogged soil. He was much impressed by the hospital for old women he saw established by the Calvinist Church in Amsterdam. Above all, he found an atmosphere and concern for toleration in religion, even in a small country threatened by a giant foe, which he saw might be translated to England. He was deeply sure that the major causes of intolerance lay in men's hearts and not in the nature of things, still less in God's word. As he noted, 'the great disputes that have been & are stil in several churches have been for the most part about their owne inventions & not about things ordeind by god himself or necessary to salvation'.[60] They were in essence philosophical disputes. All the more reason, therefore, for pressing ahead with his programme. All the more reason for supporting the cause of the English radicals. Above all,

---

[59] On the situation in England, see Harold J. Cook, *The Decline of the Old Medical Regime in Stuart England* (Ithaca, NY, 1986), *passim*. See also Simon Schaffer, 'The Glorious Revolution and Medicine in Britain and the Netherlands', *Notes and Records of the Royal Society of London*, 43 (1989), 167–90. There are many entries in Locke's journals for the Dutch years that give ample testimony of his admiration for Dutch medical practice, an admiration that was reciprocated.

[60] From Locke's journal for July 17 1684, Bodl. MS Locke f. 8.

Holland provided an opportunity for the renewal of old friendships and the acquisition of new ones in an atmosphere of toleration, exemplified in his relationship with Limborch and the ethic of the Remonstrant Church and captured in a letter where, apropos of a difference in theology, Limborch wrote: 'let our contest be in acts of sincere friendship and unfeigned affection'.[61] In contrast to the benighted of many lands *'cooped in close by the laws* of their Countries, and the strict guards of those, whose Interest it is to keep them ignorant',[62] Locke saw in Holland, and sought for his own land, a society where citizens could enjoy *'the Liberty* and Opportunities *of a fair Enquiry'*.[63] Holland we may even surmise, was the midwife to his genius.

II

The chapters in this volume cover a variety of Locke issues ranging from his early intellectual concerns to his impact, surprisingly large, on Polish society. All but one of the chapters have not been previously published and between them they not only illuminate aspects of Locke's thought but they also open up new areas of enquiry which illustrate very well his continuing relevance to the modern world.

In 'Locke at Oxford' (Chapter 1) J. R. Milton shows how careful attention to Locke's manuscripts, and, in particular attention to Locke's commonplace books which reveal his reading, throws important light on understanding Locke's intellectual development and squashes some long-standing myths. He concentrates on Locke's years at Christ Church, underlining its unique place amongst Oxford colleges in not having fellows and being governed by the Dean and Canons of the cathedral, and having 100 Students who very loosely corresponded to the fellows and scholars of the other colleges. Locke progressed up the ladder of Students from his arrival in 1652 until his expulsion in 1684, though from his move to join Shaftesbury's London household in 1667 he was rarely there. Looking at those years before the London move Milton is able to make a strong case for several important conclusions about Locke's intellectual interests from a reconstruction of his reading. He is able, for example, to demonstrate the predominant place that medicine held, and, by contrast, the very low place occupied by what is now thought of as

---

[61] *Correspondence*, ii. 756. There is some irony in the fact that the letter was written on the same day as the Revocation of the Edict of Nantes.

[62] *Essay*, IV. xx. 4.   [63] Ibid.

philosophy in Locke's intellectual concerns. Indeed, with the important exception of the Cambridge Platonists, philosophy in the modern sense was not centrally part of the English intellectual scene at this time. It is, Milton suggests, one of Locke's great contributions to have identified the issues that were to remain central to British philosophy from 1690 onwards.

In 'The Foundations of Knowledge and the Logic of Substance: The Structure of Locke's General Philosophy' (Chapter 2) Michael Ayers also makes a case for Locke's importance as an original advocate of an empiricist philosophy which is at the same time realist. Ayers sees Locke, along with Hobbes and Gassendi, as self-consciously opposed to the rationalism of Descartes in holding that the senses provide us with an authority for knowledge independent of reason. He sees Locke's commitment here as having sources in ancient Stoic and Epicurean texts and he links these with the ancient doctrine of signs, both reminiscent and indicative. Only the former can give us knowledge, whilst the latter, in going beyond experience, can only yield probabilities.

Whilst close to Gassendi in the early Draft A of the *Essay* Ayers sees Locke as diverging from him in the course of developing the argument of the published work, especially with respect to our knowledge of general truths about the world. He detects a shift away from a presumption that a kind of induction can lead us to knowledge of general truths about the world to the abandoning of this as a possibility. Ayers sees this as an important change and one which lies at the heart of Locke's account of substance. This, he believes, is still misunderstood by commentators who hold that 'the general idea of substance is for Locke the idea of a pure logical subject underlying all properties, known or unknown, and for that reason unknowable in principle', whereas Locke was only committed to the contingent unknowability of the essence of any particular example of a substance, through the empirical fact that our senses are limited in what they can perceive.

Ayers sees Locke's account of the possibility of knowledge of universals as having an influence on Kant. But it is not just this historical fact that gives importance to Locke's argument. Both he and Kant recognized the distinction between the attainable knowledge of natural history and the impossible goal of certain knowledge of the objects of natural science. Locke's insights into these matters still provide the framework, if not the detail, for a powerful realist empiricism.

In 'The Real Molyneux Question and the Basis of Locke's Answer' (Chapter 3) Martha Brandt Bolton throws new light on the question

raised by William Molyneux and Locke's response to it by a careful
examination of the context in which Molyneux raised the issue, and in
particular the context of contemporary optical theory. The question that
Molyneux posed was whether a man born blind who had learned to
distinguish a solid cube from a globe by touch, could, if he were made to
see, immediately distinguish by sight which was the globe and which the
cube. Molyneux's own answer was negative, and Locke agreed with him,
and incorporated the problem and his answer in the second edition of the
Essay. But Locke gave no detailed argument for his conclusion and Bolton offers us a reconstruction of the thinking that is likely to have lain
behind it. Before doing so, however, she considers the difficulties raised
by contemporaries to Locke's answer, including Berkeley's argument that
it conflicts with the *Essay*'s account of primary qualities. She argues that
this reading of Locke rests on a mistaken understanding of the basis of his
conclusion. Central to this is the view, widely accepted from the medieval
and Renaissance perspectivist tradition, that bodily shapes are not immediately given in sight. She traces the optical theory from John Pecham's
late thirteenth-century textbook, through the work of Kepler, Hobbes,
Gassendi, and Descartes to Malebranche, Molyneux, and Locke at the
end of the century. In rejecting innatist accounts of perceiving figure,
Bolton suggests, Locke would argue that we come to see figure by correlating sensations over time. It is not something that we could do *immediately*. Rather, it requires inductively learnt judgement. That this account
argues that Locke's simple ideas have 'logical structure', that they are not
conceptual atoms, itself illuminates aspects of Locke's notion of simple
idea.

Locke's chapter 'Of Power' was one that caused him as much trouble
as any in the *Essay*. It was in it that he gives us his thoughts about human
freedom, a subject on which his views deepened through the years following the first edition of the *Essay* and his discussions on the topic, especially in his correspondence with his Dutch friend Philippus van Limborch
in the later years of his life. Vere Chappell (in Chapter 4) provides not
only the most careful charting and analysis of Locke's changing position
to date, but also reason for seeing Locke's considered opinion to be one
of considerable strength and interest. Locke was, Chappell uncontentiously
claims, a libertarian, though his understanding of human freedom was
different from many other libertarians in that he believed that all actions
have causes. The precise nature of Locke's libertarianism is, however,
much more difficult to locate, especially as his own views changed. It is
here that Chappell adds considerably to our understanding of Locke's

position and its strengths, though he readily admits that there remain further important questions about Locke's claims that require yet further close scrutiny.

Chappell focuses particularly on one feature of Locke's discussion, the place of 'volitional determinism' in Locke's analysis: the thesis that freedom in willing is not a possible part of free agency. According to Locke, the will is an active power belonging to rational agents, and willing is the exercise of that power, directed at some end. From this beginning Chappell explores the various dimensions of Locke's claims and their links and contrasts with libertarian contemporaries such as Bramhall and the Arminians. He does so in a way which not only gives historical insight but also a deeper understanding of the nature of freedom itself, and thus stands as a model of how the examination of a text some three centuries old can be philosophically illuminating. He concludes with a statement of the central core of Locke's theory of freedom which includes the following: that freedom belongs only to rational agents, including normal mature, adult human beings; that every free action is voluntary in the sense that its causes include a volition on the part of the agent, but the volition need not itself be a free action. So that when late in his life Locke came to abandon voluntary determinism, this was not crucial to his account, for it is not inconsistent with the main thrust of his claim.

In his 'Locke on Meaning and Signification' (Chapter 5) Michael Losonsky defends a traditional reading of Book III of the *Essay* as 'the first modern treatise devoted specifically to philosophy of language'. He does so against various recent writers who have proposed other accounts, but especially E. J. Ashworth's influential claim that Locke uses 'signification' not to mean 'meaning'. Losonsky argues that she does not fully appreciate that for Locke meanings and definitions are distinct. The meaning of a term is for Locke always identified with the idea that the term signifies, whereas definitions involve the explications of words by other words.

Another aspect of Ashworth's case is drawn from the scholastic sense of 'significatio' which, she claims, does not equate with *meaning*. Losonsky does not find her arguments for this compelling and holds on to the thesis that signification and meaning can be more or less equated in Locke. He then turns to the problem of whether Locke on his theory can account for successful communication between language users. Here Losonsky argues against Hacking that Locke was well aware that we can fail to communicate successfully—fail to rouse the correct ideas in the mind of our auditor—but we can also rectify our failures and mistakes. What we mean by having the same (kind of) idea as somebody else has, in the case of simple ideas at least, a clear sense: we have the same idea (as somebody else) if our ideas have the same cause. Although communication does not reach certainty, we can nevertheless be pretty sure about the success of much of it. Finally, Losonsky claims, we must see Locke's account not as a continuation of Scholastic debates but as part of the seventeenth-century concern with the failure of public discourse. It is this context, rather than the Scholastic one, that Locke's account of meaning should be placed.

Central to much of the 'New Philosophy of the Seventeenth Century' was the reintroduction of atomistic or corpuscular accounts of matter and its properties, and Locke is famous for his espousal of the associated distinction between the primary and secondary qualities of bodies. Peter Alexander has done much to illuminate Locke's account, stressing the strong links between Locke's version and that of his mentor Robert Boyle. But there were serious problems that atomism had to meet. One was the status of the atoms themselves. Could absolutely solid atoms exist? And if they did, could such objects rebound from each other? For some, the supposed impossibility was sufficient to reject the proposed version of the atomic hypothesis completely, and this is the position that we would expect a physicist to take today. But in the seventeenth century the hard body theory was accepted by many of the leading natural philosophers, and in Chapter 6 Alexander examines why this may have been so. In exploring the argument on both sides he throws light on the relation between theory, experiment, and the deeper metaphysical beliefs of the protagonists.

Alexander begins from Locke's chapter in the *Essay* on solidity. Our idea of solidity, in so far as it is based on experience, is relative. All the objects we experience are collections of particles. But we can on this basis reach an idea of absolute solidity in which there is no gap between the particles. Absolute solidity is reached only in the case of single and unobservable corpuscles. And such particles can act singly on us, Alexander sees Locke as claiming, as is exhibited in the effects of particles of light which give rise to visual sensations.

The belief that perfectly hard bodies will rebound from one another was one accepted by Descartes, as Alexander shows. But it stood in marked contrast to the account of matter offered by Leibniz. Which of these answers was correct was not easily settled and continued to be an issue raising fundamental questions about the nature of matter and its properties well into the next century. What Alexander shows is that the question was not resolvable at the experimental level and there were powerful arguments on both sides, dependent on contrasting metaphysical assumptions about the nature of matter.

James Tully's chapter (7) brings us to Locke's political philosophy and its implications, some of which continue to have a deep effect on our contemporary moral and political concepts and categories. One aspect of Locke's theory which still exercises a powerful hold over our thinking is Locke's answer to questions of political legitimacy: What constitutes consent? When is revolt justifiable? Another, arising from Locke's account of property, concerns such questions as what constitutes the just distribution of the product of labour? What constitutes exploitation? Our contemporary answers to these questions are still largely framed from within the Lockean categories, categories which, Tully holds, are no longer appropriate. He fastens on two issues to illustrate his case: that of aboriginal self-government and how we should manage our environment. Tully sees these two matters as closely related. It is the Lockean understanding of property that legitimized the European expansion into aboriginal territory, and it is the economic system that flowed from that understanding that has been most damaging to the environment. Tully examines the context in which the Lockean conceptions were created and contrasts them with the Amerindian forms of government. In so doing he both increases our understanding of Locke's theory and also hopes to loosen its hold on our thinking. His detailed and powerful argument reveals the way in which Locke imported into his analysis, itself a sophisticated version of earlier justifications for European intervention in North America, the categories of the Old World and attempted to read them on to the quite different social and political arrangements already in place in the New. Lockean arguments were forcefully used by those seeking to justify the European colonization of land in the eighteenth century and Locke himself may well have had the rivalry between Britain and France in North America in mind when he argued for the superiority of the more intensive agriculture of the English colonies. Tully concludes that Locke's theory not only allows scope for arguments to support the injustice of colonial land acquisition, but even at this last stage, it also provides a framework for a theory of reparation. For Locke held that title to land was not destroyed by unjust invasion. Lockean theory might therefore still provide a basis for a settlement with justice of the claims of the Amerindians. If such be the case then Locke's political theory still retains important relevance to the modern world in at least this respect.

In Chapter 8, 'The Politics of Christianity', Ian Harris argues not only that Locke's politics were mediated through his theology but, more surprisingly, that his understanding of politics affected what he under-stood by Christianity. Harris begins with an examination of the Augus-tinian doctrine of original sin as transmitted from Adam to all mankind and the associated theory espoused by, for example, George Lawson, that God saw the whole human race as one person. It was a theory accepted by Robert Filmer and it was at the heart of Filmer's understanding of the transmission of political power. It was a theory that Locke had to demol-ish if his own account was to carry the day.

Locke's assault on Filmer began from a commitment to a literal inter-pretation of the text of Genesis. A literal reading gave authority to all mankind and not to Adam alone, as Filmer required. Conversely, it was Adam alone, in the singular of the biblical text, that Locke took as the correct reading in other contexts. As Harris says, 'Locke could not easily admit Adam's representative capacity at all.'

But for Locke what then of original sin? Harris argues that Locke did not see Adam's Fall as involving the kind or depth of corruption that Augustine and Calvin had claimed. Locke, in his later writings at least, was never committed to explaining human sin by the fall, merely by human nature, and these failings were not seen as insurmountable.

We may add to Locke's strong underplaying of the argument from the Fall of Adam another important reason for Locke taking the position that he did, namely his account of personal identity. For it leaves no room for the imputation of Adam's sin and punishment to mankind. And this was a position entirely consistent with that found in Locke's *Reasonableness of Christianity*: 'none are truly punished but for their own deeds'. Filmer's account of the transmission of political power was quite incompatible with Locke's theology.

In the last two chapters we have accounts of the impact of Locke's philosophy in Eastern Europe, and in particular Greece and Poland. In light of the enormous impact of Locke in north-west Europe it is perhaps surprising that nothing of his philosophy was published in Greek until 1796. In his chapter on Locke's reception in Greece Paschalis Kitromilides shows how complex that reception was and thereby advances our under-standing of how Locke's ideas spread through Europe in the eighteenth century. Locke's impact, however, anticipated the translation of his works, as many Greek scholars read him in French, but it is perhaps surprising that it was the *Essay concerning Human Understanding* rather than his political philosophy that made such an impression. It is a significant fact that the radicals of nineteenth-century Greek political philosophy never show familiarity with Locke's argument against tyranny that would have been so useful to them. In this they broadly followed a similar neglect throughout Europe, followed by a decline in the influence not only of his political theory but also of his epistemology. It was not until 1990 that the *Two Treatises* appeared in a Greek translation.

A country where Locke's influence was perhaps unexpectedly substantial was Poland, and in her chapter Janina Rosicka explains the phases of Locke's reception. It is perhaps surprising to discover that it was Locke's educational writings that first made a significant impact and it was only later that the *Essay concerning Human Understanding* became prominent. Much of this is explained in terms of the differing contexts to which Locke's thought was applicable, and in particular the way in which Enlightenment thought impinged on the social structure of Polish society, which was very different from that in England. In ways similar to other European countries, it was not Locke's political writings that had the greatest impact, even though the reformers often talked a language not dissimilar to that of the *Two Treatises*, a position comparable to the reception of Locke in North America. He was, nevertheless, a very important figure in shaping Polish thought in the eighteenth century and beyond.

I

Locke at Oxford

J. R. MILTON

John Locke's association with the University of Oxford lasted for rather more than thirty years, from May 1652, when he was elected to a Studentship at Christ Church, to November 1684, when he was expelled from the same Studentship by direct royal command. During the second half of this period his connection with the college became fairly tenuous in most respects other than the purely financial. He took great care to collect all the income due to him, but for most of the time his rooms were let and his visits to Oxford infrequent. From May 1667 until November 1675 he lived almost continuously in London, as a member of the Earl of Shaftesbury's household.[1] Even after his return from France in 1679, when his visits to Oxford became longer and more frequent, he still kept himself to himself and played little part in the life of the college.[2] What can properly be called Locke's Oxford period lasted a little less than fifteen years, from the autumn of 1652 until the beginning of April 1667.[3]

By virtue of containing both a cathedral and a university college, Christ Church remains even today a somewhat unusual institution. In the seventeenth century the differences between it and the other colleges were considerably greater than they have since become, and in 1652, when every other cathedral chapter in England had been dissolved, its position was particularly anomalous.

The internal organization of Christ Church was also unique in two

---

[1] Locke's exact movements cannot always be traced until the journals begin in Nov. 1675, but there is evidence of only two visits to Oxford in this period, in Sept. 1671 and 4–7 Feb. 1675.
[2] Locke's journal shows that he was in Oxford for a total of about ten months between Dec. 1679 and June 1683.
[3] Locke left Oxford on 2 Apr. and spent most of the month in Somerset before travelling to London via Salisbury.

respects. In contrast with all the other colleges in both Oxford and Cambridge it had no fellows. The government of both the cathedral and the college was entirely in the hands of the Dean and the eight Canons who made up the cathedral Chapter. It was also unlike any of the other colleges in that it had never been given any statutes. Residence in Christ Church would have given Locke intimate experience of living under absolute government.

In place of the scholars and fellows of other colleges Christ Church had places for 100 Students. Studentships still exist at Christ Church, but they now differ only in name from the fellowships offered by the other colleges. In the seventeenth century their status was very different, and the peculiarities of the institution are sufficiently relevant to Locke's career as to make some description of it necessary.[4]

There were two ways of becoming a Student of Christ Church. Every year a certain number (in Locke's time usually five or six[5]) were elected from among the scholars at Westminster School. This was how Locke obtained his Studentship in 1652. The other Students, rather fewer in number than those from Westminster, were nominated by the Dean and the Canons acting in turn. In complete contrast with the fellowships at other colleges, no one could be elected to a Studentship once they had taken any degree.[6]

Studentships were tenable for life, but could be forfeited on a number of grounds: failure to take a degree when qualified for it, marriage, failure to take orders when of sufficient seniority to do so, and receiving a church living of more than a certain value. The effect of these requirements was to keep the average length of tenure to less than fifteen years. It is easy to imagine the old, unreformed Oxford (and perhaps Christ Church in particular) as being populated by aged clergymen tottering between Hall

---

[4] Fox Bourne, i. 52–3 gives an entirely erroneous account of Locke holding a junior Studentship that expired after seven years, and of his consequent election to a senior Studentship on some unrecorded occasion in 1658 or early 1659. There was, however, no distinction between junior and senior Studentships until 1858 and no need for a further election of any kind. Locke's supposed election has left no trace because it never took place. It is curious to note that the date of this (literal) non-event has become more precise in more recent authors. Maurice Cranston dates it to soon after Locke graduated MA in June 1658 (Cranston, 43); W. von Leyden, most precisely of all, to six months after that date (*Law of Nature*, 15).

[5] Lists of Students elected from Westminster are contained in J. Welch (ed.), *The List of the Queen's Scholars at St Peter's College, Westminster* (London, 1852). Between 1640 and 1659 the average number elected was 5.5. In 1652 Locke was placed last in a list of six.

[6] An invaluable account of the workings of Christ Church during this period can be found in E. G. W. Bill, *Education at Christ Church Oxford 1660–1800* (Oxford, 1988).

and Chapel. Such figures undoubtedly existed, but most of the Students were in reality in their twenties or early thirties.

The Students of Christ Church were divided into three groups: twenty *theologi*, forty *philosophi* (themselves split into two equal divisions), and forty *discipuli* or *scholares* (similarly subdivided). The position of any Student on this ladder was determined solely by seniority, with the exception of one group. Four Studentships were known as Faculty Studentships— two in law, two in medicine—and their holders were not required or allowed to pass into the ranks of the *theologi*. This deprived them of a small addition to their income but, much more importantly, freed them from the obligation falling on all the *theologi* to take orders or else be deprived of their Studentships.

Gaps in the records at Christ Church mean that the earliest stages of Locke's progress cannot now be traced.[7] By the beginning of 1659 he was already among the *philosophi*—sixth in the second division. A year later he was second. The readmission in 1660 of a number of formerly extruded royalists resulted in a fall of two places, but by the beginning of 1662 Locke had risen to last but one among the first division of *philosophi*, and by 1663 he was eleventh. It was only too clear that the time when he might have to decide whether or not to be ordained was approaching fast, and a letter from his Somerset friend John Strachey shows that Locke was worried about what he should do.[8] By the beginning of 1664 he had moved up to ninth place—apart from the Faculty Students there were only four *philosophi* still above him. At the end of the year the long-awaited if undesired promotion occurred: Locke began 1665 eighteenth among the *theologi*.

The fact that Locke managed to retain his Studentship under these circumstances for nearly two years, until he was able to procure a royal dispensation from the obligation of taking orders in November 1666,[9] suggests that he was regarded with some indulgence by the Dean, John Fell. In October 1663 Fell and two of the Canons had signed a testimonial[10] stating Locke's diligence in study, moral probity, and theological orthodoxy, and it is likely that Fell still hoped that Locke would take orders. The contrast with the situation twenty years later, when Fell clearly regarded Locke with considerable suspicion and obeyed the order to expel him with very little reluctance, is striking.

Further evidence of Locke's good standing with the Dean and Chapter

---

[7] The details of Locke's rise in seniority given below are taken from the Christ Church Disbursement Books, which are missing for the years 1646–58.

[8] *Correspondence*, i. 215.   [9] Text in Fox Bourne, i. 131.   [10] Ibid. 88.

in the early 1660s can be seen from the list of College offices which he held: Lecturer in Greek for the years 1661 and 1662, Lecturer in Rhetoric for 1663, and finally Censor of Moral Philosophy for 1664. Locke's tenure of the two lectureships need not be taken as indicating any particular commitment to either rhetoric or Greek: together with the two Censorships they made up the College offices that were normally awarded to Students of his degree of seniority. Fell's own approval of Locke is shown by his making him a tutor in May 1661. This provided a modest though useful addition to Locke's income and a considerable quantity of extra work. It also necessitated fairly continuous residence in Christ Church, at least during term-time. In the early 1660s Locke gave every appearance of being a 'good College man', busy with his pupils and his College duties, and trusted and respected by the Dean and the Canons.

The archives at Christ Church enable one to reconstruct the externals of Locke's career, but as one would expect they furnish no information about the character of his thought while he was there. When Locke arrived in Oxford he was just 20; when he left he was nearly 35. These are years which one generally would expect to be crucial in anyone's intellectual development, but were they in Locke's case? How much can we now discover about what he thought, what he read, what interests he pursued? How much light does any of this throw on the works which Locke published in late middle age, almost a quarter of a century after he ceased to be an active resident member of Christ Church?

Anyone interested in trying to answer these questions is likely to turn first of all to Locke's biographers. Fox Bourne is of little use here. *The Life of John Locke* was in its time an excellent piece of work, and has still not been entirely superseded, but it was written without access to the main body of Locke's papers, on which any adequate account must necessarily rest. Cranston's biography is unfortunately only a limited improvement. It is undoubtedly an extremely useful work, but its inadequacies are no less striking. The case against it has been most vigorously expressed by Richard Ashcraft: 'Cranston's biography . . . was notable for its failure to shed any light upon the intellectual dimensions of Locke's thought.'[11] This is surely too harsh, but one can see why it was said. Cranston provides a smoothly flowing account of the externals of Locke's life, but one hardly ends up understanding very much more about what he thought, or how his thoughts evolved.

One reason for this is that Cranston's biography is based on a

---

[11] Richard Ashcraft, *Locke's 'Two Treatises of Government'* (London, 1987), 303.

disturbingly narrow range of sources. This may not be apparent to the casual reader, but anyone familiar with Locke's manuscripts is likely to be struck (or at any rate certainly should be) by just how many important sources there are which were either never cited at all by Cranston or else mentioned only once or twice in passing. These weaknesses are particularly serious for the earliest part of Locke's life. Apart from Locke's own works, Cranston relied almost entirely on Locke's journals and letters, and in the period before 1675, when there are no journals and relatively few letters, the limitations of these sources are particularly severe. From Locke's letters we can learn a great deal about Locke's sentimental friendships with the ladies of Black Hall, but very little about what he was thinking, or what the intellectual issues were that had engaged his attention.

Apart from Locke's biographers, the most accessible sources of information about his early thought are those of his works from this period which have since been published. Of these the most substantial and most well known are the *Two Tracts on Government* (1660–*c*.1662) and the *Essays on the Law of Nature* (completed 1664, but probably for the most part written rather earlier). To these one should add a short and somewhat neglected disputation *An Necesse Sit Dari in Ecclesia Infallibilem Sacro Sanctae Scripturae Interpretem?* (1661).[12] All these works are of considerable though unequal value for our understanding of Locke's early thought, but anyone who uses them as their main source of evidence for what Locke was thinking at this time will almost inevitably finish up with a severely distorted account. There can be no doubt that Locke was deeply interested in the kind of questions that arise in the area where religion, ethics, and politics mingle together, not only in the early 1660s but for the whole of his life, but he always had other concerns, and there is ample evidence to suggest that during his years at Oxford it was these that occupied the greater part of his time.[13]

The most valuable sources of information about how Locke's

---

[12] John C. Biddle, 'John Locke's Essay on Infallibility: Introduction, Text and Translation', *Journal of Church and State*, 19 (1977), 301–27.

[13] It is under these circumstances singularly unfortunate that the only one of Locke's early works which is on a scientific or medical subject, the short physiological tract *Respirationis Usus*, is only available in an exceedingly unsatisfactory edition (Kenneth Dewhurst, 'Locke's Essay on Respiration', *Bulletin of the History of Medicine*, 34 (1960), 257–73). This is marred by numerous serious omissions and gross errors of transcription, but above all an extraordinary failure to notice that the inner sheet of the MS (PRO 30/24/47/2, fo. 71–4) has been bound in back to front. The text printed by Dewhurst is therefore so badly shuffled as to make Locke's train of thought entirely unintelligible. Its replacement must be regarded as a matter of some urgency.

intellectual interests remain unpublished. These are the commonplace books in which he noted down extracts from the books he was reading, interspersed with occasional comments of his own; they can be supplemented by similar material recorded in several of the interleaved books in his library.

Locke took great care over his commonplace books. The earliest ones contain a mere jumble of material, but from about the beginning of 1660 he started organizing the entries according to one or other of a variety of closely related systems.[14] A few years later he went through some of the older unsystematized books and transcribed the material he thought worth preserving into the books he was currently using. The commonplace books were the equivalent of a modern researcher's sets of 6-by-4 file cards, not an intellectual lumber-room into which material could be thrown without adequate means of retrieval.

This material has so far been inadequately used (Cranston made no real attempt to use it at all), primarily because almost all of it is undated. Such dates as have been suggested have frequently been badly mistaken, mainly because they have been derived from the easily made but erroneous supposition that the numbers inside the front covers of some of the notebooks indicate the dates when they were first used. (They are in fact almost certainly part of a system of cross-referencing which Locke used for a while in the early 1680s.) Fortunately the great majority of the entries in Locke's commonplace books can be fairly precisely dated, though it would take too long to explain the techniques here.[15] I would, however, like to emphasize that the dates I shall be mentioning in the remainder of this paper are securely grounded and are *not* mere conjectures.

These sources when taken together cast a very considerable amount of light on Locke's intellectual development, but it is a kind of illumination that is by its nature both indirect and diffuse. We are able to see what books Locke was reading, and more particularly what passages from those books he thought it worth while to transcribe, but except in a few cases we cannot see what Locke's own thoughts were. (Like Plato's man in the cave, we can see reflections on the walls, but not the objects causing them.) Given the very considerable quantity of material that has survived we can achieve a kind of understanding of Locke's early thought that is

---

[14] The change to the new system can be clearly seen in Bodl. MSS Locke f.14, f.18, and f.20.

[15] I have described the problems involved in dating entries in one very important early notebook, Bodl. MS Locke f.14, in 'The Date and Significance of Two of Locke's Early Manuscripts', *Locke Newsletter*, 19 (1988), 47–90.

simply not available for thinkers like Hobbes or Descartes, but even so we are still not in a position to produce the kind of detailed account that becomes possible when we have precisely dated drafts and similar material.

The main series of commonplace books in which Locke recorded his reading begins in about 1658, perhaps soon after 29 June of that year, when he graduated as Master of Arts. We know very little about his thoughts up until this time. Apart from two poems and various not very informative letters we have nothing that he himself wrote; and only one commonplace book and a few other scraps of information tell us anything about what he read. He seems to have followed the usual curriculum and to have read the usual authors. In the seventeenth century undergraduates were neither expected nor encouraged to be original. If Locke found the syllabus irksome (as his own much later testimony suggests) then he seems to have found escape in reading translations of French romances, not in voyaging in strange seas of thought alone.

Once a Master of Arts Locke was free to pursue any line of study that he pleased. The main area that he chose seems to have been medicine. That Locke was interested in medicine is well known, but it is not always realized just how extensive his interests were, or how early they began. One has of course to be careful here. One of the earliest of Locke's notebooks—probably started in the early 1650s—begins with a wide range of rustic remedies for ailments of various kinds, in many cases taken from Locke's family or from his neighbours in Somerset. These are the kind of prescriptions that begin 'Hedghogs greace one pound'.[16] They are clearly not in themselves evidence of any academic or professional interest in medicine. Later on in this notebook, however, and then in a series of others, we find passages extracted by Locke from a very large number of highly technical medical works. Whether or not Locke was at this time planning a career as a physician we cannot now say, but there can be no doubt that he was equipping himself with a thorough medical education.

The most immediately obvious characteristic of Locke's early medical reading is its sheer extent. We have records of about 350 books read by Locke between 1658 and March 1667. The picture that emerges if these are classified by subject is given in the accompanying table (the figures for Locke's final library, as calculated by Harrison and Laslett,[17] have been given for comparison). These figures are inherently imprecise for several reasons: it is often impossible to be certain in the case of books read *c*.1658 and *c*.1667 whether they fall inside or outside the period in question;

---

[16] Bodl. MS Locke e.4, 2.   [17] Harrison and Laslett, 18.

TABLE I. *Locke's reading, 1658–March 1667*

Subject	Books read 1658–March 1667		Final Library
	No.	%	%
Theology and religion	55	15.4	23.8
Medicine	167	46.6	11.1
Politics and law	7	2.0	10.7
Classical literature	9	2.5	10.1
Geography and exploration	19	5.3	7.6
Philosophy	14	3.9	7.4
Natural science	59	16.4	6.6
Modern literature	19	5.3	5.8
History and biography	6	1.7	5.1
Economics	1	0.3	3.5
Reference and bibliography	1	0.3	2.7
Others	1	0.3	5.6
TOTAL	358	100.0	100.0

it is not always clear what should count as one title and what as two or more; and finally the subject-matter of many books makes their allocation to one category or another somewhat arbitrary.[18] Nevertheless, the general picture that emerges is unambiguous enough and would certainly not be significantly modified by any recalculation. Almost half the books that we have any record of Locke reading were medical. Approximately equal second, though a long distance behind, are natural science and theology, each comprising slightly less than one-sixth of the total. None of the others amounts to significantly more than 5 per cent, and one may note that in the case of travel literature Locke's interests seem generally to have been medical or botanical rather than ethnographical. If we knew of Locke only by his commonplace books we would almost certainly think of him as a physician who had wider intellectual interests—a man like Sir Thomas Browne.

Medicine led Locke to iatrochemistry and then to chemistry itself. The

---

[18] I have clearly been less ready than Harrison and Laslett to place books in the residual category of 'Others'.

main period of his chemical researches was the middle 1660s—in particular 1666–7—but he had started reading chemical authors and making notes as early as the late 1650s.[19] One writer whose works he read with great care, and from which he took extremely full notes, was Daniel Sennert.[20] It is striking that though some modern writers have been ready to speculate about the possible influence on Locke of authors whom we have no definite evidence that he ever read,[21] no one so far as I know has ever attempted to find out how much he owed to Sennert, whose works he can be shown to have studied with great care.

It seems not to have been until about 1660 that Locke began seriously to investigate the tenets of the new mechanical philosophy. By May of that year (if not before) he had made Boyle's acquaintance, and as Boyle's work came out, he read each of them carefully, starting with *New Essays Physico-Mechanical touching the Spring of Air*, and continuing with *Certain Physiological Essays, The Style of the Scriptures*, and *The Usefulness of Experimental Natural Philosophy*. At this stage of his life Locke seems to have been reading everything that Boyle was having published.[22] Later on he became rather more selective, though he continued to read a good number of Boyle's works and (when in London) to have fairly frequent personal dealings with Boyle himself.

It is in this context worth noting that Locke's surviving notebooks contain almost no sign of his reading the work which has figured so largely in most recent discussions of Boyle's influence on him—namely *The Origin of Forms and Qualities*. The disparity between the centrality of this work in modern reconstructions and its almost complete absence from Locke's notebooks (there is only one citation, dating from about September 1666[23]) is remarkable and deserves to be pointed out.

From Boyle Locke moved on to Descartes. In the years from 1660 to 1662 he read first the *Principles of Philosophy*; then the *Discourse on Method*, together with the *Dioptrics* and the *Meteors* (though not, it would appear, the *Geometry*); then the *Meditations*, at least some of the

---

[19] Bodl. MS Locke f.25, *passim* (1666–7); Bodl. MS Locke e.4, 118–21 (*c*.1658).

[20] The collection of notes from Sennert's works dating from *c*.1659 to *c*.1662 are in Bodl. MSS Locke f.18 and d.11, in BL Add. MS 32554, and in Locke's copy of Philip Ferrarius' *Lexicon Geographicum* (London, 1657).

[21] e.g. W. von Leyden's speculation about Culverwel's influence on the *Essays on the Law of Nature* (*Law of Nature*, 39–43).

[22] Locke does not appear to have taken notes from *The Sceptical Chymist* (1661) until *c*.1664–5. The early notes from Boyle's works can be found in Bodl. MSS Locke d.10, d.11, f.14, f.19, f.27, and in BL Add. MS 32554.

[23] Bodl. MS Locke f.25, 313.

Objections and Replies, and the *Passions of the Soul*.[24] A few years after leaving Oxford he was to start reading Clerselier's edition of Descartes's letters.[25] Conjectural historians may be reassured to know that Descartes is one of the major thinkers whose influence on Locke actually can be amply documented.

It is therefore all the more important to determine as accurately as we can what the influence was. The passages from Descartes's writings which Locke copied into his commonplace books are overwhelmingly concerned with what we would categorize as natural science rather than philosophy. In the case of the most heavily cited work, *The Principles of Philosophy*, they come almost entirely from Parts III and IV; there are a few from Part II but none at all from Part I. Locke made careful notes on the parts of the work which twentieth-century philosophers tend to skip, and apparently ignored the metaphysical and epistemological material which has been the subject of so much recent discussion. The same is true of the very much smaller number of notes on the *Discourse*, the *Meditations*, and the *Objections and Replies*.

There are of course various ways in which this apparent lack of philosophical interests can be explained—or else explained away. One possibility is that it is real: in the early 1660s Locke was not yet greatly interested in Cartesian metaphysics. Another is that he chose not to use his commonplace books for recording philosophical material, but rather for factual information of various kinds. A third is that he did make philosophical notes, but that the notebooks in which they were recorded have since been lost.

It is I think clear that the choice between these possibilities is not at all straightforward. A final verdict is likely to depend on the answer we give to a critical question of Locke scholarship, though one that has hardly

---

[24] There are many extracts from the *Principles* and the *Meteors* in Bodl. MSS Locke d.11 and f.14 and in BL Add. MS 32554, and others from the *Dioptrics* in BL Add. MS 32554, 49, 76, 90, 176–7, the *Discourse* in Bodl. MS Locke d.11, fo. 10ᵛ, and the *Meditations* in BL Add. MS 32554, 177. There are slightly later citations of the *Objections and Replies* in Bodl. MS Locke f.14, 64, 79, and in the interleaved Bible (Harrison and Laslett, item 309) *apud* 1 Cor. 8: 2, and to the *Passions of the Soul* in Bodl. MS Locke f.14, 25, 92. All these references are to Latin editions: there is no sign in Locke's papers of his reading anything in French before his visit there in 1675–9. Cranston's statement (p. 100) that Locke began reading Descartes in about 1666 is quite erroneous. G. A. J. Rogers, 'Descartes and the Mind of Locke: The Cartesian Impact on Locke's Philosophical Development', in Giulia Belgioioso, Guido Cimino, Pierre Costabel, and Giovanni Papuli (eds.), *Descartes: Il metodo e i saggi* (Rome, 1990), 689–97, is much more satisfactory, though I see no reason for supposing that the notes in BL Add. MS 32554 are earlier than those elsewhere.

[25] Locke was probably reading the Amsterdam 1668 edn. early in 1671. Bodl. MS Locke d.11, fos. 11ᵛ, 39ᵛ, 73ᵛ, Adversaria 1661, 1–2 (Bodl. MS Film 77).

ever been asked, let alone answered: What proportion do the surviving Locke manuscripts bear to the original total? (My own view, which is more than a guess, but certainly not yet a firm conclusion, is that most of the commonplace books have survived, though it is clear that at least a few have not.[26])

Locke's explorations of the mechanical philosophy were not confined to Descartes and Boyle. He read Spinoza's reconstruction of Descartes's *Principles of Philosophy* and at least a little (though probably not much) of Gassendi's *Syntagma*.[27] He also kept up to date with the works produced by other exponents of the new philosophy in England, reading Glanvill's *Vanity of Dogmatizing*, Power's *Experimental Philosophy*, and Hooke's *Micrographia*, in each case very soon after they were first published. He also made a good number of extracts from the *Philosophical Transactions* of the Royal Society. Even after Locke became a Fellow in 1668 he seems to have preferred reading the journal to attending the meetings.

This kind of interest in the mechanical philosophy was hardly unusual in the second half of the seventeenth century. What distinguishes Locke is the form that his interest took. He was alone among the major philosophers in coming to the mechanical philosophy from medicine. Descartes and Leibniz were first-rate mathematicians who made major contributions to dynamics. Malebranche was at least competent. Hobbes was a mathematical bungler, but he was at any rate trying to make progress in the same areas. Problems that were central to them were peripheral to Locke and vice versa.

An awareness of this is essential if we are not to misunderstand Locke's attitude to the mechanical philosophy. I can see *no* evidence that Locke was seriously interested in the kinds of problems that fascinated Malebranche and Leibniz: how motion is communicated from one body to another, what the laws of motion are, the role of conservation principles, etc. The mere fact that Locke wrote nothing about these questions signifies very little; what is decisive is that there is no sign that he was reading about them either.

The problems that engaged Locke in the 1660s lay in a very different area—in medicine, and in the borderland between medicine and natural

[26] The most conspicuous absentee is the 4to notebook 'Adversaria 62', listed in Locke's library in 1681 (Harrison and Laslett, 270) and referred to in several other MSS (e.g. Bodl. MSS Locke f.23, 14 ff.; f.28, 127; f.29, 28).

[27] Locke's notes from the *Syntagma* date from 1660–1, not from 1667 as has frequently been supposed. I have analysed the evidence for Locke's knowledge of Gassendi's philosophy in 'Locke and Gassendi: A Reappraisal', in M. A. Stewart (ed.), *Studies in Seventeenth-Century Philosophy*, Oxford Studies in the History of Philosophy, ii (Oxford, forthcoming).

philosophy. As other material besides *Respirationis Usus* shows, he was particularly interested in animal respiration.[28] This was a problem that had already attracted the attention of several of his ablest contemporaries, including Boyle, Hooke, and Lower. Locke recorded the results of their research and speculated about its significance, but there is no sign that he took any part himself. His own experimental explorations were confined to the far more accessible discipline of chemistry.

This location of Locke's interests was undoubtedly important in shaping his attitude towards the mechanical philosophy. In the physical sciences it had already become the new orthodoxy, but in the disciplines which most interested Locke, in particular in medicine and in chemistry, it faced a much harder fight. Not only were the Aristotelian and alchemical traditions still very much alive, but there was in addition a rival group of moderns. Paracelsus' own writings were notoriously obscure but the modern Paracelsians like van Helmont were considerably more intelligible. Locke read van Helmont's *Ortus Medicinae* at least twice,[29] as well as writings by other members of the school.

While the central paradigmatic example for the mechanical philosophy was the *clock*, its equivalent for the non-mechanical chemists and physicians was *fermentation*. The vigorous enzyme-catalysed reactions that so clearly manifest themselves when wine and beer are fermented were not obviously explicable in terms of the pores, sieves, and curiously shaped particles postulated by the mechanical philosophers. Locke read widely among the literature produced in the course of these debates, but seems in the end to have been undecided about which approach to adopt.[30] There is no trace in his thought at this time (or, I believe, later) of the kind of a priori commitment to mechanism so evident in Descartes.

In the years 1665–7 Locke's attention seems to have been absorbed very largely by medicine and natural philosophy. (Even during the diplomatic visit to Cleves in the winter of 1665–6 most of his reading seems to have been in these areas.) In the preceding years, however, he seems to have been more active in pursuing other interests. Politics was no longer among them: once the *Two Tracts* had been finished, his attention turned elsewhere. All the surviving records of Locke's early political reading date

---

[28] Robert Frank, *Harvey and the Oxford Physiologists* (Berkeley, Calif., 1980), 186–8.

[29] The 1648 edn. in 1660 or 1661, the 1652 edn. between 1665 and 1667.

[30] The main evidence for this is a long note entitled 'Morbus', in BL Add. MS 32554, dating from *c*.1666, printed in P. Romanell, *Locke and Medicine* (Buffalo, NY, 1984), 207–9.

from about 1659–60, and this is unlikely to be accidental.[31] He seems in general to have been drawn to politics only during periods of uncertainty and instability. Once the nature of the Restoration Settlement had become clear, he turned to other matters.

As the figures for Locke's reading which I gave earlier quite unmistakably show, Locke's main area of study outside medicine and natural science was religion. This is an aspect of his life which has received far too little sustained attention, though there are welcome signs that things are starting to improve.[32] Very little is known about his earliest beliefs. His father fought on the parliamentary side in the Civil War, and his uncle Peter seems to have been involved in ejecting recalcitrant Anglican clergy, so the family can plausibly, if imprecisely, be categorized as Puritan. Locke, however, not merely welcomed the Restoration, as many Presbyterians and future Nonconformists of course did, but wrote defending the right of the political authorities to impose forms of worship at a time when it had become quite apparent what the character of the restored Church would be.

Locke's early political writings have quite rightly received a great deal of attention. The very extensive theological reading he was doing during the same period has by contrast been almost entirely ignored. One reason for this is no doubt that the religious side of Locke's thought has in general been given insufficient attention. Another, more specific, is that the misdating of Bodleian Library MS Locke f.14 has had as baleful consequences here as it has elsewhere: the assignation to 1667 of reading undertaken in 1660 hardly assists our understanding of Locke's response to the Restoration. The main reason, however, is that by far the most important single source of information about this aspect of Locke's thoughts, his interleaved Bible,[33] has been almost entirely unexploited.

---

[31] The quotations from Milton and Filmer in Bodl. MSS Locke f.14, 6–7 (that on p. 41 is copied from p. 6), and d.10, 93, 185, are among the very earliest in those notebooks, and probably pre-date the Restoration. Those from Edward Gee, *The Divine Right and Original of the Civil Magistrate from God* (London, 1658) are a little later, probably from about the time of the first *Tract on Government* (Bodl. MS Locke f.14, 78). Laslett's ascription in App. B of his edition of the *Two Treatises* and elsewhere of this material to Locke's first years with Shaftesbury is unfortunately badly mistaken.

[32] W. M. Spellman, *John Locke and the Problem of Depravity* (Oxford, 1988) contains useful insights but unfortunately makes very little use of Locke's unpublished papers. This is not true of a valuable recent paper by John Marshall, 'John Locke and Latitudinarianism', in Richard W. F. Kroll, Richard Ashcraft, and Perez Zagorin (eds.), *Philosophy, Science, and Religion in England 1640–1700* (Cambridge, 1992), 253–82.

[33] Harrison and Laslett, item 309.

Arthur Wainwright, in his recent edition of the *Paraphrase*,[34] has been the only person to make any systematic use of it, and even he seems to have made no attempt to distinguish between notes which can be shown to have been made in the 1660s and other notes made during the final decades of Locke's life.

Locke's theological reading during the early 1660s can be loosely divided into three categories: biblical scholarship, patristics, and Anglican theology. The first of these was an area in which Locke continued to work for the remainder of his life—the *Paraphrase* was the culmination of a lifetime's study, not a late intellectual deviation. The other two areas were of course connected—the study of the Church Fathers was always an Anglican rather than a Puritan activity. Locke seems, for whatever reason, to have been interested primarily in the earlier Fathers—Justin Martyr, Tertullian, Irenaeus, Clement of Alexandria, and Origen. He may have needed to know about them for teaching at Christ Church, but whatever the explanation, it was not an area of enquiry that he pursued later in life.

Locke also spent a fair amount of time reading various Anglican theologians—notably Hammond, but also Heylyn, Pearson, Sanderson, and Hooker. He need not of course have agreed with every remark that he noted down, but there is no sign of any systematic disagreement with any of these authors. In the early 1660s Locke not merely appeared, as was only prudent, but almost certainly *was* an orthodox Anglican.

While at Christ Church Locke presumably attended services in the cathedral. It is, however, worth mentioning how little—how extraordinarily little—we know about his church-going, not merely at this period but at any time in his life. This is one reason why the successive stages of his deviation away from Anglican orthodoxy are so difficult to uncover. Richard Ashcraft has suggested that he was already moving away from the Church of England before he left Oxford, and that he may have been present at a clandestine Nonconformist service in London in January 1667;[35] I am not sure that the manuscript that he cites adequately supports that conclusion, and in any case it can be shown from Locke's weather records that he was in Oxford on the day in question.[36] Ashcraft

---

[34] *Paraphrase*, 691–5.

[35] Richard Ashcraft, *Revolutionary Politics and Locke's 'Two Treatises of Government'* (Princeton, NJ, 1986), 92–4.

[36] 20 Jan. 1667. The weather records for 1666–7 are in Bodl. MS Locke d.9, 528–31; a comparison of them with Locke's known absences from Oxford and with the records of his chemical experiments in Bodl. MS Locke f.25 shows that they can be used as a reliable guide to his whereabouts. The content and provenance of the sermon are usefully discussed by Marshall, 'John Locke and Latitudinarianism', 279, though his belief that the MS may be in Locke's hand is quite unjustified.

is, however, in my view quite right in being sceptical about Cranston's uncorroborated statement that Locke was subsequently a member of Benjamin Whichcote's congregation at St Lawrence Jewry.[37]

Locke's early reading could be analysed in far more detail than has been possible here. The resulting information would have been of some real historical value even if Locke had had the misfortune to die before publishing the works that have given him his subsequent fame. Nevertheless, it is quite unavoidable that the main interest of Locke's commonplace books is that they are *Locke's*, that the man who produced them is the same man that later wrote the *Epistola de Tolerantia*, the *Two Treatises*, and the *Essay*. The question therefore inevitably arises: How much can our understanding of these works be improved by a knowledge of what Locke was doing twenty or thirty years before?

There are a variety of methods that can be used to understand a work like the *Essay*. One is to compare its contents with the views of currently influential twentieth-century philosophers. This is for obvious reasons the dominant mode in which the history of philosophy is now written by the members of philosophy departments in universities, at least in the English-speaking world. It requires considerable analytical skills, which for professional reasons its practitioners would in varying degrees possess, and makes few demands on a historical sensitivity which they might well lack. It also requires nothing more than the survival of the main works of the author in question.

Another more recognizably historical approach requires both the original production and the subsequent survival of a body of comparable literature from the same period. These enable a work to be understood by being placed in its historical context. In practice it turns out that some works are rather more securely locatable in a context than others. The *Two Treatises* can usefully be compared with a great mass of other writings produced during the Exclusion Crisis or defending the right of William III to the throne. The *Essay* on the other hand was a far more isolated work, and a significant part of its historical importance lies precisely in that fact.

A third approach becomes possible if we possess a sufficient quantity of material in the way of personal papers. In these cases we can hope to follow the evolution of someone's thought, to discover what they read

---

[37] Ashcraft, *Revolutionary Politics*, 76. Locke was certainly acquainted with Whichcote by 1678 (*Correspondence*, i. 626) and he remarked to Lady Masham that he had heard some of Whichcote's sermons (J. Le Clerc, *The Life and Character of Mr John Locke* (London, 1706), 28), but neither of these facts shows him to have been a member of Whichcote's congregation. The most we can say is that he may have attended services there.

and what they did not, and by doing this see which problems really engaged their attention and which left them unconcerned.

None of these approaches need be pursued to the exclusion of the others. All of them, if well done, can produce increased understanding. What we should do must, however, depend on what we have got, and in Locke's case we are fortunate to possess an archive far superior to any that survives for any other seventeenth-century philosopher, except Leibniz. If this material had perished life would in many ways be easier, but we would inevitably end up understanding less, and misunderstanding more.

Locke was, like all great philosophers, an idiosyncratic thinker, in the literal sense that the mixture of elements that made up the mind and personality of John Locke was not one which he shared with anyone else. Some of the characteristics possessed by the author of the *Essay* and the *Two Treatises* can be inferred from those works themselves; others cannot, though they may in fact be just as important for our understanding of what Locke was trying to say.

What Locke was not is in some ways as important as what he was. Unlike so many of his contemporaries who wrote on politics, he cared (and knew) little about English history or the Common Law. He was neither a mathematician, nor an astronomer, nor a physicist. In 1690 Locke was a former civil servant with more recent experience of political conspiracy, an intermittently practising physician with a vast knowledge of that intimidating subject, a former chemist who still included an iron furnace among his luggage, an occasional writer on economics who had invested his money in a wide variety of speculative enterprises, a former tutor at Christ Church who had become increasingly interested in the general theory of education, a secret Unitarian interested in biblical criticism and deeply concerned with religious toleration, an irreconcilable opponent of absolute monarchy who had become deeply absorbed in highly abstract problems about the operations of the human understanding.

Locke's years at Oxford are the first period in which we can observe this amalgam being formed. (We know very little about his childhood, and so far, unlike Newton, he seems to have escaped the attentions of the Freudians.) As we have seen, many of the elements of Locke's mature intellectual personality were in place by 1667. There are, however, some significant exceptions, and it is worth saying something about two of these.

The first is that Locke's intellectual approach at Oxford was fundamentally bookish and academic. (It is striking that the literary form of all his early writings is that of a scholastic disputation.) The *Two Tracts on Government* were directed against a rival academic theorist, and in all the medical notes that pre-date 1667 I cannot recall any that show Locke treating any concrete, identifiable patient. It is therefore all the more significant that the two men who most influenced Locke in the years after 1667—Shaftesbury and Sydenham—were so markedly non-academic. Shaftesbury was a brilliant exponent of practical politics, not a political theorist. Sydenham believed that medicine should be learned at the bedside, not in the library. The world of London was very different from the world of Oxford, as perhaps it still is.

It is therefore unsurprising that while at Oxford Locke showed almost no sign of any concern with economics. (There are a few notes on one book that might be so classified: Thomas Mun's *England's Treasure by Foreign Trade*.[38]) Enquiries about the rate of interest belonged to the political and mercantile world of London, not the academic world of Oxford.

Economics is a subject quite obviously missing from Locke's early enquiries. Another more elusive and more controversial absentee is philosophy itself. There is nothing about Locke's pursuits in 1667 that makes it very appropriate to characterize him as a philosopher, as we now understand the term. His intellectual investigations, though wide-ranging, seem to have been pursued in isolation from one another: there is no discernible connection between medical and scientific work on the one hand and the writings on government and the law of nature on the other. It was only after he started on the epistemological enquiries that were to lead to the *Essay* that these areas of his work started to become indirectly (and problematically) related to each other.

This reluctance to describe the young John Locke as a philosopher would not have been immediately intelligible to Locke himself. He had, after all, when seeking entry to Christ Church, described himself as another Ulysses in search of Philosophy, a more desirable Penelope.[39] It is, however, a familiar enough point that in the seventeenth century philosophy covered a much wider field than it does now. One can see something of what it included for Locke from a list of books which he drew up at about the time that he left Oxford.[40] The entries in this list are grouped under a variety of headings: *politici, mathematici, de rebus ecclesiasticis et religione*, and so on. There are 31 in the section marked

---

[38] Read Oct.–Nov. 1664, Bodl. MS Locke f.27, 9–10.
[39] *Correspondence*, i. 8.   [40] This list is in PRO 30/24/47/30 fos. 42–3.

philosophici, but though a few of the works mentioned would now be classified as philosophical,[41] most are concerned with natural science, or even less abstract matters such as voyages of exploration or agricultural improvements. There is no sign either that Locke saw the subjects that we describe as philosophy as forming a distinct category or that he was particularly interested in them.

Further evidence for the absence of any particular concern with the discipline that we call philosophy emerges from some slightly later documents. In the early 1670s Locke seems to have become unusually interested in the classification of the various branches of human knowledge. The earliest of these analyses, dating from around 1670, divides knowledge into four areas: *theologia, politia, prudentia*, and *physica*.[42] The disciplines which we see as making up philosophy are either omitted altogether or else placed under a variety of headings—ethics under *theologia*, the study of the intellect, will, and passions under *physica*.

What these facts suggest is that the kind of intellectual explorations that Locke began in 1671 had no secure location on his own current maps of the intellectual world. This was not because Locke was a provincial or isolated thinker, cut off from the mainstream in a stagnant intellectual backwater. Oxford was no backwater, and in England no recognizable mainstream existed. Here there is a striking contrast with France, where a culture of abstract philosophical discussion conducted in the vernacular had already come into existence. Locke's ignorance of French made the greater part of this inaccessible to him, and in England there was as yet nothing comparable.[43] Hobbes's feelings of intellectual isolation once

[41] Sextus Empiricus, Francisco Sanches, and Cornelius Agrippa are mentioned in the list, though there is no evidence of Locke reading any of their works—their names were taken from Evelyn's translation of Naudé's *Instructions concerning . . . a Library* (London, 1661).

[42] Adversaria 1661 (copy in Bodl. MS Film 77), opening pages (unnumbered). This is printed in *Two Tracts*, 245–6. Abrams's dating of this to *c.*1661 is, however, almost certainly wrong. Nothing else in this MS is as early as this: the entries immediately following cannot have been made before 1668 and almost certainly date from *c.*1670–1. Another closely similar piece is Bodl. MS Locke c.28, 41, endorsed by Locke's 'Sapientia 72', presumably dating from 1672.

[43] An illustration of the paucity of philosophical books published in England before 1690 can be seen from Locke's library. Harrison and Laslett classify as philosophical 65 books published in England; 45 of these appeared in 1690 or later. Of the remainder, 2 are copies of More's *Utopia*, 8 are by Bacon, and 6 by Henry More. The others are Cudworth's *True Intellectual System* (1678), a volume containing two short treatises by Joseph Glanvill and George Rust (1682), Stanley's *History of Philosophy* (1687), and a pamphlet by Roger Coke, *Treatises of the Nature of Man* (1685). Even if we add *Leviathan* to the list, the total is not impressive, and the number of books available to Locke in 1667 or 1671 was evidently smaller still. The contrast with the plentiful philosophical literature published after 1690 is obvious.

he had come back from France were not solely the result of his abrasive temperament and objectionable doctrines, important as both of these undoubtedly were.

One major part of Locke's achievement was therefore to help create the discipline to which he made such a major contribution. Under these circumstances it is hardly surprising that the writing of the *Essay* occupied him for so many years. No doubt the time in their lives when different philosophers do their most significant work is powerfully affected by individual factors of personality as well as situation, but one cannot easily imagine an intellectual trajectory like Berkeley's in the Oxford of the 1650s and 1660s. Berkeley was an original thinker of a very high order, but he was able to write as he did because he was working within an established intellectual tradition, albeit one of quite recent origin. For the young Locke, nothing comparable was available. The tradition in which Berkeley was to work did not yet exist: a major part of Locke's achievement was to create it.

2

The Foundations of Knowledge and the Logic of Substance: The Structure of Locke's General Philosophy

M. R. AYERS

1. The Foundations of Knowledge

Gassendi, Hobbes, and Locke all categorically asserted the independent authority of the senses as knowledge-producing faculties. As Hobbes put it, '*Knowledge of Fact* . . . is nothing else but Sense and Memory, and is *Absolute Knowledge*.'[1] Locke announced the senses' immediate authority on questions of existence just as bluntly: they are 'the proper and sole Judges of this thing'.[2] On the other side, Platonistic or Augustinian philosophers such as Mersenne, Descartes, and Arnauld firmly subordinated the senses to the intellect. This division constitutes one of the great watersheds of early modern epistemology, and is well illustrated by Locke's response, as we may suppose it to be, to an argument in the Port Royal *Logic*. The *Logic* had argued, in effect, that the doctrine of transubstantiation does not contradict the senses, since even ordinarily the senses must be interpreted by reason. In the case of the Eucharist we simply have special reasons for taking the body of Christ to be behind a wafer-like

---

This chapter was written in response to a request for a broad discussion of Locke's general philosophy, and necessarily overlaps material in my more recently published monograph, *Locke*, 2 vols. (London, 1991). Nevertheless, since some of that material is here expanded (e.g. the discussion of Draft A and the Hellenistic parallels), and some compressed, while all has been taken from its various contexts and reordered, I hope that the present chapter will help to clarify (my view of) Locke's theory.

[1] Thomas Hobbes, *Leviathan* (London, 1651), I. ix. 'Absolute' by contrast with the hypothetical sentences which constitute science.

[2] *Essay*, IV. xi. 2. The phrase occurs in Draft A, in the original version of this passage (*Drafts*, i. 20 f.).

appearance.[3] Locke brought the independent authority of the senses in the Protestant cause. Because the Romanist is indoctrinated from childhood with the principle that Church and Pope are infallible, 'How is he prepared easily to swallow, not only against all probability, but even the clear evidence of his Senses, the Doctrine of Transubstantiation? This Principle has such an influence on his Mind, that he will take that to be Flesh, which he sees to be Bread.'[4]

It is well known that Gassendi's mature epistemology was built on Epicurean and Stoic sources. Locke's similar debt to ancient empiricism was less explicit and may or may not have been less direct, but it is no less certain. His treatment of 'sensitive knowledge of existence' is an example. He identified the 'evidence' of such knowledge with our immediate knowledge in sensation 'that something doth exist without us, which causes [an] *Idea* in us': accordingly 'I have by the Paper affecting my Eyes, that *Idea* produced in my Mind, which whatever Object causes, I call *White*; by which I know, that that Quality or Accident (*i.e.* whose appearance before my Eyes, always causes that *Idea*) doth really exist.'[5] This direct causal realism has much the same general structure, and is expressed by means of the same example, as the theory attributed to the Stoic Chrysippus in a work present in Locke's library: 'An impression is an affection occurring in the soul, which reveals itself and its cause. Thus, when through sight we observe something white, the affection is what is engendered in the soul through vision; and it is this affection which enables us to say that there is a white object which activates us.'[6]

Even more convincing evidence of an ancient source is provided by Locke's argument that metaphysical mistrust of the senses is mistrust of a basic cognitive faculty, and is therefore self-destructive: 'For we cannot act any thing, but by our Faculties: nor talk of Knowledge it self, but by the help of those Faculties, which are fitted to apprehend even what Knowledge is.'[7] The suggestion that the senses are the source of the sceptic's own capacity to conceive of knowledge itself echoes the Epicurean onslaught on the sceptic in *De Rerum Natura*: 'if he has never seen

---

[3] A. Arnauld and P. Nicole, *La Logique, ou L'art de penser*, ed. P. Clair and F. Girbal (Paris, 1965), IV. xii. Cf. IV. i.

[4] *Essay*, IV. xx. 10. The thought was an early one: see *Drafts*, i. 71.

[5] *Essay*, IV. xi. 2.

[6] Cited in A. A. Long and D. N. Sedley (eds.), *The Hellenistic Philosophers* (Cambridge, 1987), i. 237. The passage is from *De Placitis Philosophorum*, in Stephanus' edn. of Plutarch. As well as the similarity, there is a difference, in that Chrysippus' 'impression' not only gives notice of its cause, but reveals the intrinsic character of its cause.

[7] *Essay*, IV. xi. 3.

anything true in the world, from where does he get his knowledge of what knowing and not knowing are?' For Lucretius, the concept of (or acquaintance with) truth 'has its origin in the senses'. Since reason is the product of the senses, 'if the senses are not true, all reason becomes false as well'.[8]

A more pervasive debt, however, was to the doctrine of signs, notes, or marks through which we can have knowledge of things not evident in themselves. A distinction was widely drawn in ancient philosophy between reminiscent signs of such things as are only sometimes not evident and indicative signs of things which are by nature never evident. In the case of reminiscent or empirical signs constant experience sets up a connection between the sign and what it signifies. In the case of indicative signs, we reason to something which is such that, unless it existed, the sign would not exist: for example, sweating is an indicative sign of invisible pores in the skin, and certain motions of the body indicate the presence of the soul. The Sceptic Sextus Empiricus granted the cogency of reminiscent signs as a basis for opinion, but rejected indicative signs. Against Sextus, Gassendi argued on behalf of indicative signs that the proof of pores in the skin appeals only to principles founded on experience. Locke structured his treatment of probability around the same distinction between beliefs based on correlations falling *within* experience and inferences going *beyond* experience. With respect to the latter he agreed with Gassendi, arguing that hypotheses about what lies 'beyond the discovery of the senses' can properly be based on a 'wary reasoning from Analogy'.[9]

Trust in the senses and the doctrine of signs came together in the principle that sensory appearances are always true indicative signs. The Epicurean thought seems to have been that, even if the same thing presents different appearances in circumstances in which it has not itself changed, or appears different to different observers at the same time (as in the standard sceptical example of water appearing hot to one person and cold to another), the difference in appearance accurately reflects a difference in the conditions of perception and so is a true sign of the object in those

---

[8] Lucretius, *De Rerum Natura*, Book IV, lines 474 ff.: 'at id ipsum/quaeram, cum in rebus veri nil viderit ante/unde sciat quid sit scire et nescire vicissim/notitiem veri neque sensus posse refelli/. . . an ab sensu falso ratio orta valebit/dicere eos contra, quae tota ab sensibus orta est?/ qui nisi sunt veri, ratio quoque falsa fit omnis' (cited by Long and Sedley, *The Hellenistic Philosophers*, i. 78–9. The argument is recorded in Gassendi's *Syntagma Epicuri Philosophiae*, which was plagiarized in Thomas Stanley's *History of Philosophy* of 1655. Of these, Locke owned Lucretius and only a later (1687) edn. of Stanley.

[9] Pierre Gassendi, *Opera Omnia* (Lyons, 1658), i. 79–86; *Essay*, IV. xvi. 12.

conditions. If we wrongly place the difference in the object itself, it is that judgement which is false, not the appearance. One example, repeated by Gassendi, is the changing appearance of an object as it grows more distant: the appearance is not false, although a judgement that the object is itself growing smaller or changing shape would be false.[10] In the *Essay* this doctrine took the form of the principle that simple ideas are always 'true', 'real', and 'adequate': 'their Truth consists in nothing else, but in such Appearances, as are produced in us, and must be suitable to those Powers, [God] has placed in external Objects, or else they could not be produced in us'.[11] The final clause echoes the Stoic characterization of a 'cognitive' (or 'grasping') impression as 'of such a kind as could not arise from what is not', and there are other Stoic resonances in Locke's account of simple ideas.[12] Yet the general point here is the broadly Epicurean one that simple ideas are dependable 'distinguishing marks' which serve their purpose whatever unknown difference lies behind the sensible distinction. For that reason they can fulfil the role of 'signs' of another kind, signs in the natural language of thought which signify their unknown causes. The signs that naturally *indicate* qualities or powers naturally *stand for* them in thought.[13] This neat conjunction of epistemology and theory of representation, encapsulated in the ambivalence of the terms 'sign' and 'signify' in Locke's usage, lies at the heart of his general philosophy.

The principle of the truth of simple ideas derives from ancient empiricism, but also responds to the very different Cartesian trust in innate 'simple notions' or 'simple natures', not to speak of the Scholastic doctrine, appealed to by Arnauld in his objections to the *Meditations*, that concepts or 'simple apprehensions' are all true.[14] It plays an important

---

[10] Lucretius, *De Rerum Natura*, Book IV, lines 499–500; Gassendi, *Opera Omnia*, i. 79–86. Gassendi's source is Sextus Empiricus, *Against the Professors*, 7. 206–10, cited in Long and Sedley, *The Hellenistic Philosophers*, i. 81.   [11] *Essay*, II. xxxii. 14.

[12] Locke's account of 'clear and distinct' simple ideas corresponds to the other main features of a Stoic cognitive impression, that it 'arises from what is and is stamped and impressed exactly in accordance with what is': as Locke puts it, 'our *simple Ideas* are *clear*, when they are such as the Objects themselves, from whence they were taken, did or might, in a well-ordered Sensation or Perception, present them' (II. xxxix. 2). The expression 'clear and distinct' is, of course, Cartesian, but it echoes equivalent Stoic expressions, as Descartes was doubtless well aware. Cf. Long and Sedley, *The Hellenistic Philosophers*, i. 241–53, ii. 243–54.   [13] Cf. *Essay*, IV. v. 2–5, IV. xxi. 4.

[14] Cf. *The Philosophical Writings of Descartes*, trans. J. Cottingham, R. Stoothoff, and D. Murdoch (Cambridge, 1985), i. 44–7, ii. 145 f. (AT X 419–23 and VII 206). In Draft A Locke accepts even with respect to complex ideas of substances the Scholastic argument that a false concept of *x* is impossible because it would not be a concept of *x* but of

part in Locke's explanation of both the certainty and the limitations of sensitive knowledge: the idea of white naturally signifies the power to cause that idea, i.e. the quality whiteness, however wrong we may be in our hypotheses about what constitutes whiteness in the object. Sensitive knowledge of existence, in other words, is theory-neutral or pre-theoretical, and that is why it is secure. Moreover, the principle was readily extensible to all *powers*: by means of the idea of power the sensible change in wax can be employed as a sign both of whatever in the sun melts wax and of whatever in wax causes it to be melted. Hence, with a murmured apology, Locke could treat ideas of powers as simple ideas and knowledge of powers as effectively foundational.[15]

In one respect Locke's determination to keep the deliverances of the senses independent of reason and prior to all inference or 'judgement' led him into an even more extreme position than Gassendi's. Gassendi recognized that individual deliverances of the senses may by themselves prompt judgements which need to be corrected, falling back on the not implausible thought that the senses are here correcting themselves rather than being corrected by independent reason. His account of Epicurus accordingly placed the criterion of truth in the consensus or 'suffrage' of the senses.[16] It is possible that Locke regarded any such move as too great a concession to reason, a denial of the immediate, unreasoned 'evidence' of sensitive knowledge. That would help to explain what might otherwise seem an amazing fact: the *Essay*, dedicated to the examination of the extent and limits of knowledge, contains no direct discussion of that most hackneyed of epistemological topics, sensory illusion. Locke did mention a standard sceptical example of something like illusion in the chapter on primary and secondary qualities, but his employment of the primary–secondary distinction to explain 'how the same Water, at the same time, may produce the *Idea* of Cold by one Hand, and of Heat by the other' was in effect a denial that *either* sensation is illusory. For *each* sensation, he suggested, is an appropriately differentiated sign of what gives rise to such sensations, namely 'the increase or diminution of the motion of the minute Parts of our Bodies, caused by the Corpuscles of' other bodies. Much the same point emerges from a discussion of the possibility of

something else (*Drafts*, i. 18). In the *Essay* he affirms its traditional, more correctly Aristotelian rival, the principle that 'our ideas . . . cannot properly and simply in themselves be said to be true or false' (II. xxxii. 1). In the sense in which ideas can loosely be said to be true in relation to reality, not all ideas are true, although all simple ideas are true.

[15] Cf. *Essay*, II. xxi. 3, II. xxiii. 7–9.   [16] Gassendi, *Opera Omnia*, iii. 7.

people with reversed sensations of colour.[17] Behind these arguments lies the ancient doctrine that appearances are always true.

There is, however, a much more significant difference between Locke's mature epistemology and that of Gassendi. Epicurean philosophy seems not to have distinguished sharply between the abstraction from sense experience of concepts giving meaning to our words, and the acquisition of propositional knowledge constituting the starting-points of reasoned enquiry. As Epicurus himself put his theory of generalized images or 'preconceptions', 'First . . . we must grasp the things which underlie words, so that we may have them as a reference point . . . and not have everything undiscriminated for ourselves as we attempt infinite chains of proofs, or have words which are empty.'[18] The preconception of *man* was identified with the knowledge that 'Such and such a kind of thing is a man' and was treated, in effect, as at once an empirical summation of experience, a definition, and a foundational premiss of rational proof. Accordingly Gassendi, working within a logical tradition which laid great emphasis on the distinction between concept and judgement, term and proposition, held not only that all our concepts are acquired in experience, but also that all our knowledge derives from sensory knowledge. As he put it, 'all the evidence and certainty which attaches to a general proposition depends upon that which has been gained from an induction of particulars'.[19]

Locke himself, whether or not in imitation of Gassendi, adopted broadly the same position in his earliest extant essay in epistemology, in what is now known as *Essays on the Law of Nature*. He there claimed that knowledge of our duty to God and our fellows lies within reach of human reason employing concepts and *premisses* derived from sense experience. Like Epicurus, he supported the claim that we need empirical premisses by an appeal to the principle that all reasoning is *ex cognitis et concessis*. Like Gassendi, he extended the claim to mathematics. Not only are such mathematical notions as those of a line, a plane, and a solid drawn from experience, but 'other common principles and axioms too' are given to reason by the senses.[20] In ethics, the senses supply reason with two kinds of premiss: first, evidence of design in the world from which we can infer the existence of a Creator whose will it is our duty to obey; and, second,

---

[17] *Essay*, II. viii. 21; II. xxxii. 15–16. For fuller discussion of both these topics, see Ayers, *Locke*, i. 166–7 and 207 ff.

[18] Cited by Long and Sedley, *The Hellenistic Philosophers*, i. 87 f. See the editors' note on these passages.

[19] Pierre Gassendi, *Institutio Logica*, ed. H. Jones (Assen, 1981), 61.

[20] *Law of Nature*, 146 ff.

knowledge of various characteristics of human nature which reveal God's particular purposes in creating us, and so the content of his will for us, the law of nature. That might suggest that the law of nature is contingent, but Locke emphasized, in opposition to extreme voluntarism, that it is not arbitrarily mutable in so far as it is tied to human nature: it has a conditional necessity in that it stands or falls with human nature 'quae iam est', as it now is.[21]

Locke apparently became dissatisfied with this account of knowledge and its foundations in the course of writing the so-called Draft A of the *Essay* in 1671. At first he was still able to say that the certainty of geometrical demonstration 'can be no greater then that of discerning by our eyes, which the very name "Demonstration" how highly magnified soever for its certainty doth signifye'; and that the axioms or maxims of geometry gain assent 'only by the testimony and assureance of our senses'.[22] At the same time he asked whether axioms might not relate 'to the signification of the words them selves they being relative words'. The model is essentially Epicurean: first, 'by constant observation of our senses espetialy our eys', we find certain proportions to hold without exception; we then assume they hold universally, employing them in some unexplained way as 'standards' of measurement embodied in the meaning of our terms.[23] In effect, Locke was here offering a choice: axioms can be regarded either as straightforward empirical summaries, open to empirical refutation, or as quasi-definitions founded on experience, and so 'barely about the signification of words'. Throughout Draft A he continued to develop the thought, with particular reference to propositions about substances, that universal propositions are either, if 'instructive', uncertain or, if certain, mere assertions or denials of identity with respect to our ideas, and consequently 'only verbal . . . and not instructive'.[24] Yet very soon mathematical propositions came to be located unequivocally in the class of propositions about ideas employed as standards, so that demonstration was now explained as 'the beare shewing of things or proposeing them to our senses *or understandings* soe as to make us take notice of them' (the 'understanding' being here the imagination).[25] At the same time Locke evidently had doubts about regarding them as merely verbal, more than

---

[21] Ibid. 150–8, 190–202.   [22] *Drafts*, i. 22–3.

[23] Ibid. 22 f. Cf. Long and Sedley, *The Hellenistic Philosophers*, i. 87–8.

[24] Cf. *Drafts, i.* 55: 'Indeed all Universall propositions are either Certain and then they are only verball but are not instructive. Or else are Instructive & then are not Certain.'

[25] Ibid. 50. But the preference for this explanation of mathematical truths as 'truths of eternall verity' is fixed as early as pp. 26–7. For explicit reference to imagination, see p. 28: 'any mathematical figure imagind in our mindes'.

once hinting that mathematics has a guaranteed relation to reality. This thought was expressed, for example, in an interpolated qualification of the instructive–verbal dichotomy: 'Mathematicall universal propositions are both true & instructive because as those Ideas are in our mindes soe are the things without us.'[26] The assumption appears to be that a condition of the instructive certainty of mathematics is the existence of its objects, and it is claimed that that condition is necessarily fulfilled just because of the simplicity of the ideas with which mathematics deals. Yet a final 'memorandum' draws a sharp contrast between particular knowledge of existence (which is dependent on the senses) and universal knowledge (which is hypothetical and 'only supposes existence'), seeming to record Locke's recognition that he had more work to do.[27]

So in the shifting course of Draft A Locke moved discernibly closer to the doctrine of the *Essay* itself, in particular towards a clear decision to restrict the essential role of the senses to the acquisition of simple ideas and (apart from questions of probability) to knowledge of particular existence and coexistence. Such less extreme empiricism, however, was entirely consistent with his original and continuing purposes. For his interest in epistemology seems to have been motivated by two early concerns: first, by his dissatisfaction with arbitrary appeals to conscience and divine inspiration (not to speak of their threat to civil order); and, second, by the study of medicine and corpuscularian science. In ethics his first considered epistemological reaction was to uphold the possibility of a reasonable morality based on the light of nature, empirically conceived. In natural philosophy, however, he adopted an opposite, if similarly 'empiricist' line: the senses give knowledge of no more than the sensible effects and powers of substances, while the intrinsic properties underlying these effects remain beyond the reach of our faculties. The 'corpuscularian' theory is simply our best inadequate speculation. The combination of epistemological optimism in ethics with pessimism regarding the possibility of a proper 'science' of nature was not, of course, in the least inconsistent. Together with his claim that careful observation

[26] Ibid. 57. On p. 26 the certainty of mathematics is attributed to 'the cleare knowledge of our owne Ideas, & the certainty that quantity and number existing have the same propertys and relations that their Ideas have one to another'. Cf. pp. 25 and 28.

[27] Ibid. 82. Cf. the disclaimer on p. 75 (strictly true, but as glossed false), 'That I never said that the truth of all propositions was to be made out to us by the senses for this was to leave noe roome for reason at all, which I think by a right traceing of those Ideas which it hath received from Sense or Sensation may come to knowledge of many propositions which our senses could never have discovered.' Locke *had* said that axioms, unless merely verbal, were known only through the senses.

and experiment can yield probabilities sufficient for the direction of action, it constituted his pious thesis that the 'candle, that is set up in us', for all its limitations, 'shines bright enough for all our purposes'.[28] Certainly it answered to his actual targets, on the one hand religious dogmatists and enthusiasts immune to what Locke saw as the reasonable argument of the natural law tradition, and on the other hand scientific dogmatists who trusted too much in reason's power to penetrate to the essences of things.

The chief theoretical problem facing Locke as an epistemologist was that of developing an account of the two sorts of science, moral and natural, which would explain very clearly why the one is possible for us while the other is not. From the first an analogy between ethics and the indubitably available science of mathematics was a promising line of approach. Yet his original quasi-Gassendist view of mathematics as a science with empirical axioms was a predictable loser, and the felt need for an explanation of the *necessity* of mathematics was surely Locke's motive for the experimental departures of Draft A.[29] In consequence the analogy between mathematics and ethics was actually weakened. If mathematics is a priori, what about ethics? In 1671 he was already attracted by the thought that moral notions, unlike ideas of substances, are constructed by us without reference to reality, and are therefore clearly knowable. Yet that left or even exacerbated the problem of how we can know whether they correspond to natural law, in Locke's terms the real problem of the foundations of ethics. As he himself pointed out, that is not a question that the senses can answer. In Draft B the problem was noted and set aside.[30]

It was eventually solved by a number of changes to the accounts both of mathematics and of ethics which restored the analogy between them to its full force. Mathematics was no longer taken to have existential import,[31] and its subject-matter was accordingly reclassified as arbitrarily constructible *complex* ideas, ideas of simple modes, comparable to the mixed modes which comprise the subject-matter of ethics.[32] Locke now dealt with the problem of its informativeness by developing a distinction between trifling knowledge of *identity* and informative knowledge of *relation*, the acknowledged ancestor of Kant's distinction between analytic and synthetic a priori judgement.[33] A corollary of these changes was a

---

[28] *Essay*, I. i. 5. See e.g. IV. xii. 11.

[29] Cf. *Drafts*, i. 26: 'proportions of numbers & extensions . . . are soe ex necessitate rei'.

[30] Ibid. 41–2 and 269–70.   [31] Cf. *Essay*, IV. iv. 8.   [32] Ibid. II. xiii–xvi.

[33] Ibid. IV. i. 5 and 7, IV. viii. 8. Cf. Kant, *Prolegomena to any Future Metaphysics*, sect. 3.

much sharper, but still firmly imagist, account of abstraction, owing something (as it seems) to Hobbes.

Already presaged in Draft A was an ordering of the degrees of certainty more like Mersenne's than Gassendi's. While maintaining the independent authority of the senses almost more rigorously than Gassendi himself, the *Essay* assigned to them no more than the third degree of knowledge, after intuition and demonstration.[34] Locke did not, however, adopt Mersenne's respect for maxims, and indeed, since axioms had lost their role as empirical premisses even in Draft A, the principle that 'all Reasonings are *ex praecognitis, et praeconcessis*' was effectively abandoned.[35] In fact the *Essay* deliberately seems to tread a careful path between Mersenne's and Gassendi's views about maxims and the relation between general and particular certainty. For Mersenne the proposition that the body is larger than a finger draws certainty from the prior certainty of the general maxim that the whole is greater than a part. For Gassendi, the latter is certain only in so far as supporting judgements like the former are certain. For Locke, both are equally self-evident, and his rider, that 'if one of these have need to be confirmed to him by the other, the general has more need to be let into his Mind by the particular, than the particular by the general',[36] is not Gassendi's inductivism, but the point that the immediate objects of universal intuition are particulars abstractly considered. We need to see the relation in the particular case before us (e.g. a geometrical diagram), in order to universalize the perception to all cases relevantly like that case.

Locke approximated his conception of morality to his reformed model of an a priori science chiefly by extending and elaborating a thought already hovering in the *Essays on the Law of Nature*: the moral law is necessarily binding on all rational creatures capable of pleasure and pain.

---

[34] *Essay*, IV. ii. 14. Cf. *Drafts*, i. 45: 'all such affirmations and negations [of universal identities] are made . . . as the clearest knowledge we can have which indeed is internal and mentall demonstration as certain and evident and perhaps more then the external' ('as . . . can have' interpolated). Contrast the earlier emphasis on the senses, p. 43: 'all a man can certainly know of things existing without him is only particular propositions, for which he hath demonstration by his senses the best ground of science he can have or expect and what soe comes to his understanding, he receives as certain knowledge and demonstration'.

[35] *Essay*, IV. vii. 8

[36] Ibid. IV. vii. 11. The example of the body and a finger is discussed at IV. xii. 3. Cf. Marin Mersenne, *La Verité des sciences contre les sceptiques ou Pyrrhoniens* (Paris, 1652), 177 (cited by Susan James, 'Certain and Less Certain Knowledge', *Proceedings of the Aristotelian Society*, 87 (1987), 227–42: 232); Gassendi, *Institution Logica*, 61. For the principle that 'the immediate Object of all our Reasoning and Knowledge, is nothing but particulars', cf. *Essay*, IV. xvii. 8.

What he added to this thought in the *Essay* was the clear statement that the law is independent of any other natural characteristics of human beings: 'were there a Monkey, or any other Creature to be found, that had the use of Reason . . . he would no doubt be subject to Law'. One advantage of this emphasis, whether or not it was a motive for it, was a stronger defence against the extreme voluntarism of revelationists than had been afforded by Locke's earlier model, according to which the law is rooted in nothing more secure than an empirically known, mutable human nature. The idea of 'the *moral Man*', Locke now said, is like the idea of a mode, an 'immoveable unchangeable *Idea*', a postulate of the hypothetical science which is independent of contingent facts.[37] At the same time our own subjection to law, as satisfying this idea, is known intuitively with every thought we have, while the existence of the divine lawgiver is strictly demonstrable.

It should not be supposed that these changes related only to the a priori sciences of mathematics and ethics, since they constituted a clarification or development of Locke's conception of science in general. Since all universal knowledge is hypothetical,[38] empirical premises are unnecessary to *any* science with respect to its status as knowledge or *scientia*. Although he rejected the Cartesian understanding of geometry as explication of the essence of matter, the general model of the fully intelligible, demonstrative science suited both his mechanist sympathies and his scepticism about natural essences very well indeed. The ideal mechanics could be supposed to have a quasi-geometrical form with intuitively evident foundations, hooking on to reality through the medium of empirical existential propositions rather than by means of contingent premises or axioms of the science itself. In other words, the propositions of natural science, if we could ever achieve such a thing, would be hypothetically necessary in just the same way as those of ethics and mathematics.[39] Yet, whereas in the case of the latter hypothetical necessity is all that is aimed for by the science (and the two existential propositions necessary for the conclusion that ethics applies to *us* are known by intuition and demonstration), it would be useless to build a purported natural science unless we knew experientially that things exist with essences answering to our ideas.[40]

---

[37] *Essay*, III. xi. 16.   [38] Cf. ibid. IV. xi. 14.

[39] Cf. ibid. IV. vi. 11: if we knew real essences, 'to know the Properties of *Gold*, it would be no more necessary that *Gold* should exist, and that we should make experiments upon it, than it is necessary for the knowing the Properties of a Triangle, that a Triangle should exist in any Matter, the *Idea* in our Minds would serve for the one as well as the other'.

[40] Cf. ibid. II. i. 10, II. xxx. 5, IV. xii. 12, etc.

Employing this model, Locke could argue, on the one hand, that our sensitive knowledge of existence is at too coarse a level for the purpose; and, on the other hand, that the corpuscularians' failure to achieve geometrical intelligibility in their speculative explanations is itself enough to show that their hypotheses have failed to capture the essences or natures of material things. It was thoughts like these which underlay his arguments about substance, to which it is now time to turn.

II. The Logic of Substance

To understand Locke's claim that 'of Substance, we have no idea of what it is, but only a confused, obscure one of what it does', it is again useful to look at earlier empiricist argument. Gassendi offers an obvious precedent. In the Second Meditation Descartes had argued that it is by means of the intellect, not the senses or imagination, that we conceive of wax as 'something extended, flexible and mutable', underlying the variety of changing appearances which we perceive as it melts. Elsewhere he had claimed that further intellectual reflection allows us to identify extension as the principal attribute, or essence, of matter.[41] Gassendi's response was to agree with 'what everyone commonly asserts, *viz.* that the concept of the wax or of its substance can be abstracted from the concepts of its accidents', but to deny that this means 'that the substance or nature of the wax is itself distinctly conceived'. 'Admittedly', Gassendi remarked, 'you perceive that the wax or its substance must be something over and above such [sensible] forms; but what this something is you do not perceive. . . . The alleged naked, or rather hidden, substance is something that we can neither ourselves conceive nor explain to others.' According to Gassendi's argument here the positive content of our ideas of material substances is wholly provided by the senses, and 'the mind is not . . . distinct from the imaginative faculty'. Hence essence always escapes us. Much the same goes for our idea of the mind or 'thinking thing': 'Who doubts that you are thinking?', he asked. 'What we are unclear about . . . is that inner substance of yours whose property is to think.'[42] Consequently, Descartes 'can be compared to a blind man who, on feeling heat and being told that it comes from the sun, thinks that he has a clear and distinct idea of the sun in that, if anyone asks him what the sun is, he can reply: "It is a heating thing." '[43]

[41] Descartes, *Philosophical Writings*, ii. 20–1 (AT VII 30 ff.). Cf. p. 54 and i. 227 (AT VII 78 and IXB 46).   [42] Ibid. ii. 189–93.
[43] Ibid. 234–5.

It seems to me that whoever seriously reflects on Gassendi's meaning and motivation, and on the connections between his argument and Locke's, will be unlikely to adhere to that (to my mind) perverse interpretation of the latter, still ferociously defended in some quarters,[44] according to which the general idea of substance is for Locke the idea of a pure logical subject underlying all properties, known or unknown, and for that reason unknowable in principle.

One part of Locke's position, indeed, was common to all the 'New Philosophers', dogmatic or anti-dogmatic. That was the anti-Aristotelian point that the multiplicity of sensible qualities and powers through which we know any substantial thing is not a multiplicity in the thing itself, but a multiplicity of ways in which the thing affects the senses or sensibly interacts with other things. Hobbes called it 'a diversity of seeming', defining an 'accident' as 'concipiendi corporis modum', a way of conceiving of body (or a body). The model echoes Epicurus' account of attributes,[45] and is present throughout Locke's *Essay*, even in passages which may seem to have little to do with substance. Here is a famous sentence: 'Though the Qualities that affect our Senses, are, in the things themselves, so united and blended, that there is no separation, no distance between them; yet 'tis plain, the *Ideas* they produce in the Mind, enter by the Senses simple and unmixed.'[46]

Such an explanation of the relation between the one substance and its many accidents was a common element in attacks on Scholastic 'real accidents', in particular on the debased account of the substance–accident relation involved in the doctrine of transubstantiation. Kenelm Digby attributed the Scholastic notion to a naïve confusion:

what is but one entire thing in it self, seemeth to be many distinct things in my understanding: whereby . . . I shall be in danger . . . to give actuall Beings to the quantity, figure, colour, smell, tast, and other accidents of the apple, each of them distinct one from another, as also from the substance which they clothe; because I find the notions of them really distinguished (as if they were different Entities) in my mind.[47]

---

[44] Most recently, as far as I know, by Jonathan Bennett, in 'Substratum', *History of Philosophy Quarterly*, 4 (1987), an article which he elsewhere describes as showing that 'when Ayers gets down to details regarding Locke on "substratum", his main work is done for him not by special attention to the historical background, but by inattention to what Locke actually wrote' (in P. Hare (ed.), *Doing Philosophy Historically* (Buffalo, NY, 1988), 68).

[45] Hobbes, *Leviathan*, III. xxxiv; *De Corpore*, II. viii. 2 (*Latin Works*, ed. W. Molesworth (London, 1839), i). For Epicurus the attributes of body are individually picked out and spoken of in consequence of the way the mind perceives or focuses on the whole (*Letter to Herodotus*, 68–73, cited in Long and Sedley, *The Hellenistic Philosophers*, i. 34; ii. 27).

[46] *Essay*, II. ii. 1.

[47] Kenelm Digby, *Two Treatises: Of Bodies and Of Man's Soule* (London, 1645), 3.

In one passage in the *Essay* Locke attacked the pretensions of the
traditional doctrine of substance and accident in much the same terms as
Digby, emphasizing the mistake of taking the one–many relationship to
be a real relationship between really distinct beings: 'They who first ran
into the Notion of *Accidents*, as a sort of real Beings, that needed something to inhere in, were forced to find out the word *Substance*, to support
them.'[48] But the chapter 'Of our Complex *Ideas* of Substances' opens
with the obverse point. Because of the presumable unity of the thing, we
fail to recognize the multiplicity in our idea of it: 'we are apt afterward to
talk of and consider as one simple *Idea*, [that] which indeed is a compli-
cation of many *Ideas* together'.[49] The immediate target here is again
Aristotelian, but this time it is the notion that we can achieve simple
conceptions of substances correspondent to their real simplicity or unity.
Those who think that their would-be scientific definitions capture unitary
essences are misled. Just because in ordinary experience of coexisting
sensible qualities we naturally (and, as Locke spelt out to Stillingfleet,
reasonably and inescapably[50]) take ourselves to be perceiving a unitary
thing, we are liable to mistake our complex idea of it for a simple one. If
the doctrine of real accidents mistakes ideal for real multiplicity, Aristotelian claims to know essences mistake real for ideal unity.

This first section of *Essay*, Book II, chapter xxiii has been a main source
of the more exotically inappropriate interpretations of Locke on substance. What seems not to have been adequately noticed is that Locke was
describing an alleged process of the mind through four clearly distinct
stages. First, there is sense perception of 'a great number' of sensible
qualities; second, 'the mind takes notice also' that some coexisting qualities go 'constantly' together; third, the presumption that such recurrently
grouped qualities belong to 'one thing', i.e. one and the same kind of
thing, leads us to combine them, for convenience, in a single idea under
a single name; fourth, 'by inadvertency we are apt afterward to talk of and
consider' this complex idea 'as one simple idea'. We take this idea to
correspond to the '*Substratum*, wherein [these simple *Ideas*] do exist, and
from which they do result, which therefore we call *Substance*'.

The term 'we', it is clear, here includes the Aristotelians, as usual
accused of merely formalizing the coarse or sloppy thinking of ordinary
people. A footnote to the fifth edition, inspired by Locke if not actually
written by him, warns us that this passage is not an account of the idea
of substance in general, but an explanation of how the (general) names

---

[48] *Essay*, II. xiii. 20.   [49] Ibid. II. xxiii. I.   [50] Cf. *Works*, iv. 18–19.

applied to 'Individuals of distinct Species of Substances' have been taken
to be simple names standing for simple ideas.[51] The reference is to Aristotelian theory of definition. According to a commonplace distinction, a
'nominal' definition of man, such as 'featherless, two-footed, broad-nailed
thing', picks out men by means of a set of mutually independent features,
whereas the 'simple', 'real' definition, 'rational animal', unpacks a unitary
essence.[52] Locke wanted to say that all candidate definitions of essences
are in fact nominal, and of the first form. It should therefore be no
surprise that the four stages of his explanation of the Aristotelian mistake
correspond in close detail to the four stages which Aristotle himself had
distinguished in the achievement of the principles of scientific knowledge.

Aristotle's four stages, as set out in a famous passage,[53] can be read as
follows: first, the perception of any object (of whatever category); second,
'experience', or the memory of repeated perceptions of similar objects;
third, the formation of a universal concept or thought; and, fourth, the
understanding which comes with a scientific definition. In the case of
substances, we first perceive, and then lay up the memory of, recurrent or
repeated similarities between individuals. Third, we form a universal
notion of the same species present on all these perceptual occasions.
Finally, sustained observation and reflection enables us to pick out the
genus and specific difference and so to arrive at a definition which will
explain the concomitance of the 'properties' of the species, the cause of
their union. Locke's commentary is to the effect that the concept formed
at the third stage and associated with the specific name in fact remains
complex and sensory, while the fourth stage is nothing but the process by
which the existence of the single name, together with the natural and
proper assumption of a common, recurring substratum or explanatory
nature behind the recurrent experience, creates the illusion that our

[51] 'This section, which was intended only to shew how the Individuals of distinct Species
of Substances came to be looked on as simple *Ideas* [i.e. presumably, simple objects of thought,
objects of simple conceptions], and so to have simple Names, . . . hath been mistaken for an
Account of the *Idea* of Substance in general' (*Essay*, 295 n.). Sect. 14, giving the example
'swan', repeats the message in terms also to be found in the drafts: 'These *Ideas* of Substances, though they are commonly called simple Apprehensions, and the Names of them
simple Terms; yet in effect, are complex and compounded.' The connection is not straightforward, but Locke seems to have been assimilating the most available Aristotelian notion
of simplicity (which involves the contrast between 'simple' concepts or terms and 'complex'
propositions) to the different (although arguably related) conception according to which
scientific definitions of essences are 'simple' for other reasons.

[52] Cf. *Essay*, III. x. 17: 'Thus . . . we say, that *Animal rationale* is, and *Animal implume bipes
latis unguibus* is not a good definition of a Man.' 'We' again means Aristotelian orthodoxy.

[53] Aristotle, *Posterior Analytics*, B. 19. Cf. *Metaphysics* A. 1.

complex idea is simple. Locke has rewritten the Aristotelian account of the apprehension of natural principles as the psychological explanation of a vain delusion.

The argument of the rest of Book II, chapter xxiii develops the claim that no idea formed on the basis of experience ever in any case captures the unity of the thing itself. The latter is never represented to the enquirer by anything more than a place-marker, the idea of substance in general, embodying 'only a Supposition of he knows not what support' of the sensible qualities 'commonly called Accidents'. The corpuscularian hypothesis that colour and weight inhere in 'the solid extended parts' leaves us with the problem of what solid extended substance is.[54] For the unity of matter so defined remains mysterious to us. Here the question of the 'cause of the union'[55] of the qualities and powers of a body becomes entwined with the explanation of its physical or material unity: we do not know 'what the substance is of that solid thing . . . [i.e.] how the solid parts of Body are united, or cohere together to make Extension'. Corpuscularian explanations of cohesion by 'the external pressure of the Aether' fail to explain 'the cohesion of the parts of the Corpuscles of the Aether it self'.[56] It is evident that we lack a 'clear and distinct *Idea* of the *Substance* of Matter', and the same goes for 'the *Substance* of Spirit'.[57]

I will not now try to map all the ramifications of Locke's theory of substance, but I would like to consider a late development of his argument which has been particularly associated with the view that for Locke 'substance' is a pure logical subject, unknowable in principle. After repeating that our ideas of the sorts of substances always include, together with ideas of qualities and powers, 'the confused *Idea* of *something* to which they belong, and in which they subsist', he commented:

and therefore when we speak of any sort of Substance, we say it is a *thing* having such or such Qualities, as body is a *thing* that is extended, figured, and capable of Motion; a Spirit a *thing* capable of thinking; and so Hardness, Friability, and Power to drawn Iron, we say, are Qualities to be found in a Loadstone. These, and the like fashions of speaking intimate, that the Substance is supposed always *something* besides the Extension, Figure, Solidity, Motion, Thinking, or other observable *Ideas*, though we know not what it is.[58]

---

[54] *Essay*, II. xxiii. 2.

[55] Cf. ibid. II. xxiii. 6: 'several Combinations of simple *Ideas*, co-existing in such, though unknown, Cause of their Union, as makes the whole subsist of itself.'

[56] Ibid. II. xxiii. 23.

[57] Ibid. II. xxiii. 5. While II. xxiii concentrates on the point that the materialists are therefore no better off than immaterialists, the argument is consonant with the obverse point, notoriously made at IV. iii. 6.					[58] Ibid. II. xxiii. 3.

Locke was here bringing his explanation of the substance–accident relationship to bear on language. To put the same point another way, he was appealing to language in support of his explanation. The existence of the distinction in language between things and their qualities, and in particular the existence of primitive noun-predicates whose definitions reflect that distinction, is taken to constitute an implicit confession of our ignorance of what is really there behind the 'observable' qualities and powers: in other words, ignorance of its real nature or essence.

I think that the difficulty that many commentators have had in reading Locke in this way stems largely from the thought that he *must* have realized that, even if (say) solidity had been the essence of matter, and we knew it, 'matter' would still have been a noun-predicate definable as *thing (or substance) which is solid*. If Locke is trying to explain primitive noun-predicates and the logical primacy of the category of substance in terms of our ignorance, it may be thought, he must surely have had in mind an ignorance that is not merely contingent and remediable. Leibniz commented, 'If you distinguish two things in a substance—the attributes or predicates, and their common subject—it is no wonder that you cannot conceive anything special in this subject.' He accuses Locke of demanding 'a way of knowing which the object does not admit of'. Does this, perhaps, say it all?[59]

---

[59] Gottfried Leibniz, *New Essays on the Human Understanding*, II. xxii. 2, trans. P. Remnant and J. Bennett (Cambridge, 1981), 218 (pagination following edn. of A. Robinet and H. Schepers). Bennett claims (in Hare (ed.), *Doing Philosophy Historically*, 68) that his 'interpretation of Locke's "substratum" texts is exactly the same as Leibniz's', but Leibniz's remarks, unlike Bennett's, are consonant with his understanding the disagreement to be over the question whether we have 'clear and distinct notions' of body and spirit in a Cartesian sense: i.e. knowledge of their essences. To see this, just suppose that the present interpretation of Locke's thesis is correct, and that Leibniz so understood Locke. To present his rival explanation of substance–attribute logic Leibniz would have needed to claim that the subject–predicate form of definitions is merely formal, reflecting, not ignorance of anything, but the possibility of abstracting the formal concept of substance from our idea of any particular substance. This formal concept is not an obscure and confused thought of something behind observable qualities, but is clear and distinct in that it can be employed in abstract metaphysical demonstrations ('Yet this conception of substance, for all its apparent thinness, is less empty and sterile than it is thought to be. Several consequences arise from it . . . of greatest importance to philosophy'). To complain that 'we have no clear idea of substance in general' is therefore to fail to recognize the nature of the substance–attribute abstraction ('you have already set aside all the attributes through which details could be conceived') and to 'demand a way of knowing which the [purely formal] object does not admit of'. This is pretty much how Leibniz does argue. It is true that we do not get accurate and sympathetic exposition of Locke's claims (any more than we do of, say, his accounts of 'reflection' and identity, or his rejection of innate principles), but that does not mean that Leibniz really took Locke explicitly to hold the strange theory that beneath *essence* there lies a further and unknowable unknown called substance. It just means that Leibniz was a polemical writer.

Other passages in the *Essay,* however, make it clear that Locke proposed his epistemological explanation of the ontological category of substance with full acceptance of its implications: if we did know the true
essence of any substance, our account of it would *not* take subject–
predicate form. Since essence and substance are one and the same, there
would be no call for a noun-predicate distinct from the adjectival noun
which names the essence. For example, if Cartesian analysis of our idea
of body could reveal that its essence is extension, the two words would be
interchangeable: 'we can never mistake in putting the Essence of any
thing for the Thing it self. Let us then in Discourse, put *Extension* for
Body. . . . He that should say, that one Extension, by impulse, moves
another extension, would, by the bare Expression, sufficiently shew the
absurdity of such a Notion.' On the other hand, 'to say, an extended solid
thing moves, or impels another, is all one, and as intelligible, as to say,
Body moves, or impels'.[60] The whole argument implies that the reason
why 'extension' can stand as neither subject nor object of 'impels' is not
because it is an adjectival or abstract noun, but because it is the wrong
adjectival noun. If *x*-ness were what extension is not, the essence of body,
then to say that one *x*-ness impelled another *would* make sense. The same
argument, Locke continued, can be brought against the doctrine that
reason is the essential property of man: 'no one will say, That Rationality
is capable of Conversation, because it makes not the whole Essence, to
which we give the Name Man'.

To understand how Locke could advance such an argument, and to
recognize its historic force, we need to appreciate how he was neatly
turning Cartesian logic against Cartesian pretensions to science. Descartes
had himself warned against distinguishing between a substance and its
principal attribute in a prominent passage: 'Thought and extension can
be regarded as constituting the natures of intelligent substance and corporeal substance; they must then be considered as nothing else but thinking substance itself and extended substance itself—that is, as mind and
body.'[61] The distinction between thought or extension and the thinking
or extended substance is, on Descartes's account, a merely conceptual
distinction, a piece of abstraction.[62] To think of the substance as some-

[60] *Essay,* III. vi. 21.

[61] Descartes, *Principles,* I. 63, in *Philosophical Writings,* i. 215.

[62] Despite what Descartes says here, it has been suggested (e.g. by Nicholas Jolley,
Leibniz and Locke: A Study of the 'New Essays on Understanding' (Oxford, 1984), 78–9) that
Descartes might at least sometimes have thought of the substance as something over and
above even its essential attributes, as when he wrote, 'We do not have immediate knowledge
of substances . . . We know them only by perceiving certain forms or attributes which must

thing other or more than its nature is to make a confused division of the substance from itself. Yet this claim left an opening for those who rejected Descartes's dogmatic premiss to put his argument in reverse. Since we *can* intelligibly make just those distinctions he condemned, between extension and the thing which is extended, thought and the thing which thinks, doesn't that show that they are not, after all, cases of dividing a substance from itself? On the contrary, it was the Cartesian tendency to employ 'extension' and 'matter' interchangeably which appeared to Locke to fall into nonsense. Malebranche, for example, argued that extension is a substance or 'being', since it is not a mode of anything as roundness is a mode of extension.[63] Locke remarked sniffily, very likely with Malebranche in mind as well as Descartes's argument against a vacuum, 'That *Body* and *Extension,* in common use, stand for two distinct *Ideas,* is plain to any one that will but reflect a little. For were their Signification precisely the same, it would be as proper, and as intelligible to say, *the Body of an Extension,* as *the Extension of a Body*; and yet there are those who find it necessary to confound their signification.'[64]

Malebranche's argument appealed to the standard Cartesian claim, repeated in their own terms by other corpuscularians such as Hobbes, that the ontological relationship between substance and accident, unintelligible on the Aristotelian account, becomes perspicuous when it is identified as the relation between determinable attribute and determinate mode. There is no mystery about the relation between extension and a particular shape, as there would be between the shape and the colour of

---

inhere in something if they are to exist; and we call the thing in which they inhere a "substance" ' (*Philosophical Writings,* ii. 156 (AT VII 222); cf. p. 114 (AT VII 161); p. 124 (AT VII 176); René Descartes, *Conversation with Burman,* trans. J. Cottingham (Oxford, 1976), p. xxv). But what Descartes seems to have in mind in these passages is something like the view advanced by Epicurus and Hobbes, that attributes in the general sense (i.e. attributes and modes in the technical Cartesian sense) are not things but, as it were, aspects of things, ways of conceiving of them. The substance cannot be known 'directly', if that means its being known otherwise than via an attribute, a way of conceiving of it. The substance is what can be conceived or known in all these ways: it cannot be reduced to them, but is not something beyond them. Its unity is grasped by grasping the unity of its attributes (i.e. the necessary connections between Cartesian attributes, and the attribute–mode relation), not by abstracting it from those attributes as if they were distinct from it (cf. *Conversation with Burman,* p. xxii; *Philosophical Writings,* ii. 44 ff. (AT X 418 and 421); pp. 296 ff. (AT VIIIB 347–51); ii. 277 (AT IXA 216)).

[63] Nicolas Malebranche, *The Search after Truth,* trans. T. M. Lennon and P. J. Olscamp (Columbus, Oh., 1980), III. ii. 8.

[64] *Essay,* III. x. 6. In Draft A Locke chided Descartes for arbitrarily using the names 'extension', 'body', and 'space' for the same idea, but the significance of the grammatical difference between them was not there an issue. Cf. *Drafts,* i. 45–6.

a thing if we took colour to be irreducible to geometrical accidents.[65] In other words, substance and accidents form an intelligible unity on the corpuscularian account of matter. That is just what Locke was denying.

Malebranche stated that the crucial question is 'whether matter does not have still other attributes, different from extension', so that 'extension itself might not be essential to matter, and might presuppose something else that would be its subject and principle'. He argued that the distinction between extension and its subject is a merely conceptual distinction employing the general idea of being:

And what is said of [something else's] being the *subject* and *principle* of extension is said gratuitously and without a clear conception of what is being said, i.e. without there being any idea of it other than a general idea from logic, like principle and subject. As a result a new *subject* and a new *principle* of this subject of extension could in turn be imagined, and so on to infinity, because the mind represents general ideas of subject and principle to itself as it pleases.[66]

The immediate context of this criticism was an attack on Aristotelian matter. Because Aristotelian matter is conceived of as *subject* to extension, it is thought of as a being which is distinct from extension. Yet nothing clear can be said about this merely 'logical entity' just because it is abstracted from any attributes through which it might be conceived. It was polemical misrepresentation on Malebranche's part to suggest that the Aristotelians envisaged matter's having definite attributes underlying extension, but the immediately relevant point is simply this: Malebranche's claim that the concept of a subject of extension is a 'disordered abstraction', an abuse of 'the vague idea of being in general', represented the subject–predicate sentence 'Matter is extended' as misleading, if not ill formed, as if the tautology ought rather to be expressed in the form of an identity, 'Matter is extension'. It is therefore easy to see why Locke, who *did* want to postulate an unknown essence underlying extension, should have insisted that 'Body is extended' is evidently *not* a gratuitous solecism, but the way we all have to talk, determined by the distinct ideas we have. It would appear, at any rate, to have been after his reading of Malebranche in the early 1680s that he introduced elements into his argument not present in the drafts of 1671: not only the direct appeals to language under discussion, but the term 'idea of substance in general',

---

[65] Cf. Descartes, *Principles*, I. 61. For the possibility of clearly conceiving how modes of quantity exist in objects, and the impossibility of so conceiving of colours, see ibid. I. 70 (cf. Hobbes, *De Corpore*, II. viii. 3).

[66] Malebranche, *The Search after Truth*, III. ii. 8.

later explained to Stillingfleet as 'the general idea of something, or being'.[67]

Another Cartesian argument concerned with the alleged mistake of dividing a substance from itself had been advanced in the Port Royal *Logic*. In their explanation of predication and nominalization, its authors distinguished three kinds of objects of thought: things, modified things, and modes of things. The full theory need not concern us, but a part of it was that primitive noun-predicates directly signify things, adjectives directly signify modified things (or things as modified), while adjectival or 'abstract' nouns directly signify modes. They then denounced the practice of employing 'abstract' forms of primitive noun-predicates, *humanitas* from *homo*, *animalitas* from *animal*, and so forth. It arises, they argued, because we generally know and name things through their modifications, as modified things, so that we become accustomed to dividing our ideas of them into subject and mode (as we might distinguish, in our idea of a ball, the idea of a body from the idea of its roundness). The habit once acquired, *homo* comes often to be 'considered as the subject of humanity, *habens humanitatem*, and so to be a modified thing'. This mistake treats 'the essential attribute, which is the thing itself', as a mode, and as 'in a subject'. Hence the Scholastic solecisms 'humanitas', 'corporeitas', and 'ratio'. 'Reason' may seem an odd member of this list, but is clear enough why a Cartesian should include it, and that 'extension' would have the same right to be there.[68]

The Port Royal argument differs from Malebranche's in an interesting way. Although both deplore the division of a substance from its essence, i.e. from itself, Malebranche seems to have regretted the misleading character of primitive noun-predicates, and to have favoured the abstract noun 'extension' over 'matter', whereas Arnauld and Nicole took the reverse view. For them, the proper role of primitive noun-predicates is to name substantial things, and of abstract nouns to name modes. Locke's response to the issue is also interesting. On the one hand, he held not just that some, but that all, substantial things are known *qua* 'modified things', so that the division of our ideas of them into subject and mode (in Arnauld's sense of 'mode') is always legitimate. In effect he was suggesting that it would never occur to us to divide a substance from its true

---

[67] *Works*, iv. 19. The notion of substance was linked with the ideas (or idea) of 'Entity Being Something Existing' in Draft A (*Drafts*, I. 19–20), but that argument, dropped in Draft B, had quite a different form, turning on the claim that an idea of being cannot be separated from the ideas of particular sensible qualities and powers.

[68] Arnauld and Nicole, *La Logique*, I. ii.

essence, if ever we had knowledge of such a thing. The terms 'extension' and 'reason' are on his view, of course, entirely legitimate, and their legitimacy demonstrates that they are not true essences. On the other hand, he followed Arnauld in recognizing the illegitimacy of such abstract terms as are created by attempting to renominalize a primitive noun-predicate. His explanation of that illegitimacy, however, given in the fascinating, neglected chapter 'Of Abstract and Concrete Terms', is quite the opposite of Arnauld's and hinges on the bold claim that the proper function of abstract terms is to name known essences. Just because we know the mind-dependent real essences of non-substances, ordinary language abounds with such words as 'whiteness', 'justice', and 'equality'. On the other hand, our not ordinarily employing such terms as 'animalness' or 'manness' constitutes 'the confession of all Mankind, that they have no *Ideas* of the real Essences of Substances . . . And indeed, it was only the Doctrine of *substantial Forms*, and the confidence of mistaken Pretenders to a knowledge that they had not, which first coined, and then introduced *Animalitas*, and *Humanitas*, and the like.'[69]

Locke's logico-linguistic arguments, then, arose naturally and plausibly enough in the context of Aristotelian and Cartesian logic as an ingenious way of advancing his kind of scepticism about essences. Leibniz's criticisms raised no new issues. Nor was the Lockean doctrine a passing aberration. It made a deep impression on much eighteenth-century logic and permanently influenced the course of philosophy.[70] Kant himself drew on it, arguing *both* (with Locke) that the possibility of dividing subject from attribute indicates that the latter does not constitute the ultimate nature of the former, *and* (with Malebranche and Leibniz) that we can in principle continue dividing subject from attribute indefinitely.

> Pure reason demands that for every predicate of a thing we should look for its appropriate subject, and for this, which is necessarily in turn only a predicate, its subject and so on to infinity (or as far as we can reach). But it follows from this that nothing which we can reach ought to be taken as a final subject, and that the substantial itself could never be thought by our understanding, however deeply it penetrated, and even if the whole of nature were disclosed to it.[71]

By means of the premiss that we could always legitimately generate the concept of an underlying subject, *however much we knew*, Kant turned

[69] *Essay*, III. viii. 2.

[70] A notable example of a Lockean treatment of substance in logical theory was in William Duncan's popular *Elements of Logic* of 1748 (London).

[71] Kant, *Prolegomena to any Future Metaphysics*, sect. 46.

Locke's idea of substance in general into something he never intended, the pure concept of a logical subject which exists in us solely as an intimation of a 'thing in itself' which is in principle unknowable. For later idealists, it became an intimation of the Absolute, the ultimate subject of all predication.

III. Conclusion

To stress Locke's influence on later philosophy—even on Kant—is not quite the same as to establish his excellence. The standard English estimation of the greatest English philosopher is perhaps illustrated by the comment, made in a public discussion of his philosophy in which I recently took part, that no other philosopher 'has had a greater influence in proportion to his merits'. Such faint praise, I feel, is entirely inappropriate. That examination of Locke's arguments in relation to their context which reveals their meaning and point also reveals the theoretical ingenuity, quality of judgement, and pertinacity in the search for consistency and comprehensiveness which is characteristic of the very greatest philosophers—all of whom have used and responded to the tradition within which they have worked. The question no doubt arises whether Locke's contributions to seventeenth-century debates, despite their high quality, are irremediably dated. Speaking as an unregenerate realist, I would suggest that philosophical thought is now in dire need of the rich context of recognized explicanda and suggestive (if, just as they stand, untenable) explanations supplied by the *Essay*.

The present imperfect sketch of the skeleton of Locke's general philosophy has left out a number of important bones, if not whole limbs. I hope, nevertheless, that it will be seen how its two halves, one centred on the mind of the knower, the other on the objects of knowledge, fit together and presuppose each other. Both are structured round two related divisions. The first division is between, on the one hand, a priori, abstract science concerned with ideal, constructed objects and, on the other hand, enquiry into the real world of naturally unitary, given objects, enquiry which cannot for us achieve the status of 'science'. The second division is a division of levels between, on the one hand, the level of coarse experiential or pre-theoretical knowledge of natural things and, on the other hand, the level of speculative hypothesis or theory about the ultimate nature of those things. This second division is presupposed in Locke's conception of the authority and limitations of sensitive knowledge.

It also corresponds to his distinction between the nominal and the real essences of substances, the former constituting the objects of natural history, the latter, the unattainable objects of natural science.

It is easy to assume that this epistemology is utterly outdated, partly because the barriers Locke perceived to lie in the way of natural science seem to have been bypassed, partly because his perception of them was in any case based on a misguided geometrical ideal of what a science should be, and partly just because we hear so much didactic rhetoric from relativistic conceptualists against both divisions, between the a priori and the empirical and between experience and theory (not to speak of foundations of knowledge), that it is easy to assume that there must be something wrong with them. How could so many, so voluble, so confident writers be completely wrong?

Now I do not suppose that Locke's conception of 'sensitive knowledge', neatly hinging as it does on a purely causal understanding of the relation between sign and significatum, satisfactorily defines the scope of perceptual knowledge. It leaves us, implausibly and incoherently, with no more than perceptual knowledge of a world of powers. Nor do I find tenable the conception of infallible knowledge-delivering faculties which Locke took over, in common with other philosophers of his time, from the ancient debates over the existence of criteria of truth. But I do suppose that, unless the senses naturally and normally presented the world to us at a conscious level, and we naturally and normally accepted their deliverances, we would have no knowledge at all; and I am no more impressed than most opticians by the curious modern thought that what we see or otherwise perceive by the senses is a direct function of our theories, scientific or 'folk'. Moreover, we need to recognize that the unfashionable notion of 'evidence', purged of its implications of infallibility, still has valuable work to do in characterizing that central and primary kind of knowledge, typified by ordinary perceptual knowledge, which we possess when belief is engendered in circumstances of full awareness of its source and basis. In the context of perception we normally not only acquire beliefs, but do so in such a way that there is no mystery to us how and why we have come to have just those beliefs. We believe what the senses make evident to us. Without an understanding of 'evidence' in this sense, we shall never achieve a satisfactory philosophical account of what knowledge is. Fortunately it looks as if philosophers will be nudged in this direction by psychology, which has begun to take a fresh interest in the role of consciousness in cognition.

Furthermore, while I do not suppose that Locke's distinction between constructed modes and natural substances satisfactorily captures and explains the undoubted difference between geometry or political theory on the one hand and chemistry or biology on the other, his assumption does seem right that a horse is a naturally unified thing as a gallop or a procession is not, and that this is connected with the role of primitive noun-predicates in our language. For such predicates give names to natural, material individuals whose individuality is prior to their individuation by us or by 'our concepts'. I do not accept Locke's claim that the role of such noun-predicates serves as a confession of our ignorance of natural essences, but at least one feature of that claim strikes me as extremely suggestive. The New Philosophy tore traditional ontology and logic apart just because it proposed that science requires knowledge, not of the essences of those material objects which natural language treats as the fundamental objects of predication, horses, oak trees, and the like, but of the essence of such an abstract or hypothetical entity as corpuscularian matter. Most philosophers felt the need to adapt the notion of substance to fit the new physics. Consequently the theory of substance tended to lose its direct connection with the logic of natural language, while the metaphysics or ontology of science remained to an extent trammelled with inappropriate logical baggage. Locke, on the other hand, kept his explanation of the category of substance to the level which is relevant to an understanding of natural language: not the level at which reality might become fully intelligible to us, but the level at which it actually impinges on us in experience.

I could go on, but my point is simply that Locke is one of the great dead from whom, for all the differences, philosophers still have much to learn. He knew where he was going and he argued and theorized in an informed, intelligent, ingenious and powerful way about issues which have long been unfashionable, and to which we should return.

3

The Real Molyneux Question and the Basis of Locke's Answer

MARTHA BRANDT BOLTON

I

William Molyneux, who was dedicated to the experimentalism of the Royal Society, had no use for a priori speculation,[1] but he was fond of posing his question about the newly sighted man. The question concerns a man born blind who has learned to distinguish a solid cube from a globe by touch. If he were made to see, could he immediately distinguish those figures by sight alone? Neither Molyneux nor those to whom he posed this question had closely observed the behaviour or someone cured of congenital blindness.[2] Nevertheless, Molyneux thought he knew the answer to the question. The once-blind man would *not* be able to distinguish the figures by sight alone.

When he related the problem to Locke in a letter of 1693, Molyneux explained his answer:

For though he has obtain'd the experience of, how a Globe, how a Cube affects his touch; yet he has not yet attained the Experience, that what affects his touch so or so, must affect his sight so or so; Or that a protuberant angle in the Cube, that pressed his hand unequally, shall appear to his eye, as it does in the Cube.[3]

---

[1] For example, he praised the 'method of Investigating Nature' practised by 'the Societies lately Instituted in several of the most noted parts of Europe' and said 'I might proceed on, and fill a Volume with Instances . . . of the usefullness of an Active Experimental Philosophy' (dedication of *Sciothericum Telescopicum* (Dublin, 1689)).

[2] Treatments for cataract were not unknown in the 17th cent. but improved methods were discovered early in the 18th cent. Even then it is unlikely sight was given to anyone totally blind from birth. It was Molyneux's query that stimulated others to observe the behaviour of persons treated for cataract, e.g. the famous Cheselden case reported to the Royal Society in 1728. See Michael Morgan, *Molyneux' Question* (Cambridge, 1977), esp. ch. 2.

[3] To Locke, 6 Mar. 1692/3, *Correspondence*, iv. 651, quoted in the 2nd edn. of the *Essay*, II. ix. 8, p. 146.

This is not a powerful argument. The *claim* is that the character of the novice's visual presentations will not suffice to indicate which figure is which. But this is far from obvious and Molyneux does not defend it. The full defence may not have been given in the letter to Locke because it depended on tenets of Locke's own philosophy. In his letter, Molyneux wrote that he had persuaded 'diverse very ingenious men' of his negative response to the query, and he suggests the *Essay* had a role in his success.[4] Although he knew Locke only from published work, Molyneux anticipated that his correspondent would be disposed to agree with the negative answer to the question.

Locke did agree. When he inserted the problem of 'that very Ingenious and Studious promoter of real Knowledge . . . Mr. *Molineux*' into the second edition of the *Essay*, he included the answer given by 'this thinking Gent. whom I am proud to call my Friend' and endorsed it. But as far as I have been able to discover, there is no place where Locke elaborates on his friend's meagre explanation. My aim in this chapter is to reconstruct the grounds that Locke, and presumably Molyneux, used to decide the question. Then I want to consider briefly some details of Locke's account of the psychology and epistemology of vision.

A suggestion on how to proceed can be derived from some historical information. Molyneux's 1693 letter was not his first communication of the query to Locke. In 1688 he relayed it through a publisher in a note addressed: 'To the author of the "Essai Philosophique concernant L'Entendement Humane"'. This is the abstract of Locke's views on human understanding, which appeared in the *Bibliothèque Universelle* more than a year before publication of the *Essay*. Although the note was found in Locke's papers, he seems not to have answered it nor to have mentioned it in later exchanges with Molyneux. In any case, the early note asks for Locke's opinion on two questions about a newly sighted man. One is virtually the same as the later question. The other asks whether the man would say his first objects of sight were within his reach, even if they were considerably farther away.[5] Molyneux linked the question about

---

[4] Molyneux introduced the question with: 'upon Discourse with several, concerning your Book and Notions, I have proposed [the question] to Divers very Ingenious Men, and could hardly ever Meet with One, that, at first dash, would give me the Answer to it which I think true; till by hearing My Reasons they were Convinced' (*Correspondence*, iv. 651).

[5] The note reads: 'A Man, being born blind, and having a Globe and a Cube, nigh of the same bigness, Committed into his Hands, and being taught or Told, which is Called the Globe, and which the Cube, so as easily to distinguish them by his Touch or Feeling; Then both being taken from Him, and Laid on a Table, Let us Suppose his Sight Restored to Him; Whether he could, by his sight, and before he touch them, know which is the Globe and which the Cube? Or Whether he could know by his sight, before he stretched out his Hand, whether he could not Reach them, tho they were Removed 20 or 1000 feet from

perception of figure with a question about distance perception. I will have more to say about that. Further, Molyneux was moved to pose his questions by reading the summary 'Essai'. Comprehensive on main points of the *Essay*, the abstract does not mention the chapter on perception, where Molyneux's problem was later placed.[6] It seems Molyneux found Lockean grounds for resolving the question apart from the specific views on perception that surround it in the *Essay*, Book II, chapter ix.

We should also bear in mind that Molyneux was author of an expert treatise on dioptrics, as well as husband to a woman who went blind within a few months of their marriage.[7] He had an abiding interest in the psychology of vision. Shortly before his first note to Locke, he sent the Royal Society a report critical of recent attempts to explain why the sun and moon appear larger on the horizon than in the meridian.[8] It is likely the Locke–Molyneux answer to the question about the newly sighted man depended on shared views on the physics and psychology of the visual process, as well as Locke's distinctive account of human understanding.

II

There may seem to be an easy explanation of Locke's position on the Molyneux question. One finds in the literature the view that it is explained by Locke's commitment to a radically atomistic theory of sense experience.[9] The outline of this theory is that experience consists of sensory units, called 'simple ideas', and simple ideas have no discoverable relations other than their co-occurrence in experience. According to this

Him?' (Bodl. MS Locke, *c*.16, fo. 92). The note is quoted in full by Desirée Park, in 'Locke and Berkeley on the Molyneux Problem', *Journal of the History of Ideas*, 30 (1969), 254. The note is mentioned by W. von Leyden in *Seventeenth Century Metaphysics* (London, 1968), 277 n. 1, and more recently quoted by Menno Lievers in 'The Molyneux Problem', *Journal of the History of Philosophy*, 30 (1992), 406.

[6] See Lord King, *The Life and Letters of John Locke* (London, 1884), 365–99. The abstract published in 1688 is a French translation by Pierre Le Coste. Although the abstract omitted it, the chapter on perception is included in Draft C (written in 1685) virtually as it appeared in the 1st edn. of the *Essay* (1690). The only significant change in the chapter introduced in later edns. is Molyneux's question.

[7] For details, see the *Dictionary of National Biography* entry on William Molyneux.

[8] Presented in 1687, the report argued that the explanations offered respectively by Descartes, Hobbes, and Gassendi are incorrect. Molyneux proposed no alternative, but enjoined the Fellows to examine the problem (see *Philosophical Transactions*, 16 (1686), 314).

[9] See John Heil, 'The Molyneux Question', *Journal for the Theory of Social Behavior*, 17 (1987), 228–33. M. R. Ayers suggests Locke's tendency to regard simple ideas as 'blank effects' may have affected his stand on the question, but cites other considerations as possibly having influenced his answer, in *Locke*, 2 vols. (London, 1991), i. 65.

theory, the once-blind man cannot know how his visual ideas are related to figures he knows by touch until he has had a chance to note recurring spatio–temporal relations within his visual–tactual experience. We need look no further than his atomistic doctrine of simple ideas to explain Locke's response to Molyneux's question.

Locke does not clearly explain his notion of simple idea.[10] As we will see, it contains some surprises. But it is a mistake to think he takes simple ideas *as such* to be totally lacking in what we might call conceptual connections. Some of these connections depend on idea–content, others on the reception or existence of ideas. In the first category, Locke counts ideas of figure and extension as simple, and certainly we do perceive the shapes and sizes of objects.[11] Ideas of these sorts are the materials of the science of geometry, for, as Locke has it, these ideas have demonstrable 'permanent Relations and Habitudes'.[12] In the second category, the fact that a particular sense idea exists carries important implications, according to Locke. For instance, simple ideas are 'designed to be the Marks, whereby we are to know, and distinguish Things'.[13] That simple ideas are indicators of the distinctive qualities of things is something we naturally understand, not something we discover entirely from repeated idea-patterns. This is closely connected with the knowledge we have by sense: 'when our Senses do actually convey into our Understanding any *Idea*', we can know 'that there doth something at that time really exist without us, which doth . . . actually produce that *Idea*'.[14] Finally, simple ideas, or their associated sensible qualities, have a necessary tie to a substance in which they inhere.[15] So Locke is far from maintaining in general that the simple ideas that constitute sense perception are completely bare of conceptual connections. Some other explanation is needed for his rejection of a conceptual connection between shapes as we see them and feel them.

III

It is useful straight off to confront two objections to Locke's negative answer, because they failed to have weight with Locke. Edward Synge,

---

[10] It has often been remarked that Locke's effort to explain in general what a simple idea is at *Essay*, II. ii. 1, p. 119 is deficient. Nor do the important general claims about simple ideas in II. xxx. 2, p. 373 and II. xxxi. 2, pp. 375–6 help to provide a criterion for simple ideas.

[11] See *Essay*, II. v, p. 127 and II. viii. 9, p. 135; ideas of figure are also classified as simple modes, e.g. II. xiii. 5, p. 168 and II. xxxi. 3, p. 376.

[12] e.g. ibid. IV. iii. 18–19, pp. 548–52.   [13] Ibid. II. xxx. 2, p. 372.

[14] Ibid. IV. xi. 9, p. 635.   [15] e.g. ibid. II. xxiii. 1, p. 295.

one of the 'ingenious gentlemen' of Molyneux's acquaintance, wrote a letter arguing for the affirmative view. Although his argument is some-what longer, the crux of his reasoning is this: 'The *Image* which upon the first View such a man will frame of a Cube, must needs be this, that it is a body which is not alike in all the parts of its Superficies which conse-quently must be agreeable to the *idea* which before he had of it and different from that *idea* which he had of a globe.'[16] Synge's letter found its way to Molyneux, who was not persuaded. Molyneux sent the solution on to Locke, saying only 'you will easily see by what false steps this Gentleman is led into his Error'. Locke wrote back that the incident showed 'how hard it is, for even ingenious men to free themselves from the anticipations of sense'.[17] Nothing more said.

The second objection is *ad hominem*. As Berkeley suggested, and more recently J. L. Mackie and others, Locke's handling of the Molyneux question conflicts with his doctrine of primary qualities.[18] They are supposed to be real qualities that exist in things whether we perceive them or not and thus, Locke reasoned, the ideas they cause in us *resemble* the bodies that cause them. This claim is difficult to understand in detail, but its rough meaning is that shape-ideas provide information about the features of their causes. Now according to the objection, a cube, for example, causes both tactual and visual ideas of shape. Given that both ideas resemble the same cause, it would be difficult for Locke to deny that their contents have significant overlap. But then there seems no princi-pled reason to insist that the visual novice would not be able to say which of the objects he sees is a cube. Locke's doctrine of primary qualities is thus inconsistent with his stand on the Molyneux question, or so the objection goes.

These two objections both assume that the man born blind perceives, or has ideas of, the *shapes* of his two first objects of sight. Since Locke dismissed the one pretty obvious objection and was oblivious to the alleged inconsistency, it is likely he rejected their shared assumption. He may well have thought a man just made to see would not receive any ideas of the figures of bodies he looked at.

This suggestion not only explains Locke's attitude to these objections, but also finds support in the text. The Molyneux question is introduced

[16] *Correspondence*, v. 496.   [17] Ibid. v. 493 and 596.

[18] See George Berkeley, *An Essay towards a New Theory of Vision*, in *The Works of George Berkeley*, ed. A. A. Luce and T. E. Jessop (London, 1948), i. 136, p. 226; J. L. Mackie, *Problems from Locke* (Oxford: 1976), 28–30. Also Morgan, *Molyneux' Question*, 15; Michael Ayers, *Locke*, 2 vols. (London, 1991), i. 65.

into a section where the main point is that 'the Ideas we receive by sensation are often in grown People alter'd by the Judgment, without our taking notice of it'.[19] For instance, we become accustomed to the appearances of colour and light presented by convex bodies as compared to concave ones: 'So that from that, which truly is variety of shadow or colour, collecting the Figure, [the judgement] makes it pass for a mark of Figure, and frames to it self the perception of a convex Figure, and an uniform Colour; when the *Idea* we receive from thence, is only a Plain variously colour'd, as is evident in Painting.'[20] This suggests the *novice* will be aware of light and colour, but will not yet have formed visual ideas of bodily shapes.

There is further evidence that this is Locke's view. In his examination of Malebranche, Locke wrote: 'he says, that when we look on a cube, "we see all its sides equal." This, I think, is a mistake; and I have in another place shown, how the idea we have from a regular solid, is not the true idea of that solid, but such an one as by custom (as the name of it does) serves to excite our judgment to form such an one.'[21] Further, it is not just bodily shapes that we learn to judge by variations in colour and light. Locke said in the *Essay*: 'Sight . . . conveying to our Minds the *Ideas* of Light and Colours, which are peculiar only to that Sense; and also the far different *Ideas* of Space, Figure, and Motion, the several varieties whereof change the appearances of its proper Object, *viz.* Light and Colours, we bring our selves by use, to judge of the one by the other.'[22] (By 'the idea of space', Locke presumably meant the ideas of distance between the perceiver and the object seen, as well as the distances between bodies or their extremities.) These passages, plus Locke's dismissive attitude toward certain objections, indicate he assumed the man cured of blindness would not at first receive visual ideas of the shapes of what he looks at.

---

[19] *Essay*, II. ix. 8, p. 145.

[20] Ibid. It is not obvious what painting is supposed to make evident. Certainly it does not show that perception of planar figures in perspective is more immediate or basic than perception of figures in three dimensions. It does show that solid figures and figures drawn in perspective, when seen in suitable circumstances, look alike. So I take it Locke's argument is this: If the things we look at caused visual ideas of bodily contours apart from acts of judgement, then objects with different contours would cause different visual ideas; a cube and a painting of a cube have different contours, yet they cause exactly similar visual ideas; so we do not receive visual ideas of bodily contours apart from judgements. The argument is unconvincing, however. For objects with different contours may sometimes, but not always, cause different visual ideas and the circumstances in which a painting of a cube looks just like a cube are unusually bad for seeing three-dimensional contours; so painting does not show that in better circumstances we must make judgements in order to have vision of shapes.   [21] *Works*, ix. 218.

[22] *Essay*, II. ix. 9, p. 146.

One might question this, because Locke said in this same section: 'When we set before our Eyes a round Globe, of any uniform colour, *v.g.* Gold, Alabaster, or Jet, 'tis certain, that the *Idea* thereby imprinted in our Mind, is of a flat Circle variously shadow'd . . .'.[23] But Locke surely did not mean that we receive, without judgement, the idea of a circular body with plane surface (such as a coin). Round flat bodies produce their own distinctive patterns of colour and light depending, for example, on their orientation with respect to the viewer. One cannot see that a surface is circular and planar without apprehending how the parts of the surface are related in space. Locke's point that the positions of the parts of concave and convex surfaces are judged by variations in colour and light is surely meant to apply as well to the parts of plane surfaces.

Still one might suggest Locke meant that a globe causes an idea of its projection on a plane at right angles to the line of sight. This, of course, describes the retinal images produced by a globe. But Locke was describing the *idea* produced *by* those retinal images, not the physical images, although commentators are often careless on this point. And the suggestion that the idea is of a two-dimensional figure at right angles to the line of sight is not consonant with Locke's overall view. In passages already quoted, he claimed entirely without restriction that we see figures by judging colour and shading. This is reinforced in the *Elements of Natural Philosophy*, where Locke observed that 'The rays reflected from opake bodies, always bring with them to the eye the idea of colour' and went on to say: 'Besides colour, we are supposed to see figure; but in truth that which we perceive when we see figure, as perceivable by sight, is nothing but the termination of colour.'[24] Another reason for thinking Locke supposed even vision of the two-dimensional outlines of bodies is achieved by judgement is that otherwise he could not easily dismiss the reasoning of Edward Synge.

But if Locke did not mean that a globe causes the idea of a two-dimensional circle, what did he mean by saying it causes 'the idea of a flat Circle variously colour'd'? It seems he was struggling to describe a pattern of light and colour that has no reference to figures in two- or three-dimensional space. As he put it elsewhere, the 'circularity' pertains, not to a surface, but to the 'termination of colours'; and we can suppose that the idea is 'flat' in that it specifies nothing about spatial relations among parts of a surface. We have seen that the phrase 'flat Circle' *cannot* be taken

---

[23] Ibid. 145; also note the reference to 'a Plain variously colour'd' from the same section (quoted above).   [24] *Works*, iii. 324.

literally; further, nothing but the mistaken assumption that Locke meant to describe a retinal image supports the non-literal reading of a two-dimensional projection on a perpendicular plane. The wholly non-spatial reading I am suggesting has the advantage of being consistent with Locke's other remarks about vision, as well as his stand on the Molyneux question.

The point is important, because it determines how Locke understood the issue at stake in Molyneux's question. If my contention is right, many others have failed to understand it as Locke and its propounder did. Most philosophers who subsequently discussed it took the question to presuppose that the once-blind man can see the shapes of things, or at least two-dimensional outlines or retinal images.[25] Although some insisted he would not be able to see the figures of things at once, their interest focused on how he would behave when he did. If this is stipulated, then the issue becomes roughly whether the man would identify the shape of the cube he saw for the first time and the shapes of cubes he formerly touched as instances of the same *kind*. This question concerns how cognition of tactual and motor space is correlated with visual cognition and it has, not surprisingly, attracted attention from a long line of philosophers and psychologists.

However, if the issue does concern recognition of visual and tactual shapes as instances of the same kinds, then Molyneux's statement of the question is sadly inadequate. One wants to know, for instance, just what the man has been told about his situation, how much he knows about geometry, what degree of warrant he is supposed to have for his classification. Most philosophers who have discussed the Molyneux question have first amended it in more or less extensive ways, for example: Leibniz, Diderot, Condillac, and much more recently Mackie and Gareth Evans.[26] More important, if classification is the issue, it is extremely difficult to see why Locke answered the question in the negative. No principle of Locke's philosophy precludes the possibility that a blind man should have formed

---

[25] Recent authors who say Locke assumes the newly sighted man would see shapes as soon as he can see anything include Morgan, *Molyneux' Question*, 7 and Heil, 'The Molyneux Question', 230. Ayers says Locke supposed we immediately see two-dimensional shapes (*Locke*, 66). Mackie correctly notes that Locke's answer to the Molyneux question is based on the doctrine that visual perception of three-dimensional shape involves interpretation of patterns of shading, but ignores it, taking the more interesting issue to be whether the once-blind man could immediately recognize two-dimensional shapes as instances of his tactual concepts of shape (*Problems from Locke*, 30–1).

[26] On treatments of the question subsequent to Locke, see Morgan, *Molyneux' Question*. Also see John W. Davis, 'The Molyneux Problem', *Journal of the History of Ideas*, 21 (1960), 392–408. For recent treatments of the problem, see Mackie, *Problems from Locke*, 30–1, and Gareth Evans, 'Molyneux's Question', in *Collected Papers* (New York, 1985), 364–82.

an idea of a globe sufficiently abstract to represent a globe were he to see one. Indeed, commentators who suppose Locke was dealing with the classification issue have gone to amazing lengths to explain his stand on it.[27]

In fact, this was not the issue for Locke. When he considered Molyneux's question, he assumed that bodily shapes are not immediately given to sight. This sort of theory of vision was widely accepted in Locke's time as part of optical theory. It was inherited from the medieval and Renaissance perspectivist tradition, which flowered in the seventeenth century in the optical treatises of Kepler, Huygens, Newton, and others.[28] Accepted theory left scope for different explanations of the function from visual cognitions of one sort to those of another, and seventeenth-century theorists had proposed several very different accounts of this psychological process. I want to look briefly at the way it was handled by some of Locke's predecessors and contemporaries in order to identify the network of considerations that grounded the Locke–Molyneux answer to the famous question.

IV

One important Latin medieval work on optics was John Pecham's textbook *Perspective Communis*. It was written in the late thirteenth century, widely used in medieval universities, and still read up to the beginning of the seventeenth century.[29] There are, Pecham says, twenty-two intentions (*intentiones*) comprehended by sight, including light, colour, distance, position, shape, size, motion, corporeity, transparency, beauty, ugliness, and so on.[30] Of these, only light and (generic) colour are comprehended

---

[27] For example, Morgan claims that if Molyneux's man had the ability immediately to identify visual shapes as instances of his concepts of tactual shapes, that would imply 'an innate supra-sensible structure to the mind' (*Molyneux' Question*, 14); later he argues that because Locke is a 'nominalist', he holds that the once-blind man cannot extend his application of the word 'cube' from tactual presentations to visual ones and, indeed, that Locke's doctrine of abstract general ideas is inconsistent with his answer to the Molyneux question (p. 88).

[28] There are several fine studies of this tradition: A. C. Crombie, 'The Mechanist Hypothesis and the Scientific Study of Vision: Some Optical Ideas as a Background to the Invention of the Microscope', in S. Bradbury and G. L'E. Turner (eds.) *Historical Aspects of Microscopy* (Cambridge, 1967); David C. Lindberg, *Theories of Vision from Al-Kindi to Kepler* (Chicago, 1976). Also Vasco Ronchi, *Optics: The Science of Vision*, trans. Edward Rosen (New York, 1957).

[29] See David C. Lindberg, *John Pecham and the Science of Optics* (Madison, Wis., 1970), 29–32. Quotations and references to *Perspective Communis* are taken from the translation in this volume.   [30] *Perspective*, prop. I. 55 [58], p. 135.

by 'naked sense'; the rest require co-operation from 'argumentation', the 'discriminitive faculty', and acquired knowledge, i.e. 'received species disposed in memory'.[31] These last three faculties, or something like them, were often listed as 'internal senses' in medieval Scholastic discussions of the soul.[32] Optical theorists maintained that the power of sight is located in the 'glacial humour' of the eye, but completion of the visual act requires that species be transmitted beyond this humour through channels that lead eventually to the brain.[33] Although each internal sense was said to be located in a specific region of the cranium, Pecham does not venture to trace the path taken by species through the organ. But he does describe the cognitive operations by which several of the visual intentions are apprehended, including distance, shape, position, and size of the object.

His theory is that vision of an object requires that species from every point on the viewed surface of the object be transmitted through the various humours of the eye on to the anterior surface of the glacial humour. The species must be ordered on this surface as they were ordered on the surface of the object from which they came.[34] Generic colour and light, as well as certain facts about the order, size, and arrangement of the species, are apprehended immediately by the presence of ordered species in the sensitive part of the eye. Other visual intentions require cognitive operations performed on these basic data by one or more co-operating faculty.

Perception of distance is said to be essential to apprehension of several other visual intentions, but Pecham seems undecided how to explain it. One proposition asserts that distance can only be 'determined by reasoning'. An object's distance is apprehended from perception of intervening bodies and 'certified', only if the distances between the intervening bodies are already known. But in a later proposition, we find that 'the lengths of rays can be perceived by sight'. Here Pecham seems to assume that distance is a basic apprehension accomplished without aid of argument, discrimination, or acquired knowledge.[35]

Other visual intentions are known by co-ordinating several other apprehensions. For instance, the shape of an object is perceived by discerning

---

[31] Ibid., props. I. 56 [59], 58 [61], and 61 [64], pp. 137 and 139.

[32] On medieval accounts of the common sense, and the internal senses in general, see Harry A. Wolfson, 'The Internal Senses in Latin, Arabic, and Hebrew Philosophic Texts', *Harvard Theological Review*, 28 (1935); Nicholas Steneck, 'Albert the Great on the Classification and Localization of the Internal Senses', *Isis*, 65 (1974), 193–211. Pecham himself gave a somewhat different list of the internal senses in his *De Anima* (*Tractatus de Animal Ioannis Pecham*), ed. P. Gaudentius Melani (Florence, 1948), ch. 10).

[33] See e.g. *Perspective*, props. I. 32 [35] and 36 [39] pp. 117–18 and 121.

[34] Ibid., props. I. 36 [39] and 37 [40], p. 121.

[35] Ibid., props. I. 63 [66], 64 [67], and 67 [70], pp. 141–3; see translator's note 153, p. 253.

the distances and order of its various parts: 'concavity is perceived when the distance to the middle is greater than that to the extremes, and convexity vice versa'.[36] Perception of an object's size requires a process of inference, which Pecham described in terms of certain technical notions. 'Rays' are sent in straight lines from the object of sight to the eyes of the perceiver; the 'radiant pyramid' is a pyramid whose vertex is at the eye and base at the surface of the object seen; the 'angle under which the object is seen' is the angle at the vertex. As Pecham explained it:

Perception of the size [of an object] derives from perception of the radiant pyramid and comparison of the base to the length and to the size of the angle. . . . Indeed the angle is apprehended from the disposition of the form in the eye; but because the rays themselves are also perceived by the eye . . . certain knowledge of size can be obtained only by a comparison of equal angles having rays of unequal length to unequal bases, for it is manifest that lines proceeding from an angle diverge in proportion to their extension and consequently contain a proportionately large base.[37]

From a psychological or epistemic perspective, the account leaves much unexplained. One wonders, for instance, how the argumentative faculty has come to understand what rays and radiant pyramids are, how it apprehends the geometrical proportion, and why it uses that proportion in determining an object's size. But the motivation for the account is clear: the reasoning gets the right *result*, according to Pecham's theory of the way species are transmitted from objects to the eye.

In 1604 Johann Kepler published a treatise on optics that superseded the medieval optical texts, *Ad Vitellionem Paralipomena*. Kepler used the notion of a pencil of rays to explain how all the rays that enter the eye from a visible object have an effect on vision. He insisted that the retina, not glacial humour, is the sensitive part of the eye and demonstrated for the first time that an image of the object of sight is formed on the retina. It followed that the image reverses the object top to bottom and left to right. Since the basic data of vision were supposed to be apprehended from the 'order of species', the inversion posed an acute problem for cognitive aspects of traditional optical theory. Kepler declined to explain how the reversed image travelled to the faculty of sight, saying this was outside the domain of geometrical optics.[38]

---

[36] Ibid., prop. I. 71 [74], p. 145.   [37] Ibid., 147.

[38] See Gerard Simon, 'À propos de la théorie de la perception visuelle chez Kepler et Descartes', in *13th International Congress on the History of Sciences, Moscow, 1971*, sect. vi (Moscow, 1974). Also Crombie, 'The Mechanistic Hypothesis' and 'Early Concepts of the Senses and the Mind', *Scientific American*, 210 (1964), 108–16.

Yet Kepler was not uninterested in the psychology of sight. In particular, he aimed to understand how we determine the positions of objects seen, because that was important in his investigations of reflection and refraction. He explained monocular distance perception in terms of adjustments made by the eye to the angles at which pencils of rays enter it from objects at different distances. Modified slightly by Descartes and others, this explanation became standard.[39] For binocular perception, Kepler accepted an explanation from the medieval tradition.[40] As he puts it, the 'sense of sight' uses the length of a line between the two eyes to judge the location of objects: 'Given two angles of a triangle and the side between them, the remaining sides are given. In vision, common sense grasps the distance between the eyes from habituation and by feeling that the eyes are turning, takes note of the angles associated with the distance of the object.'[41] 'Common sense' is one of the traditional faculties of internal sense. Kepler invoked a psychology similar to Pecham's. Certain immediate visual data are available to a faculty of inner sense, which employs a geometrical proportion to determine the distance of the object seen. Kepler did not explain how common sense gets its basic data or knows what geometrical theorem to apply, but he does describe an inference that correctly determines distance according to his optical theory.

Scholastic psychology was rejected later in the seventeenth century, in part because of Kepler's discoveries, but more generally due to acceptance of mechanist theories of the corporeal world. Some of the new accounts of vision retained an inferential model, revised in accord with new theories of the mind and its cognitive powers. The range of available alternatives included visual theories offered by Descartes, Gassendi, Malebranche, and Hobbes. All were mechanists, who rejected the transmission of intentional species from objects to the visual faculty. They agreed instead that objects of sight emit or reflect particles that enter the eye, are refracted as Kepler described, and cause motions on the retina; they in turn produce motions or impressions in the brain. But modern philosophers had radically different views of how cerebral motions are related to vision.

Descartes said in the *Optics* that vision involves corporeal events that terminate in pineal motions that are 'ordained by nature' to prompt specific sensory ideas in the incorporeal mind. It is simply the nature of the mind to supply certain sorts of sensory ideas on the occasion of

[39] See Ronchi, *Optics*, 43–4, and Crombie, 'The Mechanistic Hypothesis', 62–3.
[40] Molyneux attributes it to Alhazen and Witelo (*Dioptrica Nova* (London, 1692), 113).
[41] Johann Kepler, *Opera Omnia*, ed. C. Frisch, 8 vols. (Frankfurt, 1859), ii. 167.

certain sorts of pineal motions.[42] For Descartes, the retinal image presented no problem; he simply supposed the mind naturally responds to the inverted pattern of motion by forming perceptions of objects in their true positions.[43] Sensations of colour and light also result from these direct psychophysical transactions. A number of other sorts of apprehensions occur in the same immediate way, e.g. (1) kinaesthetic awareness of the positions of limbs, hands, eyes, etc., (2) awareness that the object of sight is located on a line projected from the eyes to infinity, and (3) awareness of the distance between perceiver and object seen, for relatively short distances.[44] As mentioned, Descartes also explained (3) by a modified version of Kepler's monocular theory.

For depth perception at greater distances, Descartes offered some traditional explanations involving inferences from other data. One is the medieval binocular theory repeated also by Kepler, but now expounded within Cartesian theory of mind. Descartes's famous illustration of this method compared it to the way a blind man could determine the distance of an object by holding a stick in each hand and making them meet at the object: 'knowing only the distance between his two hands and the size of the angles [made by the sticks and the line between his hands], [he] can tell from this knowledge, as if by a natural geometry, where the point [at which the sticks meet] is'.[45]

Although the notion of a 'natural geometry' is not developed in *Optics*, it is linked to the innatist doctrines in Descartes's other works.[46] Cartesian innate ideas are particularly associated with clear and distinct perception, certainty, and operations of the intellect, but also play a role in sense perception. In the Fifth Replies, Descartes said that we use innate geometrical ideas to understand presentations of sense.[47] Because mathematical

---

[42] See *Optics*, in *The Philosophical Writings of Descartes*, 2 vols., trans. J. Cottingham, R. Stoothoff, and D. Murdoch (Cambridge, 1985), i. 167 (also see pp. 152–4 and 164–6); also *The World*, pp. 81–2 and *Comments on a Certain Broadsheet*, p. 304.

[43] Descartes, *Philosophical Writings*, i. 169–70.

[44] The account of visual perception in the *Optics* contrasts with a passage from the 'Sixth Replies'. There Descartes gives a list of things we apprehend immediately by sense 'which arise from the union and, as it were, mingling, of mind and body'; the list is not said to be inclusive, but it makes no mention of position or distance.

[45] Descartes, *Philosophical Writings*, i. 170. On Descartes's theory of visual perception, see Nancy L. Maull, 'Cartesian Optics and the Geometrization of Nature', in Stephen Gaukroger (ed.), *Descartes: Philosophy, Mathematics, and Physics* (Brighton, 1980) and John W. Yolton, *Perceptual Acquaintance from Descartes to Reid* (Minneapolis, 1984), ch. 1.

[46] The phrase 'ex geometria quadam omnibus innata', quoted by Berkeley in the *Essay towards a New Theory of Vision*, is in the Latin translation of the *Optics* by Étienne de Courcelles, approved by Descartes.

[47] Descartes, *Philosophical Writings*, ii. 262.

ideas are innate and the mind, prompted by pineal motions, supplies its own sensory ideas, Descartes freely supposed that geometrical concepts are available to structure visual perception from the start. When we are very young, he said, we perceive distance by making the geometrical calculation just described. Later the reasoning has become so familiar that we usually seem to see the distances of things directly.[48] Descartes probably did not mean that we *understand* the geometrical reckonings we make when very young. He held that sometimes a person brings to mind an innate idea without clearly understanding what the idea is (e.g. when a pagan or atheist thinks of God).[49] The situation is similar, it seems, when we first calculate distance by triangulation. Referring to this process, Descartes said: 'And this is done by a mental act which, though only a very simple act of the imagination, involves [*enveloper en soi*] a kind of reasoning quite similar to that used by surveyors . . .'.[50] This suggests that when we first use the geometry of distance perception, the imagination grasps something simple that *includes*, or as one translator puts it 'implicitly contains',[51] the geometrical argument.

Descartes mentioned several other methods of determining distance, also similar to ones given by the medievals. These further methods are based on experience and memory: we detect distance from previous knowledge of an object's size and colour, or the strength of the light coming from it, or the perception of intermediate objects. For vision of size and shape, Descartes continued to follow the outline of Pecham's accounts. The shape of a visual object is said to be judged from apprehension of the distances of its various parts. An object's size is determined as a function of its distance and 'the size of the image imprinted on the back of the eye'.[52] Within his radical dualism, Descartes adapted much of the traditional theory that vision of objects sometimes involves rational operations performed on basic data.

A different approach to the visual process was offered in François Bernier's abridgement of Gassendi's philosophy.[53] Bernier said that retinal images cause motions in the brain, which excite sensations of colour, and so on, but unlike Descartes, he did not distinguish between certain

---

[48] Ibid. 295–96.   [49] Ibid. 257.   [50] Ibid. i. 170.

[51] René Descartes, *Discourse on Method, Optics, Geometry, and Meteorology*, trans. P. J. Olscamp (Indianapolis, 1965), 106.

[52] Descartes, *Philosophical Writings*, i. 172; also see ii. 295.

[53] The French abridgement first appeared in 1678 and thereafter was more widely read than Gassendi's massive *Syntagma Philosophici* (1658). John Milton, in 'Locke at Oxford' (Ch. 1 of this volume), reports that Locke read something of *Syntagma* in the 1660s.

corporeal motions and apprehensions of sense.[54] The Gassendist view was that sense and imagination are entirely corporeal although the faculty of 'understanding' is incorporeal.[55] As a mechanist, Gassendi held non-rational animals to be nothing but aggregates of material particles. But because he took sense and imagination to be corporeal faculties, he rejected the Cartesian contention that beasts have no sentient faculty.

Bernier wrote that the 'understanding' is immaterial, because it performs operations impossible for a material thing, e.g. apprehension of insensible entities, God, universals, one's self, infinity, and mathematical abstractions.[56] Accordingly sense perception is possible without cognition of universals, geometrical proportions, and the like. On the Gassendist view, there are three main cognitive operations of corporeal imagination. (1) It performs acts of simple (non-propositional) apprehension; e.g. it perceives things and retains vestiges of them. Imagination also represents collections of things by assembling particular vestiges on the basis of their resemblances. (2) Imagination forms propositions; as Bernier put it: 'It assembles two apprehensions, as having agreement between them, or separates them, as not having it, so that it imagines them as one, not as two things.' (3) Imagination engages in a type of argumentation, 'sensitive reasoning' or 'reasoning by analogy', in which perception of one particular thing serves as a sign of another. This is possible 'only because it has memory of many similar cases'.[57] Thus the only type of inference required for rudimentary sense perception is apprehension of signs established by experience and memory.

As Bernier put it, we see the *distances* of objects simply by perceiving intervening bodies, e.g. seeing that one body partially covers another.[58] Indeed, Gassendi rejected the traditional triangulation account of binocular depth perception as involving a fundamental error. He maintained

---

[54] *Abrégé de la philosophie de Gassendi . . . par F. Bernier*, 2nd edn., 7 vols. (Lyons, 1684), vi. 111–12; compare Pierre Gassendi, *Opera Omnia* (1658), 3 vols., fac. edn. (Stuttgart, 1964), ii. 377*b*.

[55] See *Abrégé* vi. 182–93 and 201–9; compare Gassendi, *Opera Omnia*, ii. 398*a*–401*b* and 403*a*–405*b*. On Gassendi's psychology and theory of mind, see the introduction to Pierre Gassendi's *Institutio Logica* (1658), trans. Howard Jones (Assen, 1981), pp. li-lvi and the following articles by Emily Michael and Fred S. Michael, 'Gassendi on Sensation and Reflection: A Non-Cartesian Dualism', *History of European Ideas*, 9 (1988), 583–95; 'Corporeal Ideas in Seventeenth-Century Psychology', *Journal of the History of Ideas*, 50 (1989), 31–48.

[56] *Abrégé*, vi. 328–46; compare Gassendi, *Opera Omnia*, ii. 446*b*–454*b*.

[57] *Abrégé*, vi. 218–47 and 251; compare Gassendi, *Opera Omnia*, ii. 409*a*–414*b* and 415*a*.

[58] *Abrégé*, vi. 147–9.

that the axes of our two eyes never converge on the object of sight, but rather always remain parallel. We nevertheless see only one object, Gassendi reasoned, because we never see out of both eyes at once. Bernier recounted a number of experiments to support these claims.[59] This theory had quite a significant following, including Marin Mersenne.[60]

In explaining perception of *size*, Bernier cited the long-recognized relation between the size of an object, its distance, and the size of the angle under which it is seen, but without ever suggesting that ordinary perceivers understand what an optic angle is. Instead, an object is said to take up a certain portion of the viewed hemisphere, i.e. the entire array of things one sees when gaze is fixed on one object. The inference from apparent size to distance is grounded entirely in past experience, the fact that we have observed 'from infancy' that apparent size is greater when distance is smaller.[61]

The *Abrégé* suggested conflicting accounts of visual perception of *shape*. The topic is not directly addressed although it is mentioned in the polemic against intentional species. The suggestion there breaks with tradition, indicating that both colour and shape are seen without processing more immediate data: 'Thus the image of the sun is nothing but the light that comes from that star and represents its brilliant colour with its roundness. Thus the image of a man is only the light that comes from the man and represents his colour borne by his proper figure and intermixing the traits of lineaments proper and particular to him'.[62] But since perception of figure requires perception of bodily contour, it is difficult to see how this can be reconciled with the view that distance perception depends on perception of intervening bodies. In fact, we find in another context that figure is apprehended only by the co-operation of memory, reasoning, and other faculties.[63]

Malebranche propounded yet another radically different visual psychology. He discussed vision at some length in the first book of the *Recherche de la verité*. His dominant thesis is that the senses are wonderfully suited 'for the preservation of our body', but are not faculties for knowing truth. Neither do they engage in inference or reasoning, which

[59] Ibid. 167–181; compare Gassendi, *Opera Omnia*, ii. 393a ff.

[60] See Marin Mersenne, *L'Optrique et catoptrique* (Paris, 1651), 63 (prop. xxvi). The theory was initially proposed by John Baptiste Porta in a treatise on refraction published in 1593 (see Crombie, 'The Mechanistic Hypothesis', 53).

[61] *Abrégé*, vi. 147–60.   [62] Ibid. iii. 281.

[63] Ibid. vi. 90; compare Gassendi, *Opera Omnia*, ii. 342a.

are functions of the will.[64] Malebranche held that reasoning and inference have *no* part in ordinary sense perception.

To be sure, he began in traditional fashion to explain the various ways we determine distances, sizes, and shapes of objects by sight. He repeated Descartes's several methods of determining distance, and even wrote: 'it might be said . . . that the soul . . . avails itself of a natural geometry'.[65] He said that sight alone cannot tell whether the bodies we see are circles or ellipses, squares or parallelograms: 'Since painters, in order to make them appear natural, are almost always forced to change them and to paint circles, for example, as ovals, we have a sure sign that the way we see non-painted objects is erroneous.' But these errors are 'corrected by new sensations that ought to be regarded as a kind of natural judgment, and that can be called judgments of sense'.[66] For example, if the visual sensation of an oval is accompanied by other sensations that indicate a certain variation in the distances of its parts, then these sensations *in combination* constitute a natural judgement, or visual perception, of a circular surface.

But it is not strictly true for Malebranche that *we* correct one sensation by another, or arrive at natural judgements by inference. As he explained in a passage clearly meant as an objection against Descartes:

God through his general law gives us precisely all those perceptions we would give ourselves *a*) if we had an exact knowledge, not only of what takes place in our brain and in our eyes, but also of the situation and movement of our bodies, *b*) if in addition we knew optics and geometry perfectly, and *c*) if we could [on this basis] . . . instantaneously produce an infinity of precise inferences, and at the same time act in ourselves according to these precise inferences and give ourselves all the different perceptions . . . that we have of objects we see at a glance . . .[67]

Malebranche concluded that none of this is possible for anything but an infinite intellect and power.[68]

In spite of the fact that natural judgements issue immediately from God, Malebranche insisted, they are strictly false. As one illustration, he produced a fascinating list of optical illusions.[69] Although our 'voluntary'

---

[64] Nicolas Malebranche, *The Search after Truth*, trans. T. M. Lennon and P. J. Olscamp (Columbus, Oh., 1980), 24 and 8–10.

[65] Ibid. 41–2.   [66] Ibid. 34.   [67] Ibid. 733–4.

[68] For a more complete discussion of Malebranche's views on the psychology of vision, see Norman Smith, 'Malebranche's Theory of the Perception of Distance and Magnitude', *British Journal of Psychology*, 1 (1905), 191–204.

[69] Malebranche, *The Search after the Truth*, 60.

judgements usually follow the natural ones, which are nearly irresistible, it is in our power to doubt and even deny the truth of presentations of sense. But even if, for example, astronomy convinces us that the moon is hundreds of thousands of miles away and of constant size, we *see* it differently: 'I do not think there is anyone in the world who in looking at the moon does not see it about a thousand feet away, and who does not find it larger when it is rising or setting than when it has risen well above the horizon . . .'[70] Malebranche, unlike Descartes and Bernier, can easily account for the persistence of optical illusions, for on his theory the visual process is completed independently of cognitive operations performed by the perceiver.

Hobbes, of all seventeenth-century writers on the psychology of vision, departed from tradition most radically. On Hobbes's materialist view, both the motions of bodies and the operations of minds are explained in terms of connatus, a sort of motion or striving for motion. In his critique of Thomas White, Hobbes applied this doctrine explicitly to vision:

The action of a shining object, when propagated to the fundus of the eye and thence to the brain, is the cause of the reaction by which motion is transmitted back from the brain, through the eye, to the objects outside. The latter motion, however, is experienced not as motion, but as the fantasy or image of the sun or of some shining body.[71]

Visual images are composed of colour and light (sometimes Hobbes adds figure). An image is merely 'an *apparition* unto us of the *motion*, agitation, or alteration, which the *object* worketh in the *brain*, or spirits, of some internal substance of the head'.[72] But we naturally tend to suppose that the image is the object and displays the object as it really is. Hobbes said in his late work *De Homine*:

It is instituted by nature [*natura insitum*] that all animals initially suppose this image is the thing, itself, that is seen, or at least a similar body with parts exactly corresponding to the thing itself. Even men, except the very few who correct

---

[70] Malebranche wrote: 'we have no sensation of external objects that does not include some false judgement' (*The Search after the Truth*, 67). Other instances of falsity include the opinion that colours, heat, cold, and the like are modifications of bodies, which is false according to mechanism, and, according to Malebranche, the all-pervasive error that we see particular bodies (rather than ideas in the mind of God).

[71] Thomas Hobbes, *Thomas White's 'De Mundo' Examined*, trans. H. W. Jones (London, 1976), 102, also see pp. 331 and 364–5. A similar account of sense perception is given elsewhere, e.g. Thomas Hobbes, *Concerning Body*, Part IV, ch. 25, sect. 2 (*The English Works of Thomas Hobbes*, ed. William Molesworth, 11 vols. (London, 1893–45; repr. 1992), i. 389–91.

[72] Thomas Hobbes *Human Nature*, in *English Works*, iv. 4–9.

sense by reason, take the image to be the object itself; and not without study can they be persuaded that the sun and stars are larger, or farther away, than they are seen to be.[73]

Hobbes went to some length to argue that visual images are not external objects and that the apparent colours, figures, sizes of images do not belong to the objects of sight. In some places, he simply cited familiar facts: we see the sun beneath the surface of a pool in which it is reflected, we see an object double when one eyeball is pushed out of position, we see light when hit on the head.[74] But in the chapters on optics in *De Homine*, he proceeded to argue on more theoretical grounds that the apparent visual qualities of things inevitably diverge from their real ones. As he put it: 'In all direct vision, the apparent place of the object, or the place of the image (*locus objecti apparens sive locus imaginis*) is on this side of the true place and smaller than it is.'[75] The argument depends on two assumptions: that a single ray of light enters the eye from each point on the viewed surface of an object (*contra* Kepler) and the thesis that the light entering the eye from an object must exceed a certain threshold in order to produce vision.[76] For any viewed object, there will be an area around its boundary such that the light coming from that region does not reach the threshold; it is only when the light from that area is joined by that from adjacent areas that the threshold is exceeded. Thus, Hobbes concluded, the object appears smaller and closer than it actually is. He was supposing that an object appears to occupy that region of space in which the rays coming from it reach threshold strength. For Hobbes, then, distance and size are not determined on the basis of other data; instead, an object immediately appears to have a certain position and size, which happen not to be its true ones. We may discover the discrepancies between bodies and their visual appearances, but Hobbes, rather like Malebranche, held that this has no effect on the process of vision.

For our purposes, it is important to note the similarity between Hobbes and Malebranche, as compared to Descartes, Gassendi, and the medieval optical theorists. According to the latter, vision involves cognitive processes that begin with data of other sorts and end with visual perception of things with sizes, shapes, and locations in space. The result is (generally)

[73] Thomas Hobbes, *Opera Philosophica quae Latine Scripsit*, ed. William Molesworth, 5 vols. (London, 1839–45; repr. Aalen, 1961), ii. 7.

[74] e.g. Hobbes, *Human Nature*, in *English Works*, iv. 3–9.

[75] Hobbes, *Opera Philosophica*, ii. 20.

[76] See Vasco Ronchi's preface to Hobbes's *Traité de l'homme*, trans. Paul-Marie Maurin (Paris, 1974), 24.

accurate perception of these properties of things, but on these views the persistence of visual illusions is difficult to explain. In contrast, according to Hobbes and Malebranche, vision is completed without rational operations on more basic data. The visual process makes things appear to have certain sizes, shapes, and positions, but these appearances are systematically false (in ways that differ, according to the two theories). When we discover the falsity, our visual images are unaltered. With this background, we can return to Locke, Molyneux, and the newly sighted man.

V

Molyneux agreed with those who held that vision involves processing of basic data. *Dioptrica Nova* deals mainly with refraction, but this topic leads him to a brief account of ordinary distance perception. It is 'rather the Act of our *Judgement*, than of *Sense*', he argued. 'For *Distance* of it self, is not to be perceived; for 'tis a Line (or a Length) presented to our Eye with its End towards us, which must therefore be only a *Point*, and that is *Invisible*.'[77] He mentioned the several methods of determining distance described by Descartes, including monocular perception due to changes in the conformation of the eye and the method of triangulation.[78] (Here he mentioned and rejected Gassendi's single-eye theory of vision.) Molyneux did not discuss perception of size and shape. But since they presuppose apprehension of the distances of the parts of objects, he no doubt thought they, too, result from cognitive operations on other data.

Locke shared this view, as we have seen. The chapter on perception in the *Essay* made this plain to Molyneux when he proposed his query to Locke for the second time. But Molyneux had seen no summary of this chapter when he sent his first note to Locke. Even so, it is not difficult to explain how he might have correctly surmised what Locke thought on the issue. For one thing, both Hobbes and Malebranche stressed the falsity of visual perception, and Molyneux could have seen the importance Locke placed on the reliability of sense perception. In any case, Hobbes and

[77] Molyneux, *Dioptrica Nova*, 113.
[78] Molyneux is non-committal on the psychological issues, e.g. whether the sizes of these angles are apprehended as part of Cartesian calculations, or whether the sense of the turning of the eyes is correlated through experience and memory with the distances of objects seen. None the less, he is accused of giving an account of distance perception in his dioptrics inconsistent with his answer to the Molyneux question by Colin M. Turbayne in 'Berkeley and Molyneux on the Retinal Image', *Journal of the History of Ideas*, 16 (1955), 341 and p. 344 n. 37.

Malebranche derived their positions from controversial premisses, respectively, an outdated theory of light rays and the doctrine of occasionalism.

For Locke and Molyneux, then, the issue posed by the newly sighted man concerns the *nature* of the cognitive process that issues in visual perception of bodily shape. Descartes and Gassendi offered two distinct alternatives to the unacceptable Scholastic psychology. On the Cartesian view, nothing in principle prevents the Molyneux-man from seeing the globe and cube at once, provided their distances are in the range we perceive by triangulation; the tendency to make this calculation is innate. In contrast, a view like Gassendi's implied that time and experience would be required for the man to see the shapes and distances of things. Why did Locke reject the Cartesian account, and how did Molyneux think that was justified by Locke's philosophy?

Part of the answer may be Locke's conviction that all animals are sentient.[79] But this probably had little to do with Molyneux's initial expectations, because this opinion of Locke was not explicit in the 'Essai'. The answer to both questions seems to lie in Descartes's natural geometry, for Locke was certainly opposed to *that*. But the significance of the dispute over innatism tends to be elusive. Just what is it about Descartes's account of visual cognition that is unacceptable to Locke?

One point of conflict between Cartesian psychology and a tenet of Locke's philosophy is particularly clear and central. Descartes's account might be taken to imply that the very young are aware of optical and geometrical principles, and this is the sort of claim Locke ridicules in the *Essay*, Book I. But, as we saw, Descartes probably did not suppose our earliest reasonings involve distinct awareness of mathematical principles, but rather thought that we use principles without being clearly aware of them. Now both philosophers held that in order to use a theorem, a child must have in mind ideas by which it is an object of thought. But whereas Descartes supposed one can have in mind an idea and not be fully conscious of what the idea is, this is inimical to Locke's notion of idea. For Locke, an idea simply is what one immediately perceives or is 'conscious of within himself'.[80] Ideas are the paradigm of intuitive knowledge; a man has the greatest certainty 'that any *Idea* in his Mind is such, as he perceives it to be'.[81] So a fundamental tenet of Locke's philosophy does rule out the Cartesian account of depth perception.

Molyneux could easily have seen this from doctrines stated in the

---

[79] *Essay*, II. ix. 11–14, pp. 147–9.   [80] Ibid. I. i. 8, p. 48.
[81] Ibid. IV. ii. 1, p. 531; also IV. iii. 8, p. 544.

'Essai'. Although it scarcely mentions innate ideas and entirely omits the polemical Book I, it stresses that all ideas are derived from experience.[82] More important, it explicitly states the crucial anti-Cartesian thesis that all ideas are intuitively known.[83]

The alternative, a view like Gassendi's, sets the cognitive operations of vision apart from the optical demonstrations that explain why those procedures generally work. We learn to see figures by correlating various sorts of sensations in ways inculcated and ratified by repeated experience. This is, I think, the main story of the Locke–Molyneux answer to the question about the once-blind man.

VI

In this last section, I want to consider briefly how Locke integrates this theory of visual cognition into his broader philosophy. Two central issues emerge in his short chapter on perception. One concerns the causal and epistemic ground of visual inference; the other, the formation of visual ideas. The key to the first issue is the role given to the faculty of judgement. It converts the ideas caused in us by objects into perceptions of their shapes, etc. As Locke said, 'the Ideas we receive by sensation, are often in grown People alter'd by the Judgment'.[84] Judgement is said later in Book IV to be a faculty 'conversant about Truth and Falsehood', and thus similar to knowledge; but whereas we know a proposition only if we perceive its truth, we judge a proposition when we presume it true with some reason.[85] Visual inferences are apparently grounded, causally and epistemically, in the sources of reasonable opinion (as opposed to knowledge) specified in Book IV.[86]

---

[82] See King, *The Life and Letters of John Locke*, 365. Innate maxims are given derogatory mention in the section summarizing *Essay*, IV. vii (p. 394).

[83] The summary of Book IV says: 'It is the first and fundamental act of our understanding to perceive the ideas it has, to know each what it is, and perceive wherein it differs from any others; without this, the mind could neither have variety of thoughts nor discourse, judge or reason about them' (King, *The Life and Letters of John Locke*, 389).

[84] *Essay*, II. ix. 8, p. 145 (italics omitted).   [85] Ibid. IV. xiv. 4, p. 653.

[86] As far as I can see, this produces no conflict in Locke's epistemology. The suggestion in *Essay*, II. ix that visual determinations of shape etc. are *merely* well-grounded opinions is quite consistent with Locke's well-known insistence that we have sensitive *knowledge*. For what we are supposed to know, when we receive ideas of sense, is just that something then exists outside us that causes these ideas in us. Beyond the thing's powers to cause those specific ideas, we have no strict knowledge of its nature or properties (see e.g. *Essay*, IV. xi. 9, pp. 635–6).

In particular, it seems they are warranted by what Locke called 'conformity of any thing with our own Knowledge, Observation, and Experience'. He gave various illustrations, some of which fit a standard inductive pattern: if one has observed in many cases that certain features go together, then one has *reason* to judge that those features go together in other cases.[87] It is natural to assume Locke construed perceptual inference on this model. A person experiences many instances of a certain pattern of light and colour that come, say, from bodies that are convex; then when she receives an idea of a pattern of this sort, she judges that it comes from a convex body and has reason for this.

Since visual judgement depends on this sort of induction, Locke must have thought everyone learns to see bodily shapes as the Molyneux-man does. We all begin by perceiving that various colour-patterns are associated with (caused by) objects of various shapes. To do this, we must perceive the shapes of things. Locke cannot suppose we *see* figures until we have noted at least a few correlations between light–colour patterns and the perceived shapes of things. So for Locke, visual competence to determine figure must always presuppose competence in some other sensory mode, namely, touch.[88]

The function assigned to judgement in Book IV is to form and affirm propositions. There are some questions about how Locke thought this function applies to visual perception. For one thing, perceptions that result from judgement should be expressed propositionally (e.g. 'I am looking at a globe', or 'Here is a globe'). In fact, Locke tends to describe judgemental perception by *de re* locutions; e.g. '[judgement] frames to it self the perception of a convex Figure, and an uniform Colour'. But Locke could, I think, accept a propositional formulation. Another question arises from Locke's tendency to say that in vision, judgement produces an *idea*: 'we take that for the Perception of our Sensation, which is an *Idea* formed by our Judgment; so that one, *viz.* that of Sensation, serves only to excite

---

[87] For example, we have reason to judge that a certain fire will warm a man, if in all our experience (and that of others), it has been observed that fire warms; see *Essay*, IV. xv. 6, p. 656.

[88] Locke never discussed such questions as whether there is a special suitability between how a cube, for example, looks and how it feels, or whether how a cube looks could have been different than it is without detracting from the information we have by sight. Locke's position allows one to ask whether certain colour–light patterns (vs. visual presentations of figure) have a special fitness for conveying the shape of a cube. But the position implies that the visual idea *of a cube* could not have been the idea of any other figure, for it is a sign of a cube only because we have found it to be an idea typically caused by cubes. This has sometimes been taken to be the sort of issue posed by Molyneux's question; see Judith Jarvis Thomson, 'Molyneux's Problem', *Journal of Philosophy*, 71 (1974), 637–50.

the other'.[89] But Locke might have regarded this as an elliptical description of an operation in which one idea excites judgement to form a
proposition one of whose terms is a different idea. There is another, more
worrisome question. The operations of judgement described in Book IV
are *affirmations*. This fits well with situations in which, so to speak, we
believe what we see; but it conflicts with the persistence of illusions, e.g.
the size of the moon on the horizon. Because the moon looks relatively
close and large, Locke must say that judgement is responsible for this
appearance (the moon does not *cause* ideas of location and size in us). But
perceivers familiar with the illusion do not judge, or affirm, that the
moon on the horizon is relatively close and large. The second issue raised
by Locke's discussion of perception concerns the mixed nature of ideas of
sight. He insists that visual ideas of bodily shape are *not* received by sense,
but imported by judgement, e.g. in the last passage quoted above. Twice
Locke offers a linguistic analogy to illustrate this: the sight of a word
excites us to form the idea of what it signifies, and often we hardly notice
the visible mark.[90] The analogy underlines the non-visual character of
visual shape-ideas: when we see a word, we form an idea of what it
signifies without *seeing* what it signifies.

It is natural to ask if this is consistent with Locke's doctrine that ideas
of figure are simple ideas we get from both sight and touch.[91] An idea may
be derived from sight even though it is not directly received. Ideas of
colour and light are caused immediately in accord with psychophysical
laws, but visual ideas of figure may require further operations of mind.
However, this is not clearly consistent with Locke's doctrine that the
'reality' and 'adequacy' of simple ideas are guaranteed, because it rests on
the claim that simple ideas are passively received.[92] Further, it is clear
visual ideas of figures must have a certain complexity. They are not just
visual images, but also marks of the shapes of things. The visual idea of
a cube is a light–colour pattern plus the understanding that it is caused
by a cube, which can only be represented by a second, tactual idea. The
content of visual ideas of figures must involve at least two separable
elements. Perhaps it should not surprise us that some of Locke's *simple*
ideas have logical structure, for we saw that these ideas are not conceptual

---

[89] *Essay*, II. ix. 9, p. 146.

[90] Ibid. 146–7 and 'Examination', in *Works*, ix. 218 (cited above, n. 21).

[91] *Essay*, II. v, p. 127.

[92] Ibid. II. xxx. 2–3, pp. 372–3 and II. xxxi. 2, pp. 375–6. The importance of this doctrine
is discussed in M. R. Ayers, 'The Foundations of Knowledge and the Logic of Substance'
(Ch. 2 in this volume).

atoms and, moreover, that all simple ideas serve as marks of the qualities of their causes. This sort of complexity is not inconsistent with Locke's essentially undefined notion of simple idea, but it does illustrate its latitude.

4

Locke on the Freedom of the Will

VERE CHAPPELL

Locke was a libertarian: he believed in human freedom. To be sure, his conception of freedom was different from that of many philosophers who call themselves libertarians. Some such philosophers maintain that an agent is free only if her action is uncaused; whereas Locke thought that all actions have causes, including the free ones. Some libertarians hold that no action is free unless it proceeds from a volition that is itself free; whereas Locke argued that free volition, as opposed to free action, is an impossibility. On the other hand, Locke agrees with the typical professed libertarian that free actions depend on volitions—or, as he often puts it, that an agent is free only with respect to the actions she wills, to those that are voluntary. And he also refuses to make voluntariness sufficient for freedom, whereby a free action is merely one that is willed. The free agent, Locke insists, must also be able or have been able to do something other than she does or did. Thus both Locke and the libertarian professor require indifference as well as spontaneity for freedom. But Locke's freedom is not contra-causal; and he denies that it extends to volition.

In this chapter I want to focus on just this last component of Locke's view of freedom: that freedom in willing, far from being required for free agency, is not even possible. I call this the thesis of volitional determinism. Locke presents an argument for this thesis in the *Essay*, but scholars have never paid much attention to it: I want to examine it. But I also have a further concern. It is well known that Locke's views on freedom and motivation changed considerably after he first presented them in the chapter 'Of Power' in the first edition of the *Essay*. This chapter was

A version of this chapter was presented at the Clarendon Locke Conference in Oxford in Sept. 1990. More-distant ancestors of it were read at Dartmouth College and to the Seventeenth-Century Study Group at the Institute for Advanced Study. I am grateful to my auditors on those occasions, and especially to Martha Bolton, Willis Doney, Robert Sleigh, and James Tully, for helpful questions and suggestions.

extensively rewritten for the second edition of 1694, and Locke made significant further additions to it both for the fourth edition, published in 1700, and for the fifth, which came out after his death in 1706. These subjects are also discussed in his correspondence with his Arminian friend Philippus van Limborch in 1701 and 1702. One of the most striking features of Locke's 'second thoughts' on freedom appears in the middle of the revised version of Book II, chapter xxi that was included in the *Essay*'s second edition. This is the observation that an agent may, while deliberating what to do, '*suspend* the execution and satisfaction of any of [his] desires',[1] and so keep his will from being determined to any action. This doctrine of suspension at least appears to conflict with the volitional determinism that Locke affirms and argues for earlier in the chapter, in its revised no less than in its original version. But not only did Locke at first fail to see that there might be a conflict between the two doctrines; he refused to acknowledge the problem of reconciling them when van Limborch pointed it out to him. Eventually, it appears that Locke did see the problem, and he altered his views and made some adjustments in the text of the *Essay* accordingly. Even so, he did not make all the adjustments that a full change of view would have called for. Hence doubts remain, both as to the actual bearing of these doctrines on one another and as to Locke's understanding of their relationship. My further purpose, therefore, is to consider Locke's volitional determinism in relation to his doctrine of suspension, and to ascertain his final position concerning it.

I begin with a more exact statement of Locke's view of freedom. The idea of freedom (or liberty) is introduced early in chapter xxi of Book II, the official subject of which is power. Power in general, Locke says, is an attribute of an individual substance, by which it is able to do or suffer something. The power is active when it enables the substance possessing it to perform an action of some kind; it is passive when it makes the substance liable to be affected in some way. Will is an active power belonging to rational agents; volition or willing is the exercise of this power, i.e. the action that having a will enables an agent to perform. Volitions are actions in their own right, but every volition is ordered or directed to some further action of the same agent—what might be called the *target* of the volition. A volition, more specifically, is either a volition to do or a volition not to do something—to forbear doing it.

When an agent wills to do something, and does it, and does it because

---

[1] *Essay*, 2nd to 5th edns., 263; original edns. are indicated only when that information matters.

she has willed it, she is said to have acted in accord with her will, and her action (i.e. the target action) is voluntary. When an agent doesn't do something she wills to do, or does something else instead of that, then her forbearance or alternative action is involuntary, and she is said to have forborne or acted against her will. Also involuntary are actions performed merely without being willed, though these are not done against the will of the agent. Only the actions of rational agents are voluntary, since only such agents are capable of willing. But involuntary actions are performed by non-rational as well as by rational agents. Indeed, all of the actions of beings without reason or thought are involuntary.

Locke first defines freedom as the property of a rational agent whereby he has the power to act or not to act 'according to the preference or direction of his own mind',[2] i.e. in accord with his will. It might appear from this that Locke identifies free with voluntary agency—that being free for him just consists in doing or being able to do what one wills. And so a number of commentators have taken him to do.[3] But in fact his position is that voluntariness is merely a necessary condition of freedom. This is the point of his famous example of the man locked in a room with someone he longs to be with. The man 'stays willingly' in the room, i.e. his doing so is voluntary. But his staying is not free because, being locked in, 'he is not at liberty not to stay, he has not freedom to be gone'.[4] Hence 'where-ever any performance or forbearance are not equally in a Man's power; where-ever doing or not doing, will not equally follow upon the preference of his mind directing it, there he is not *Free*, though perhaps the Action may be voluntary'.[5] And again, 'where-ever . . . compulsion takes away that Indifferency of Ability on either side to act, or to forbear acting, there *liberty* . . . presently ceases'.[6] Locke's freedom, therefore, includes this liberty of indifference as well as the liberty of spontaneity: freedom means having a choice in addition to choosing. To be free an agent must not only do something because she has willed it, and thus be able to do what she wills; she must also be able, by willing, to do something other than that—her action must be avoidable, she must have an alternative to it.

Things that lack freedom, for Locke, are necessary; the word 'necessary',

[2] *Essay*, 237.
[3] See e.g. Edmund Law, in his edn. of William King's *The Origin of Evil*, 5th edn. (London, 1781), 186 n. 42; John W. Yolton, *Locke and the Compass of Human Understanding* (Cambridge, 1970), 144; D. Locke, 'Three Concepts of Free Action', *Proceedings of the Aristotelian Society*, supp. vol. 68 (1975), 96; and J. O'Higgins, *Determinism and Freewill* (The Hague, 1976), 119.
[4] *Essay*, 238.   [5] Ibid. 237.   [6] Ibid. 238.

at least in the chapter on power, just means 'not free'. Necessity, like freedom, is properly an attribute of agents; but Locke sometimes calls actions with respect to which an agent is 'under necessity' 'necessary actions'.[7] An action may be necessary because it is done by an inanimate or otherwise non-rational agent; or because its (rational) agent either is compelled by some irresistible internal or external force to do it against his will, or else merely fails to exercise his will with respect to it. Thus all involuntary actions are necessary for Locke. But likewise necessary are those voluntary actions which an agent cannot avoid doing because of internal or external constraints which prevent him from performing any alternative action, including that of merely forbearing the action he does.

It is important to note that no action is necessary for Locke simply by being the effect of antecedent causes. Locke's use of 'necessary' thus differs from that of certain 'compatibilist' philosophers with whose views on freedom his is often associated—Hobbes and Hume, for example. For the latter, 'necessary' means 'causally determined'; and in this sense, they maintain, an action can be necessary *and* free: this is what makes them compatibilists. For Locke, on the contrary, since 'necessary' means 'not free', the same action cannot be both free and necessary. Is Locke then an incompatibilist? In one way he is; but in another not. For his disagreement with Hobbes and Hume is only verbal. He believes, as they do, that all human actions are causally determined, and hence that all free actions are. So Locke accepts the substance of the compatibilists' view: his incompatibilism concerns 'necessity' only in *his* sense of the word.

Locke claims that it follows from his view of freedom that the 'long agitated' question, 'Whether Man's Will be free, or no', is 'unintelligible'. It makes no more sense to say that the will is, or is not, free than to say that one's sleep is swift or one's virtue square. This is so because '*Liberty*, which is but a power, belongs only to Agents, and cannot be an attribute or modification of the *Will*, which is also but a Power'.[8]

Later on, however, Locke concedes that those who dispute 'Whether the *will* be free' may have a different question in mind. What they may mean to ask is not whether the will itself has the property of freedom, but whether an agent having a will is free to exercise it upon occasion: 'Whether a man be free to will'.[9] This question, Locke allows, is perfectly intelligible,

---

[7] Though he never, I think, makes the parallel move from 'free agent' to 'free action'. But since there is no reason for him to avoid the latter expression, I shall myself use it in expounding Locke's position.

[8] Ibid. 240.   [9] Ibid. 245.

and he proceeds to provide his own answer to it. It is in the course of doing this that he puts forward his doctrine of volitional determinism.

In fact Locke construes the question here in two different ways. What he actually considers, therefore, are two distinct questions. In the one case, the question is whether a man is free 'in respect of willing any Action in his power once proposed to his Thoughts'. In the other, the question is whether 'a Man be at liberty to will either Motion, or Rest; Speaking, or Silence; which he pleases'. Locke takes up the first of these questions in section 23, the second in section 25.

His answer to the first question is negative. Once a man considers an action, or starts deliberating about it, he 'cannot be free' in respect of willing it, since it is 'unavoidably necessary' that he will either to do it or not to do it. Locke argues for this position as follows:

Willing, or Choosing being an Action, and Freedom consisting in a power of acting, or not acting, [1] *a Man in respect of willing any Action in his power once proposed to his Thoughts, cannot be free.* The reason whereof is very manifest: For [2] it being unavoidable that the Action depending on his *Will*, should exist, or not exist; and its existence, or not existence, following perfectly the determination, and preference of his Will, [3] he cannot avoid willing the existence, or not existence, of that Action; it is absolutely necessary that he *will* the one, or the other, *i.e. prefer* the one to the other: since one of them must necessarily follow; and [4] that which does follow, follows by the choice and determination of his Mind, that is, by his *willing* it: for [5] if he did not *will* it, it would not be. So that [1] in respect of the act of *willing*, a Man is not free: Liberty consisting in a power to act, or not to act, which, in regard of Volition, a Man has not: it being necessary, and unavoidable (any Action in his power being once thought on) to prefer either its doing, or forbearance, upon which preference, the Action, or its forbearance certainly follows, and is truly voluntary.[10]

Locke's reasoning here has the form of a constructive dilemma. A more perspicuous statement of it, with suppressed premisses and lemmas filled in, is the following (numbers in square brackets refer to the text just quoted):

(1) [2] Every action a man considers doing must either exist or not exist.

(2) [5] If the man considering such an action did not will it to exist, it would not exist.

So (3) [4] If such an action exists, the man wills it to exist.

[10] *Essay*, 1st to 3rd edns., 245; bracketed numbers added.

(4)   If the man considering such an action did not will it not to exist, it would not not exist.

So (5)   If such an action does not exist, the man wills it not to exist.

So (6) [3] Every such action must either be willed to exist or be willed not to exist by the man considering it.

(7)   If a man wills an action to exist, he wills.

(8)   If a man wills an action not to exist, he wills.

So (9)   A man considering an action must will.

(10)   If a man considering an action must will, then he is not free in respect of the act of willing: he cannot avoid willing.

So (11) [1] A man considering an action is not free in respect of the act of willing: he cannot avoid willing.

This argument, clearly, is valid. But equally clearly, it has a false premiss. The obvious offender was spotted by Leibniz. Here is Theophile's response to Philalethe's summary of section 23 in the *Nouveaux essais*:

I would have thought that one can suspend one's choice, and that this happens quite often, especially when other thoughts interrupt one's deliberation. Thus, although it is necessary that the action about which one is deliberating must exist or not exist, it doesn't follow at all that one necessarily has to decide on its existence or non-existence. For its non-existence could well come about in the absence of any decision.[11]

Leibniz's point is directed against premiss (4) of Locke's argument. This premiss is not stated explicitly, but clauses 3–5 in the text quoted above plainly imply it; and in any case the argument requires it. So if Leibniz is right—as surely he is—then Locke's reasoning fails to establish its conclusion.

But if Locke is thus guilty of accepting an evident falsehood, that is not the whole of his fault in this matter. For he also expressly acknowledges the very ability to 'suspend one's choice' that Leibniz uses to refute his argument in section 23. That agents have such an ability is precisely the point of his doctrine of suspension, stated in section 47 of the same chapter of the *Essay*. Thus, not only is premiss (4) of Locke's argument

---

[11] Gottfried Leibniz, *Nouveaux essais sur l'entendement humain*, II. xxi. 23, p. 181. I quote from the translation by Peter Remnant and Jonathan Bennett (Cambridge, 1981); the page number is that of the Akademie edition, whose numbering also is used by Remnant and Bennett.

false, it is directly contradicted by something he himself affirms. Indeed, the doctrine of suspension contradicts the argument's conclusion also. It is true that these inconsistencies are not to be found in the first edition of Locke's work. For though the argument of section 23 was present from the outset, the doctrine of suspension did not appear until the second edition. But the inconsistencies did exist then, and they continued to do so thereafter. For Locke made no changes in the doctrine of suspension in subsequent editions of the *Essay*, nor did he excise or amend the (false) premiss of his argument in section 23—although he did finally, in his revisions for the fifth edition, qualify the argument's conclusion.

There is more to be said about Locke's position here; but to say it would take me away from my central concern in this paper. For the thesis that a man who thinks about doing something is unavoidably bound to will one way or the other regarding it—call this the unavoidability thesis— is not volitional determinism; nor is there any logical relation between this thesis and that. Volitional determinism applies to concrete acts of willing, and it ascribes necessity *de re* to all of them. It says of every volition that it is a necessary action on the part of its agent. The unavoidability thesis, by contrast, ascribes necessity *de dicto* to a propo- sition about agents, agents operating, furthermore, under a special con- dition. It says that if an agent thinks about doing something x then it is necessary that either he will to do x or else he will not to do x.[12] Not only does this thesis attribute necessity to no individual volition, but it is less than universal in scope, since not all of the actions that agents perform, or even their voluntary actions, are 'proposed to their thoughts' before being done. We often do things, and will to do things, quite spontaneously, without first thinking about them.

To discover Locke's volitional determinism, then, we must look to the second of the two questions he considers in sections 23–5. This second question is whether a man is free to will what he does will—free to will to move, for example, as opposed to willing to stand still, or willing not to move, or not willing to move, or even not willing at all. Locke's imme- diate response is that

This Question carries the absurdity of it so manifestly in it self, that one might thereby sufficiently be convinced, that Liberty concerns not the Will in any case. For to ask, whether a Man be at Liberty to will either Motion or Rest; Speaking,

---

[12] This is one possible way of construing Locke's unavoidability thesis, as a conditional necessity. Another is to take it as a necessary conditional: it is necessary that if an agent thinks about doing x then either he wills to do x or he wills not to do x.

or Silence; which he pleases, is to ask, whether a Man can *will*, what he *wills*; or be pleased with what he is pleased with. A Question, which, I think, needs no answer: and they, who can make a Question of it, must suppose one Will to determine the Acts of another, and another to determinate that; and so on *in infinitum*.[13]

What is Locke's position here? The question, he says, has an 'absurdity' in it. But he does not say that it is an 'insignificant' or an 'unintelligible' question. Furthermore, he pronounces the absurdity 'manifest'; but then, as if not trusting us to see it, takes steps to locate it. He suggests that the absurdity lies not in the question itself, but in an affirmative answer to it; that it consists in some sort of viciously infinite succession of wills; and that it arises somehow from the idea of iterated willing, of willing to will. It seems plain that Locke is urging a substantive, albeit negative answer to the question at issue, and that he is basing it on an argument of the *reductio ad absurdum* form. This negative answer is in fact the thesis of volitional determinism.

But what exactly is the reasoning by which Locke seeks to establish this thesis? His argument is barely adumbrated in the text I have quoted from section 25; and in the fifth edition of the *Essay* the section ends with the words '*in infinitum*'. But in the first four editions these words are immediately followed by a reference to an earlier statement of the same argument: 'an absurdity before taken notice of'. This earlier statement occurs in section 23—or did in the first four editions, after which it too was dropped, along with the reference to it. This section originally contained two distinct arguments, both ostensibly in support of the unavoidability thesis. The second of these is indeed the *reductio* argument of section 25, more fully and more explicitly set forth. (The fact that the unavoidability thesis is logically distinct from the thesis of volitional determinism may explain why, assuming he realized it, Locke cut this passage out of the fifth edition.) Here is the earlier statement:

Besides, to make a Man free after this manner [sc. free with respect to the act of volition], by making the Action of *willing* to depend on his *Will*, there must be another antecedent *Will*, to determine the Acts of this *Will*, and another to determine that, and so *in infinitum*: For where-ever one stops, the Actions of the last *Will* cannot be free . . .[14]

This statement enables us to identify three of Locke's premisses:

---

[13] *Essay*, 247. [14] *Essay*, 4th edn., 245.

(1) An agent's action of willing must, to be free, 'depend on his Will': i.e. it must be voluntary. This is just the general requirement that free actions be voluntary applied to the special case of actions of willing.

(2) To say that an action 'depends on a will' is to say that the will 'determines' that action. When the action determined is a volition, then there is a will to which that action belongs: a volition just is the act of a will. It might be supposed that the will by which a voluntary volition is determined is the same as that to which the volition belongs, or at least that it could be the same. On this supposition, a will would be capable of determining itself, i.e. of determining its own acts of willing. Locke, however, is clearly denying such self-determination on the part of the will. His position is, in fact, that a voluntary action of willing can only be determined by 'another antecedent will'—a will distinct from the will to which it belongs. (That the will can determine itself is what I shall call the 'autonomy principle'; its denial is then the 'heteronomy principle'.)

(3) Given that a voluntary volition requires a second will, distinct from the one it belongs to, why should any third will be required, let alone the infinite series of wills invoked by Locke's argument? Locke holds that when a will determines an action it does so by acting, i.e. by performing one or more volitions. Let us say that the volition by which a will determines an action 'produces' the action, to distinguish the relation the volition bears to the action from the relation the will bears to it. If a volition, belonging to a will, is voluntary, then there is another volition, belonging to a second will, which produces it. But there is so far no need for this second volition to be voluntary also: that is, the fact that the first volition is *voluntary* does not require this. What does require it, according to Locke, is the fact that the first volition is *free*, besides being voluntary. For in this passage he embraces what I shall call the 'inheritance principle' of free action. This is the principle that a free action must 'inherit' its freedom from the volition which produces it. More precisely, it is the principle that an action is free only if the volition which produces it is free; or, contrapositively, that if a volition is necessary then any action produced by it also is necessary. By this principle, a free volition requires a second volition that is free, and not merely voluntary; and this in turn requires a third free volition; and so on without end. 'For where-ever one stops, the Actions of the last Will cannot be free.'

It appears, then, that the argument of section 25—and of section 23 in editions 1–4 of the *Essay*—can be represented as follows.

(1) Acts of willing are acts.

(2) Every act with respect to which an agent is free is voluntary.

(3) An act is voluntary iff there is an act of willing which produces it.

(4) An act of willing is voluntary iff there is a will which determines it.

(5) Every act of willing belongs to a will.

(6) The act of willing which produces a voluntary act of willing belongs to the will which determines that act.

(7) No will determines itself, i.e. determines the acts of willing which belong to it. (Heteronomy principle)

(8) An agent is free with respect to an act, only if he also is free with respect to the act of willing which produces that act. (Inheritance principle)

(9) If an act of willing is such that (*a*) there is an act of willing which produces it, and (*b*) there is a will which determines it, and (*c*) the act of willing which produces it belongs to the will which determines it, and (*d*) no will determines its own acts of willing, and (*e*) an agent is free with respect to an act only if he also is free with respect to the act of willing which produces that act; then there is an infinite series of wills running back from the will to which the first act of willing belongs.

(10) An infinite series of wills running back from the will to which a specified act of willing belongs is an absurdity.

(11) There are no absurdities.

So (12) No agent is free with respect to an act of willing.

Locke's argument, as I have rendered it, is valid. The task of evaluating it is therefore reduced to that of assessing its premisses. We need not reach the question of the truth of these premisses, however. For one of them turns out to be such that it cannot have been held to be true by the argument's own author, i.e. by Locke himself, which means that he cannot consistently have used the argument against its intended victims. The premiss in question is (8), the inheritance principle, which specifies a necessary condition for an action's being free: the action is free only if the volition that makes it a voluntary action itself is free. That such a condition holds is a fundamental doctrine of the very philosophers who were Locke's opponents on this issue. It is these philosophers who pronounce that 'Man's will is free', although what they must mean is that 'Men are free to will'. And it is at them that Locke's sarcastic jab in section 22 is directed: 'It passes for a good Plea', he remarks, 'that a Man is not free at all, if he be not as free to will, as he is to act, what he wills'.[15] This remark by itself might convince us that Locke would not have accepted premiss (8). But beyond that, there is a passage farther on in chapter xxi in which he explicitly rejects it. A prisoner, Locke writes,

> that has his Chains knocked off, and the Prison doors set open to him, is perfectly at *liberty*, because he may either go or stay, as he best likes; though his preference be determined to stay, by the darkness of the Night, or illness of the Weather, or want of other Lodging. He ceases not to be free; though the desire of some convenience to be had there, absolutely determines his preference, and makes him stay in his Prison.[16]

In any case, the conjunction of premiss (8) with Locke's own libertarianism directly contradicts the conclusion of his *reductio* argument. Locke begins his discussion of freedom in chapter xxi with the declaration that 'every one finds in himself' the power of acting freely. But if the volitions by which free actions are produced also has to be free, it would follow that some volitions are free, which is just the position that Locke's argument is directed against.

There is, to be sure, another way of using a *reductio* argument against an opponent.[17] Instead of reaching an absurdity via premisses that he himself would accept, the author of a *reductio* may reason *ad hominem*, seeking to show that the absurdity follows from the opponent's own premisses. The conclusion then drawn is that some part of the opponent's position is faulty, no matter whether it be the proposition originally tagged for 'reduction' or some other premiss, since in any case the position is damaged. It might then be suggested that Locke's *reductio* argument was meant to be used in this *ad hominem* way, with libertarians such as Bramhall and the Arminians the intended targets. There is no doubt that premiss (8) of the argument had a crucial place in the credo of these thinkers.[18] Most of the other premisses, as well, would have been acceptable to the philosophers that Locke was attacking.

But the *ad hominem* use of a *reductio* argument can succeed only if *all* of its premisses would be accepted by the *homine* against whom it is

---

[15] *Essay*, 245. [16] Ibid. 266.

[17] This point was suggested to me by Martha Bolton, who heard an earlier version of this paper.

[18] See e.g. Bramhall's *Defence of True Liberty* (London, 1655), 13–16; and van Limborch's letter to Locke dated 8 July 1701 (*Correspondence*, vii. 368, no. 2953).

directed. For otherwise the intended target can disarm the argument simply by rejecting any premiss that fails to accord with his overall position. And there is one premiss of Locke's argument which most of his opponents indeed would have rejected, namely (7), the heteronomy principle, that no will is self-determining. These thinkers subscribed, on the contrary, to the autonomy principle: for them, the power of self-determination is the central feature of the will. It is also the key to the will's freedom, and thence the basis of all human freedom, freedom with respect to acts other than volitions as well as volitions themselves. William King, for example, in a direct comment on section 23 of (the first edition of) the *Essay*, says of the claim 'that there must be an antecedent will to determine this will and so in infinitum', that 'this were true if the will were a passive power'. But in fact, King maintains, the will 'is an active power [that] determines it self in its choice and is not determined by another', adding that 'he that doth not understand this understands nothing of liberty'.[19] And Bishop Bramhall, in his *Castigations of Mr. Hobbes*, declares that it 'is a truth not to be doubted of' that 'the will doth determine itself'.[20] It is extremely unlikely, therefore, that Locke's *reductio* was intended to show the absurdity of his opponents' position upon their own premisses. But even if it had been so intended it would not have succeeded.

But if Locke's argument fails, it does not follow that its conclusion, the thesis of volitional determinism, is false. We have not shown even that any of its premisses are false—we have not raised any question as to their truth—only that their relation to other positions held by Locke and by his opponents is such that effective use of the argument is barred. Perhaps, after all, the thesis is true; and perhaps there is some other argument that Locke could have used to establish it.

Perhaps indeed. But the fact is, as I have noted, that Locke's view of freedom and motivation changed considerably after he published it in the *Essay*'s first edition. One significant new element in the position set forth in the second edition is the doctrine of suspension. This doctrine, far from providing support for volitional determinism, seems rather to undermine it: and Locke himself seems, near the end of his life, to have given it up.

I turn now to consider this doctrine. It is stated in section 47 of the revised version of chapter xxi that Locke wrote for the second edition. At

---

[19] King's comment is made in a letter to William Molyneux, who conveyed it to Locke with his own letter of 15 Oct. 1692 (*Correspondence*, iv. 540, no. 1544).

[20] *The Works of John Bramhall, D.D.* (Oxford, 1842), iv. 221.

this point in the chapter Locke is presenting his new view of 'what determines the will'. His exposition here is subtle and intricate, and to do justice to it I should have to lay out at length not only what the new view amounts to, but how it differs from the old one, what led Locke to give up the one and develop the other, and what it is to 'determine the will' in the first place. In this chapter, however, a rough sketch is all that is needed, to indicate the context in which the doctrine of suspension is introduced.

According, then, to Locke's second thoughts on the subject, what determines the will of an agent who is set to do something 'is not, as is generally supposed', and as he himself used to think, 'the greater good in view: But some . . . *uneasiness* [the agent] is at present under'.[21] This uneasiness is the troublesome feeling that constitutes, or at least is a part of, desire. Since 'desire' is defined as 'an uneasiness of the Mind for want of some absent good',[22] we cannot say that 'uneasiness' has simply, in Locke's later view, been substituted for 'the greater good in view' as the one factor that makes agents will as they do. Originally, the mere perception of something as good was deemed sufficient to determine the will to an action, an action designed to attain the good so perceived; and desire and volition were hardly distinguished. In Locke's revised view, 'desiring and willing are two distinct Acts of the mind',[23] related as cause and effect. The will, moreover, is not actually affected, we are not 'set on work', unless our desire for the good we perceive 'makes us uneasy in the want of it'.[24] For ' 'tis uneasiness alone [that] operates on the will';[25] only uneasiness 'immediately determines' its choice.[26] Still, 'Good and Evil, present and absent', do 'work upon the mind',[27] even if they do not do so directly. Indeed, they are always involved in the motivational process.

A simple example may help to convey Locke's position. Suppose a man to be hungry. Hunger is a form of desire, a desire either for food or for the relief that eating will bring. Relief is pleasant, and food produces pleasure; but the hunger itself is painful, an uneasy state. Depending on his situation and his beliefs, our hungry man wills to go to the fridge or a restaurant, or to pick a strawberry, or to perform some other action which is apt to satisfy his desire, bring relief from his pain, remove his uneasiness. Now the object of our agent's desire, food or relief, being pleasant or productive of pleasure, is good, at least in his eyes. The target of his volition is the action he opts for, e.g. to go to the fridge. And his

[21] *Essay*, 250–1.   [22] Ibid. 251.   [23] Ibid. 250.
[24] Ibid. 253.   [25] Ibid. 254.   [26] Ibid. 252.   [27] Ibid.

desire determines his will, meaning that his desire causes his will to settle upon the action chosen, in the sense both of eliciting an actual volition and of specifying it as a volition to perform precisely that action.

The agent in our example has only one desire, hunger. In real life, however, Locke observes, we are 'beset with sundry *uneasinesses*, distracted with different *desires*',[28] all clamouring for attention, the will being incapable of being determined to more than one action at once.[29] Locke then asks himself which of these competing desires 'has the precedency in determining the *will* to the next action'.[30] It is in addressing this question that he introduces the doctrine of suspension.

There being in us a great many *uneasinesses* always solliciting, and ready to determine the *will*, it is natural . . . that the greatest, and most pressing should determine the *will* to the next action; and so it does for the most part, but not always. For the mind having in most cases, as is evident in Experience, a power to *suspend* the execution and satisfaction of any of its desires, and so all, one after another, is at liberty to consider the objects of them; examine them on all sides, and weigh them with others. . . . we have a power to *suspend* the prosecution of this or that desire, as every one daily may Experiment in himself. . . . [And] during this *suspension* of any desire, before the *will* be determined to action, and the action (which follows that determination) done, we have opportunity to examine, view, and judge, of the good or evil of what we are going to do . . .[31]

Two features of Locke's position are worth noting. The first is that the doctrine of suspension is not a logical consequence of any element of his (revised) view of motivation. He presents it rather as an empirical datum. Second, the point of suspending one's desires, for an agent, is to effect some change in their content or relative strength. The doctrine of suspension does not presuppose, but it nicely supports, Locke's conviction that an agent may, through diligent effort and (especially) rational consideration, control his desires. Thus 'due, and repeated Contemplation' is capable of bringing some absent good, which we have recognized as such but have not judged to be essential to our present happiness, 'nearer to the Mind', of giving 'some relish' to it, and raising 'in us some desire; which then beginning to make a part of our present *uneasiness* . . . comes in its turn to determine the *will*'.[32] In this way, Locke continues, 'by a due consideration and examining any good proposed, it is in our power, to raise our desires . . . whereby [that good] may come to work upon the *will*, and be pursued'.[33] It follows, he later notes, that it is within 'a Man's

---

[28] Ibid. 257. [29] Ibid. 254. [30] Ibid. 257.
[31] Ibid. 263. [32] Ibid. 262. [33] Ibid.

power to change the pleasantness, and unpleasantness' of things.[34] This is not the position Locke had taken in his original version of chapter xxi. Indeed, he had explicitly maintained the contrary, saying that it is not 'in [anyone's] choice, whether he will, or will not be better pleased with one thing than another'.[35]

Locke's doctrine of suspension, I said earlier, appears to conflict with his volitional determinism. I said 'appears to conflict' because I believe that although there is some reason to think that the two positions do contradict each other, there is also some reason to think that they do not.

Volitional determinism is the thesis that no volition is free. This thesis is inconsistent with the doctrine of suspension if the latter entails that some volitions are free. According to Locke's view of freedom, a volition is free for an agent if two requirements are met: first, the volition is voluntary—the agent wills to perform it—and second, it is avoidable—the agent can forbear from performing it by willing not to do so.

The case for holding that Locke's two positions are in conflict is this. If one is able to suspend all of one's desires then the second requirement is met: that one can avoid performing some volition. For suppose that agent m has several desires, the most pressing of which is about to determine her will to action s. Thus m is about to perform the volition of willing s. Now suppose that m suspends these desires, and thereby keeps her will from being determined to s. It is plain that m has avoided willing s; but has she done so by willing not to will s? That depends on whether suspension is a voluntary action on the part of its agent, whether suspending one's desires is something one does in consequence of willing to do it. But Locke surely did hold that suspension is voluntary, although he never says so explicitly.[36] And if so, then m suspends her desires by willing to do so. And thus it is by willing also that she forbears from willing s. Hence there is a volition that m is able to avoid by willing.

As for the first requirement, that some volitions are voluntary, the doctrine of suspension entails that it too is met, provided we make a small and plausible addition to Locke's actual statement of the doctrine. Locke says that an agent can suspend all of her desires during deliberation and so avoid performing the volition that the desires would otherwise have

---

[34] Ibid. 280–1.   [35] *Essay*, 1st edn., 248.

[36] It is worth noting, however, that two professed followers of Locke, Anthony Collins and Jonathan Edwards, do explicitly say that suspension is a voluntary act on the part of its agent: see Collins's *Philosophical Inquiry concerning Human Liberty*, in O'Higgins, *Determinism and Freewill*, 73–4; and Edwards's *Careful and Strict Enquiry into the . . . Freedom of Will*, ed. Paul Ramsey (New Haven, Conn., 1957), 210.

caused. It is plausible to add to this that an agent also has the power of lifting or rescinding a suspension once imposed, thus reinstating the suspended desires and allowing them, or the most pressing among them, to proceed to determine her will. But if any suspension is voluntary, so too must its rescission, or the desuspension, if I may so call it, of the suspended desires, be voluntary. It is true that most volitions that are or could have been avoided because of a suspension would not have been or were not the result of a rescission of a previous suspension by their agent, or of any other voluntary action on her part. But those that do follow (voluntary) rescissions are themselves voluntary: their performance is consequent upon the will. Since all such volitions follow suspensions as well, they are also such as could have been avoided. Hence both requirements for free volitions are met in their case. So there are free volitions if agents have the power of suspending (and subsequently desuspending) their desires.

So goes the case for holding that the doctrine of suspension is in conflict with volitional determinism. The case for the contrary proposition runs as follows. It is true that an agent who suspends her desires, or desuspends desires previously suspended, exercises control over her will; and that, since suspending and desuspending are voluntary actions on her part, she does so by willing: she wills or forbears from willing at will. But her (first-order) willing or not willing is not the direct or immediate target of her (second-order) willing in such cases. (I use Harry Frankfurt's terminology to distinguish the two willings here involved.[37]) The precise and immediate target of someone who wills to suspend her desires is the action of suspending such and such desires. The forbearance from willing that then ensues is only the consequence or result of that action, a distinct event that is brought about by it. This is so even if the agent wills the suspension for the purpose of preventing the first-order volition, if suspension is the means employed by the agent in order to bring about the end of keeping her will from being determined. But Locke's view of freedom limits free actions to those that an agent wills, and whose forbearance she could will, directly, i.e. to those whose performance and forbearance are themselves targets of the agent's willing. Volitions which an agent manages to accomplish or prevent by willing something else which in turn brings about their existence or non-existence do not meet this condition, and hence are not free actions. The doctrine of suspension,

---

[37] See Harry Frankfurt, 'Freedom of the Will and the Concept of a Person', *Journal of Philosophy*, 68 (1971), 5–20, repr. in *The Importance of What We Care About* (Cambridge, 1988).

therefore, poses no challenge to volitional determinism: the two positions are perfectly compatible.

In my view, neither one of the two lines of reasoning just sketched is conclusive. The issues whereover they differ have been discussed by philosophers for centuries, without ever, to my mind, having been definitely settled. There surely is a difference between direct and (what we might call) instrumental willing—between the things we simply will to do and those we can only accomplish by willing to do other things that cause the former to occur. But just where and how is the line dividing these two to be drawn? Clear cases exist on both sides: on the one hand, I move my right arm; on the other, I turn on the light by flipping the switch. But suppose I scratch my left elbow (by moving my right arm), or (Descartes's example) enlarge my pupils by looking at a far-distant object? These cases seem to fall between the first two, but is it still clear that the one is, whereas the other is not, an instance of direct willing? And even if it is clear with these actions, are there not others which fall between them, and whose position with respect to the direct-instrumental divide is not clear? Furthermore, even in the clear cases of direct willing, as when I move my right arm, can we not treat the action here as a kind of result brought about by other things I do—more 'basic' things such as intending or trying to move my arm, or moving various muscles? And in the clear cases of instrumental willing, such as turning on the light by flipping the switch, is there not a sense in which the one action just *is* the other differently described, so that there is really only one action being performed? Or if there really are two, is not their relation such—that of the means to an end—that willing carries over from the one to the other? Some philosophers at least would agree with St Thomas that 'when you will the means to an end you thereby also [*eodem actu*] will the end'.[38]

In the absence of definitive answers to these questions, there is, I believe, no certain basis for pronouncing that Locke's doctrine of suspension either does or does not entail the denial of his volitional determinism. That is, there is no basis for any pronouncement concerning the relationship of these two positions considered in and of themselves. It is of course a different question what Locke thought about that relationship. And as to that, there is no evidence in the text of the second, third, or fourth editions of the *Essay* that he had any thought about it at all. To be sure, since he explicitly affirms both volitional determinism and the

---

[38] St Thomas Aquinas, *Summa Theologiae*, trans. Thomas Gilby *et al.* (London, 1964), 1a2ae. 8. 3, xvii. 58 and 59.

doctrine of suspension in all three editions, we might ascribe to him the implicit view that the two positions are consistent. But it is probably more accurate to say that he simply had no view whatsoever about their relationship, not having perceived it to be a matter one needs to have a view about.

Some time after the publication of the fourth edition in 1700, however, Locke's perception changed. Not only did he come to see a conflict between the doctrine of suspension and volitional determinism, but he repudiated the latter because of this conflict, thus opting for the one position at the expense of the other. The result is set forth in a passage Locke wrote to be added to the *Essay*'s fifth edition, which was actually published, as it turns out, after his death.

Liberty 'tis plain consists in a Power to do, or not to do; to do, or forbear doing as we *will*. This cannot be deny'd. But this seeming to comprehend only the actions of a Man consecutive to volition, it is farther enquired, whether he be at Liberty to *will*, or no? and to this it has been answered, that in most cases a Man is not at Liberty to forbear the act of volition; he must exert an act of his *will*, whereby the action proposed, is made to exist, or not to exist. But yet there is a case wherein a Man is at Liberty in respect of *willing*, and that is the chusing of a remote Good as an end to be pursued. Here a Man may suspend the act of his choice from being determined for or against the thing proposed, till he has examined, whether it be really of a nature in it self and consequences to make him happy, or no.[39]

Locke indicates here that he takes the doctrine of suspension to conflict with his unavoidability thesis, defended in section 23 of chapter xxi, as well as with the volitional determinism of section 25. But he plainly abandons the latter as well as the former of these two positions: the admission of 'a case wherein a Man is at Liberty in respect of *willing*' is all that is needed to refute the proposition that 'Liberty concerns not the will in any case'.[40]

What accounts for this change in Locke's outlook? The answer lies in several letters that passed between Locke and Philippus van Limborch in 1701 and 1702. Van Limborch found much to dispute in Locke's account of liberty, not only as presented in the *Essay*, but especially as Locke restated and elaborated it in response to his friend's criticisms. One major point of difference is just Locke's refusal to admit free volitions—his thesis of volitional determinism. In one of his letters Locke insists that liberty 'consists solely in the power to act or not to act consequent

---

[39] *Essay*, 5th edn., 270.   [40] *Essay*, 247.

on ... the determination of the will'.[41] To this van Limborch replies, 'altogether to the contrary, that liberty consists solely in a power by which a man can determine, or not determine, an action of willing'.[42] He goes on to claim that this power of determining the will is manifested in a man's ability to 'suspend his action' of willing on occasion, and declares that he 'thought that [Locke's] opinion was the same' on this, citing section 47 of the chapter on power.[43] He also says that though he agrees with several of the things set forth in section 47, he 'cannot reconcile them with' certain other features of Locke's position, including, presumably, his denial of free willing.[44]

At first, Locke either failed or refused to grasp the significance of van Limborch's point here—more likely the latter, in view of the blustery manner of his initial reply.[45] But van Limborch pressed the matter in his next letter; and in responding to that Locke did acknowledge the problem at issue, albeit not directly. For in lieu of a direct answer to several of van Limborch's criticisms, Locke sent along with his letter a set of 'explications' to be inserted at various places in chapter xxi of the *Essay*. Among them was the passage I quoted a moment ago, in which Locke affirms the incompatibility of the doctrine of suspension with volitional determinism. It is past doubt that this passage was written because of van Limborch's efforts. But as further confirmation of van Limborch's role I would note that Locke did at last, in a letter written a year later, inform his friend directly of his change of mind. 'Generally', Locke writes,

in my opinion a man is free in every action, as well of willing as of understanding, if he was able to have abstained from that action of willing or understanding; if not, not.

More particularly, as regards the will: there are some cases in which a man is unable not to will, and in all those acts of willing a man is not free because he is unable not to act. In the rest, where he was able to will or not to will, he is free.[46]

Locke's final position, therefore, is that the doctrine of suspension is incompatible with the thesis of volitional determinism, and that, since the former is true, the latter is false: there are free volitions, cases in which a man is indeed free with respect to his willing this or that. The last question I wish to discuss concerns the consequences of this about-face on Locke's part for his overall view of human free action. It seems clear that he himself did not go very far in working out these consequences: for

---

[41] *Correspondence*, vii. 329, no. 2925.   [42] Ibid. vii. 368, no. 2953.
[43] Ibid. vii. 370, no. 2953.   [44] Ibid.
[45] Ibid. vii. 402 ff., no. 2979.   [46] Ibid. vii. 680, no. 3192.

example, he made no change in the text of that portion of section 25 in which volitional determinism and the argument supporting it are stated (although he did, as I noted earlier, drop another statement of the same argument from section 23). Furthermore, whereas some of Locke's readers have judged his doctrine of suspension, along with the free volitions he took it to entail, to be inconsistent with the main thrust of his theory of freedom, others have made the contrary claim.[47]

The central core of Locke's theory of freedom comprises the following propositions:

(1) Freedom is a property only of rational agents.

(2) Human beings are free agents; i.e. they are free with respect to some of their actions.

(3) The human will is not an agent; hence the will is not a free agent.

(4) A free action is an action whose agent is free with respect to it.

(5) Every action is the effect of antecedent causes.

(6) Every free action is voluntary; i.e. its causes include a volition on the part of its agent.

(7) Every free action is avoidable; i.e. its non-occurrence can be effected by a volition on the part of its agent.

(8) The volition that causes a free action need not itself be a free action.

Now it is obvious that it doesn't follow from any of these propositions, or from all together, that no volition is a free action. Hence volitional determinism is not a logical consequence of them. Hence the denial of volitional determinism is perfectly consistent with the essential core of Locke's theory of freedom. Locke's admission, therefore, late in his life, that there are free volitions neither conflicts with the main thrust of his original thoughts on the subject, nor produces an incoherent new body of thought.

In particular, Locke is not, by allowing free volitions, joining forces with libertarians of the Bramhallian or the Arminian stripe. To give up on volitional determinism is not to give in to the inheritance principle. Nor does the admission of some free volitions commit one to holding that

---

[47] One reader who has taken the former position is Edmund Law, in his edn. of King, *The Origin of Evil*, 214–16 n. 48. On the other side, both Collins and Edwards maintain that there is no conflict between the doctrine of suspension and the rest of the Lockean theory of freedom, which is also the theory (more or less) that each of them wishes to defend. See Collins, *Philosophical Inquiry*, 73–4; and Edwards, *Careful and Strict Enquiry*, 209–11.

all volitions are free. Surely the right view, on empirical grounds, is both that most of the volitions that agents perform are not free, and that very few of their free actions are brought about by free volitions. And this is the view, one presumes, that Locke in the end held as well.

On the other hand, if there are free volitions, then Locke's *reductio* in section 25 of chapter xxi is unsound. But the loss of this argument does no damage to his overall theory. Indeed, as I hope to have shown, it could not have fulfilled the purpose he intended it for in any case.

As for the doctrine of suspension, I have not myself endorsed Locke's final view that it entails the admission of free volitions. But nor have I rejected it. In my judgement, the correctness of that view is an open question, pending further investigation. But it is clear that the doctrine of suspension itself is perfectly compatible with the central core of Locke's theory—although it is not, as I remarked earlier, entailed by it. And I agree with Locke, again on empirical grounds, that the doctrine is true.

If there are free volitions, then there are second-order volitions, i.e. willings whose targets are other willings, these being volitions of the first order. There may even be volitions of the third and fourth orders. Some philosophers, Hobbes and Leibniz for two, have objected to the very idea of such iterated willing.[48] But no solid argument has ever been offered, to my knowledge, in support of these objections. To be sure, the capacity of human consciousness is limited, in such wise that we can be sure that seventeenth-order volitions, say, never occur, and that even third-order willing is exceedingly rare. But the warrant for our assurance here is empirical; and not only is the idea of willing to will coherent, but it can be used to provide valuable light in moral psychology, as recent work by Frankfurt and others has shown.[49]

Nothing that I have said in this chapter, however, should be taken to imply that I accept, or even that I understand, the general theory of will and volition that underlies Locke's view of freedom. I have tried to work around this theory, taking Locke more or less at his word with regard to it, and leaving his meaning, for the most part, unexplored. But I am well aware that a full account of Locke's thought would have to include a detailed examination and critical assessment of this theory also.

---

[48] See Hobbes's *Of Liberty and Necessity*, in *The English Works of Thomas Hobbes*, ed. William Molesworth (London, 1839), iv. 240; and Leibniz's *Nouveaux essais*, 182.

[49] See Frankfurt's *The Importance of What We Care About*; also, for example, Susan Wolf's 'The Importance of Free Will', *Mind*, 90 (1981), 386–405, and Eleonore Stump's 'Sanctification, Hardening of the Heart, and Frankfurt's Concept of Free Will', *Journal of Philosophy*, 85 (1988), 395–420.

5

Locke on Meaning and Signification

MICHAEL LOSONSKY

I. Introduction

Chapter ii of Book III of John Locke's *Essay* is called 'Of the Signification of Words' and this is the main topic of Book III. What is signification? A simple answer is that Locke is concerned with linguistic meaning. If that is correct, Book III of Locke's *Essay* is 'the first modern treatise devoted specifically to philosophy of language' and Locke's theory of signification is a 'semantic theory'.[1]

Signification and linguistic meaning appear to be identical in the writings of Locke's immediate predecessors. Thomas Hobbes appears to be writing about the meaning of words when he writes that 'words so and so connected signify the cogitations and motions of our mind'.[2] The Port Royal *Grammar* is divided into two parts: one is concerned with grammar while the other is devoted to 'the signification of words'. Words, according to the authors, were invented to signify our thoughts.[3]

John Wilkins's *Essay towards a Real Character, and a Philosophical Language*, contains 'a *Dictionary* of the English tongue' that attempts to capture 'all of the words of this Language' and 'the various equivocal senses of

Research for this chapter was inspired by Hans Aarsleff's seminar in 1988 sponsored by the National Endowment for the Humanities of the United States. Completion of this chapter was made possible by an additional NEH Summer Stipend in 1990. I wish to thank the NEH for their financial support.

[1] Norman Kretzmann's essay on the history of semantics in *The Encyclopedia of Philosophy*, ed. Paul Edwards (New York, 1967), vii. 379. Also see Kretzmann's essay 'The Main Thesis of Locke's Semantic Theory', *Philosophical Review*, 77 (1968), 175–96. Michael Ayers also assumes that Locke's discussion of signification was a discussion of linguistic meaning. See his *Locke*, 2 vols. (London, 1991), i. *Epistemology*, 269–76.

[2] Thomas Hobbes, *De Corpore* (London, 1655), ch. ii.

[3] Antoine Arnauld and Claude Lancelot, *General and Rational Grammar: The Port-Royal Grammar*, trans. J. Rieux and B. Rollin (The Hague, 1975), 63.

them'.[4] The title of this dictionary is 'An Alphabetical Dictionary Wherein all English Words According to their Various Significations, Are Referred to their Places in the Philosophical Tables, or explained by such Words as are in those Tables'. Dictionaries try to give the meanings of words, and so Wilkins's use of 'signification' here seems synonymous with 'meaning'. In his *Real Character* Wilkins explicitly characterizes 'meaning' in terms of signification: 'Those particular *sounds* or *Characters*, which are agreed upon to *signifie any one thing or notion*, are called by the general name WORD. . . . *That which is intended by any such sound or character*, is called MEANING, *Sense, Signification, Purport, Acception, Import, tenor, denote, moral*'.[5]

So signification appears to be linguistic meaning. However, we need to be careful that we are not just interpreting the past, in Locke's words, 'by the Notions of our Philosophy'.[6] In this chapter I will examine some important arguments for the view that Locke's theory of signification was not meant to be a theory of linguistic meaning, and I will defend the traditional reading of Locke on signification.

II. Definitions, Ideas, and Meanings

E. J. Ashworth is a careful proponent of the revised reading of Locke.[7] Her overall argument has two prongs. First, she argues that Locke uses 'signify' in the same way late sixteenth- and early seventeenth-century scholastics used 'significare', and 'significare' and its cognate 'significatio' are not about meaning.[8] Second, she offers revised readings of passages where Locke seems to use 'meaning' and 'signification' synonymously. I will consider the second prong first.

An important passage from Locke's *Essay* that undermines Ashworth's interpretation is in Book III where Locke writes that '*the defining of Words* . . . is nothing but declaring their signification'.[9] Later in the same section he writes: 'For Definition being nothing but making another understand by Words, what *Idea*, the term defined stands for, a definition is best made by enumerating those simple *Ideas* that are combined in the

---

[4] John Wilkins, *Essay towards a Real Character, and a Philosophical Language* (London, 1668), 1–2. [5] Ibid. 46.

[6] *Paraphrase*, i. 114.

[7] E. J. Ashworth, ' "Do Words Signify Ideas or Things?" The Scholastic Sources of Locke's Theory of Language', *Journal of the History of Philosophy*, 19 (1981), 299–326; and 'Locke on Language', *Canadian Journal of Philosophy*, 14 (1984), 45–73.

[8] Ashworth, 'Do Words Signify Ideas or Things?', 309–11, and 'Locke on Language', 59–63. [9] *Essay*, II. iii. 10, p. 412.

signification of the term Defined.'[10] Ashworth grants that 'what a word means according to Locke just is a series of ideas', but she distinguishes between the original complex idea a word signifies and the series of ideas enumerated by the definition.[11] A term signifies the complex idea, but giving the meaning of a term 'must involve a psychological progression from the original [complex] idea to its components listed separately'. A word, as used by a particular speaker, has meaning only if the speaker can 'break down his complex idea into its component parts'.[12]

Ashworth is correct in assuming that for Locke complex ideas are not mere aggregates of simple ideas, but are simple ideas *unified* in a certain way.[13] Moreover, it is also true that when we define or give the meaning of a term we give a list of simpler ideas. However, Ashworth does not take seriously enough that meanings and definitions are distinct. Although a definition does give or, as Locke puts it, show the meaning of a word, definitions are not meanings. Locke makes this clear in the following passage:

> *a Definition is* nothing else, but *the shewing the meaning of one word by several other not synonymous Terms.* The meaning of Words, being only the *Ideas* they are made to stand for by him that uses them; the meaning of any Term is then shewed, or the word is defined when by other words, the *Idea* it is made the Sign of, and annexed to in the Mind of the Speaker, is as it were represented, or set before the view of another; and thus its Signification ascertained.[14]

A definition shows the meaning of a term, and the meaning of a term is explicitly identified by Locke with the idea that the term signifies.[15] The definition shows the speaker's meaning of a term to others by giving the words for the simple ideas that constitute the complex idea. Hearers can then use those words to ascertain what the term signified for the speaker by constructing the same kind of idea in their minds. I will discuss this feature of Locke's theory below in Section V.

There are other passages where Locke appears to use 'meaning' synonymously with 'signification', and in fact Ashworth lists the passages she found.[16] But Ashworth maintains that 'it is doubtful whether much

---

[10] Ibid. 413.
[11] Ashworth, 'Do Words Signify Ideas or Things?', 326.   [12] Ibid.
[13] See my 'Locke on the Making of Complex Ideas', *Locke Newsletter*, 20 (1989), 35–46.
[14] *Essay*, III. iv. 6, p. 422.
[15] Also see III. iii. 10, p. 413, where Locke writes that 'Definitions [are] . . . only the explaining of one Word, by several others, so that the meaning, or *Idea* it stands for, may be certainly known.'
[16] Ashworth, 'Locke on Language,' 54–5. Ashworth gives ten references.

can be concluded from any of these passages'.[17] She maintains that Locke's identification of meaning and signification is casual and infrequent, and that Locke's 'technical semantic vocabulary . . . centres on the words "sign", "signify", and "signification",' not on 'meaning'.[18]

Although 'signification' is indeed Locke's preferred term,[19] a close look at the *Essay* shows that Locke's use of 'meaning' is not as infrequent or casual as Ashworth suggests.[20] A search of the electronic text (including the two Epistles) shows that as a matter of fact 'meaning' occurs sixty-eight times in the *Essay*, and it occurs sixty-one times as a term referring to what he in other places calls the 'signification of words'. Thirty-two times it occurs in passages where in close proximity Locke also uses either 'signification' or one of its cognates synonymously with 'meaning'.[21] He uses grammatical variants of 'meaning' in the relevant sense thirty-three times, and eight times it occurs in passages together with 'signification' and its cognates.[22]

Moreover, Locke uses 'meaning' to denote signification in important passages. For example, he uses it in his discussion of definitions mentioned above, and also in the concluding remarks of Book III.[23] Locke uses 'meaning' twice (not once, as Ashworth maintains) in the crucial second chapter of Book III, where he introduces signification. The first occurrence is in section 3 of chapter ii, where Locke writes:

This is so necessary in the use of Language, that in this respect, the Knowing, and the Ignorant; the Learned, and Unlearned, use the *Words* they speak (with any meaning) all alike. They, *in every Man's Mouth, stand for the* Ideas *he has*, and which he would express by them.[24]

---

[17] Ibid. 55.

[18] Ashworth also argues that these passages may be ignored because 'one of the standard uses of the word "meaning" in Locke's day was as a synonym for "signification" [*OED*]' ('Locke on Language', 55). This argument is relevant only if signification is not linguistic meaning, which is the question at hand.

[19] See R. M. Malpas, 'An Electronic Text of the *Essay* and Wordlist', *Locke Newsletter*, 21 (1990), 57–110.

[20] *An Essay concerning Human Understanding*, Oxford Electronic Text Library (Oxford, 1990). I want to thank John Schmitt of Colorado State University's Morgan Library for his help with the electronic text.

[21] Ibid. II. viii. 11, p. 171; II. xxviii. 18, p. 360; III. ii. 8, p. 408; III. iii. 10, p. 413 (twice); III. iv. 6, p. 422 (three times); III. iv. 10, p. 423; III. vi. 19, p. 449; III. ix. 2, p. 476; III. ix. 8, p. 479; III. ix. 9, p. 480 (three times); III. ix. 11, p. 481; III. ix. 18, p. 487; III. ix. 20, p. 488; III. x. 4, p. 492; III. x. 6, p. 493; III. x. 6, p. 494; III. x. 12, p. 496; III. x. 22, p. 503 (three times); III. xi. 5, p. 510; III. xi. 12, p. 515; III. xi. 13, p. 515; III. xi. 25, p. 522; III. xi. 27, p. 524 (twice); and IV. iv. 14, p. 570.

[22] Ibid. I. ii. 5, p. 50; I. iii. 19, p. 78–9; II. xiii. 11, p. 171; II. xxxii. 9, p. 387; III. vi. 50, p. 470 (twice); III. vii. 4, p. 472; and IV. v. 2, p. 574.

[23] Ibid. III. xi. 27, p. 524; see also III. xi. 26, p. 523.

[24] Ibid. III. ii. 3, p. 406.

The second occurrence is in the last sentence of this chapter:

But whatever be the consequence of any Man's using of Words differently, either from their general Meaning, or the particular Sense of the Person to whom he addresses them, this is certain, their signification, in his use of them, is limited to his *Ideas*, and they can be Signs of nothing else.[25]

Ashworth notices this second occurrence, but she takes it to show that Locke distinguishes meaning and signification.[26] She maintains that here Locke is *contrasting* meaning and sense, on the one hand, and signification, on the other, and that Locke is excluding meaning and sense from his discussion of signification. I think this is an incorrect reading of the passage. Locke is distinguishing between the ideas that people usually have when using a word, the idea a hearer may have upon hearing a word, and the idea a speaker has when using it. Locke's point is that a speaker is always limited to signifying her own ideas.

'Meaning' also occurs in his discussion of the abuse of words. Locke writes that one way in which people abuse words is when they '*imagine so near and necessary a connexion between the names and the signification* they use them in, that they forwardly suppose one cannot understand what their meaning is'.[27] A consequence of this is that they 'never trouble themselves to explain their own, or understand clearly others meaning', and are surprised if you ask them for 'the meaning of their Terms'. Locke suggests that if one departs from common use, 'it is sometimes necessary for the ascertaining the signification of Words, to *declare their Meaning*'.[28]

In short, Ashworth's textual analysis is not sufficient to overturn the traditional reading of Locke. But there is another prong to her argument. Scholastic discussions of *significatio*, Ashworth argues, were not about meaning, and Locke's use of 'signification' mirrors Scholastic usage. In the next section I will address the claim that the Scholastic's 'significatio' was not about meaning, and in my concluding remarks I will respond to the suggestion that Locke's use of 'signification' is synonymous with Scholastic 'significatio'.

III. Meaning and *Significatio*

The following are Ashworth's reasons for denying that 'significare' and its cognates are not to be equated with meaning:

[25] Ibid. III. ii. 8, p. 408. Locke added the terms 'meaning' and 'sense' in this passage in the 4th edn. (1700) of the *Essay*.   [26] Ashworth, 'Locke on Language', 55.
[27] *Essay*, III. x. 22, p. 503.   [28] Ibid. III. xi. 12, p. 515.

1. 'Significatio' covered both the sense and the reference of a term.[29]

2. The traditional medieval question and the question that underlies Locke's discussion of language in Book III of the *Essay* 'Do words signify things or concepts (or both)?' ceases to be a sensible question if we replace 'signify' with 'mean'.[30]

3. 'Significatio' is transitive. If a term x signifies a concept, and a concept signifies an object y, then x signifies y. 'Meaning' is not transitive.[31]

4. It was perfectly correct to say that a term signifies its 'total denotation', e.g. 'man' signifies Plato, Socrates, Cicero, and so forth, but this cannot be said of the meaning of a term.[32]

5. 'Significatio' was a 'psychologico-causal property'; to mean something [*significare*] was 'to represent something or some things or in some way to the cognitive power'. Thus, 'significatio' and its cognates were about 'psychological states as opposed to abstract entities such as meanings'.[33]

I am not persuaded by these reasons.

First, the fact that 'significatio' was ambiguous between sense and reference, connotation and denotation, or intension and extension does not suggest that it cannot be equated with our concept of *meaning*. It is certainly true that 'significatio' cannot be equated with Frege's technical notion of a sense or the intensions of intensional semantics,[34] but it is also true that these technical concepts cannot be equated with the ordinary, pre-theoretical concept of 'meaning'. Theories of sense and reference, for example, aim to distinguish what is not explicitly distinguished when we ask for the meaning of a word or sentence. This pre-theoretical concept of meaning is ambiguous, and the fact that it is far from settled whether an adequate account of the linguistic meaning must involve senses, what speakers have in mind, referential relations, referents, or all of the above

---

[29] Ashworth, 'Do Words Signify Ideas or Things?', 310. Also Ashworth's 'Chimeras and Imaginary Objects: A Study in the Post-Medieval Theory of Signification', *Vivarium*, 14 (1977), 57–79.

[30] Ashworth, 'Do Words Signify Ideas or Things?', 311, and 'Locke on Language', 62.

[31] Ashworth, 'Locke on Language', 62.   [32] Ibid. 61.

[33] Ibid. 60–1, and Ashworth, 'Mental Language and the Unity of Propositions', *Franciscan Studies*, 41 (1984), 65–6. Also see Paul Vincent Spade, 'The Semantics of Terms', *The Cambridge History of Later Medieval Philosophy* (Cambridge, 1982), 188. Ian Hacking also suggests that signification is a causal relation between signs and mental states, and thus cannot be meaning, see n. 49.

[34] Gottlob Frege, 'Über Sinn und Bedeutung', *Zeitschrift für Philosophie und philosophische Kritik*, 100 (1892), 25–50, trans. as 'On Sense and Reference', in *Translations of the Philosophical Writings of Gottlob Frege*, ed. P. Geach and M. Black (Oxford, 1960); Alonzo Church, 'The Need for Abstract Entities', *Proceedings of the American Academy of Arts and Sciences*, 8 (1951), 100–13; Rudolf Carnap, *Meaning and Necessity* (Chicago, 1956).

illustrates this ambiguity. In short, the ambiguities of 'significatio' seem to track the ambiguities of our own concept of 'meaning'.

Second, it is true that the question 'Do words mean ideas or things (or both)?' seems awkward, but I think this is due to the fact that in twentieth-century technical discussions of meaning it is an orthodoxy that meaning is not a relation and 'the meaning of *s*' is not a name of an individual.[35] However, from this we cannot conclude that the question 'Do words mean ideas or things (or both)?' is meaningless. If we hold that a word's meaning something is not a relation between the word and some other meaning-endowing entity, then we will not be interested in this question because it makes what we take to be a false presupposition.[36] The question nevertheless remains meaningful unless it is a conceptual truth that meaning is not a relation. But that meaning is not a relation is not a conceptual truth. After all, it was an interesting and novel move of twentieth-century theories of meaning to maintain that the surface structure of 'means', which in fact is relational, is misleading because to mean something is not to be related to something. Moreover, it is still possible that meaning turns out to be a relation between signs and some meaning-endowing entities, and that the prevailing view is false. If this is possible, the question 'Do words mean ideas or things (or both)?' still makes perfect sense.

Granted, our beliefs about linguistic meaning have changed since the seventeenth century. However, just because we changed our beliefs about the nature of water in 1750 and certain questions ceased to be acceptable after 1750 does not mean that English speakers using 'water' before 1750 and English speakers today are talking about different things. The same holds for meaning. The dominant beliefs about the nature of meaning today are different from the views that dominated in the seventeenth century, but this does not mean that we are discussing different things.[37]

Third, 'signify' and 'mean' in fact do share important logical features, particularly transitivity. In certain contexts 'mean' is also transitive. If

---

[35] Ashworth endorses this in 'Locke on Language', 54. For some clear statements of this orthodoxy, see M. Black, *The Labyrinth of Language* (London, 1968), 162, or W. V. O. Quine, 'Ontological Relativity', *Ontological Relativity and Other Essays* (New York, 1969), 26 ff.

[36] The situation here is analogous to the question 'Have you stopped beating your dog?' If you have never engaged in this activity, the question is uninteresting, but it is not without meaning.

[37] It is of some interest that C. I. Lewis uses the term 'signification' to refer to a mode of meaning, namely that 'property in things the presence of which indicates that the term correctly applies, and the absence of which indicates that it does not apply'; see *Analysis of Knowledge and Valuation* (La Salle, Ill., 1946), 35–70.

'snow' and 'Schnee' mean the same thing, and 'Schnee' and 'snih' mean the same thing, then 'snow' and 'snih' mean the same thing. This feature is preserved if we use the locution '*x* means *y*' rather than '*x* means the same thing as *y*'. If 'snih' in Czech means 'snow' and 'snow' in English means 'particles of water vapour which when frozen in the upper air fall to earth as soft, white, crystalline flakes', then the Czech word 'snih' means 'particles of water vapour which when frozen in the upper air fall to earth as soft, white, crystalline flakes'.

Fourth, it would not be senseless to maintain that the meaning of a kind term, say, 'horse', is its denotation, namely the class of horses. Perhaps this is an incorrect account of meaning for such terms, but such extensional accounts were once in vogue, and now have come into vogue again with direct theories of reference.[38]

Finally, the fact that *significatio* was a psychological and causal property does not preclude its being meaning. Linguistic meaning could very well turn out to be a psychological and causal property. In fact, Hobbes, for whom signification clearly is a causal relationship, has been cited as the father of contemporary attempts to naturalize mind and meaning.[39] It should also be noted that abstractness does not distinguish meanings from psychological states. Psychological states, especially if functional accounts of psychological states are correct, are no less abstract than meanings.

IV. Meaning and Communication

My discussion assumes there is some minimal, pre-theoretical conception of meaning that we have, and that we, as well as seventeenth-century philosophers, try to explain and develop in our philosophical accounts of meaning. This minimal, pre-theoretic conception of meaning can be characterized as follows: meaning is whatever makes language intelligible to us as well as others. Locke rightly maintains that language has two functions, namely to record our own thoughts and to communicate our thoughts to others,[40] and a theory that accounts for these functions has the earmarks of a theory of linguistic meaning.

A simple and straightforward account of what makes communication

[38] On recent theories of direct reference, see e.g. N. U. Salmon's work *Reference and Essence* (Princeton, NJ, 1981) and *Frege's Puzzle* (Cambridge, Mass., 1986).

[39] John Haugeland, 'Semantic Engines', in J. Haugeland (ed.), *Mind Design* (Cambridge, Mass., 1981), 1. See Thomas Hobbes, *Leviathan* (London, 1651), ch. v, and *De Corpore*. chap. i.   [40] *Essay*, III. ix. 1, p. 476.

possible is Locke's own account, namely that we can record our own thoughts and communicate them *because* our language is made meaningful by signifying our thoughts. If language is made meaningful to me in virtue of my signified ideas, then obviously I can use my language to record my thoughts and order my thoughts.[41] As long as a person associates words and ideas in a constant manner, 'he cannot fail of having his meaning understood [by him]'.[42] Although this assumption was not universally shared in the seventeenth century, Locke did not believe that there are any major problems with the view that we can endow language with our own meanings and use it 'as it were . . . [to] talk to ourselves'.[43]

The headache, for Locke, comes with 'the communicating of our Thoughts to others'. Locke again relies on signification to account for the possibility of communication with others. He writes: 'The Comfort, and Advantage of Society, not being to be had without Communication of Thoughts, it was necessary, that Man should find out some external sensible Signs, whereby those invisible *Ideas*, which his thoughts are made up of, might be made known to others.'[44] Words were 'well adapted to that purpose' and so they came to be used by human beings 'as *the Signs* of their *Ideas*. . . . The use then of Words, is to be sensible Marks of *Ideas*; and the *Ideas* they stand for, are their proper and immediate Signification.'[45] Signification is what makes human communication possible.

But a few lines later we find Locke's famous and disturbing claim that '*Words in their primary or immediate Signification, stand for nothing, but the* Ideas *in the Mind of him that uses them.*'[46] How can Locke hope to explain communication with other people in terms of signification if we can only signify our own ideas? Was Locke's theory totally inadequate to its appointed task?[47]

[41] Locke was not only concerned with communication with oneself at different times, but also with the fact that language is intelligible to me at the very moment I am using it. D. M. Armstrong, 'Meaning and Communication', *Philosophical Review*, 80 (1971), 427–47, assumes that Locke's theory of signification is only based on the use of language in communication with others and ourselves at different times (pp. 427–8).

[42] *Essay*, III. ix. 2, p. 476.

[43] Kant echoes this view in his *Anthropology from a Pragmatic Point of View*: language is 'the most important way we have of understanding ourselves' (*Kants gesammelte Schriften*, ed. Preussische Akademie der Wissenschaften, vol. vii, sect. 39, p. 192).

[44] *Essay*, III. ii. 1, p. 405.   [45] Ibid.   [46] Ibid. III. ii. 2, p. 405.

[47] See J. Bennett, *Locke, Berkeley, Hume* (Oxford, 1971), 4–6. This is also called the 'communicational puzzle' by T. J. Talbot, 'Linguistic Origins: Bruner and Condillac on Learning how to Talk', *Language and Communication*, 4 (1984). Karl-Otto Apel, 'The Transcendental Conception of Language-Communication and the Idea of First Philosophy', in Herman Parrett (ed.), *History of Linguistic Thought and Contemporary Linguistics* (Berlin, 1975), 42–3, argues that Locke could only account for private languages.

It is obviously possible that a philosopher advances a theory that is severely flawed, but perhaps this theory of communication is so terrible that we should give Locke the benefit of the doubt and re-evaluate the assumption that his theory of signification was intended to account for human communication. This is what motivates Ian Hacking's revision of Locke. Hacking claims that if Locke really thought his theory of signification was a plausible theory of communication, he was 'unusually unreflective'.[48] Hacking argues that 'theories of meaning have to do with the essentially public features of language', and since Locke really did not have a serious theory of public discourse, he did not have a theory of meaning.[49]

The only time Locke touches on the concept meaning, Hacking argues, is when Locke mentions 'the common acceptation of . . . [a] language' wherein people assume 'that the *Idea*, they make it a Sign of, is precisely the same, to which the Understanding Men of that Country apply that Name'.[50] But Locke, according to Hacking, neither has an account of how different people can have the same ideas nor does he have an account of how we can know that we have the same ideas. Since Locke himself admits that 'unless a man's words excite the same ideas in the hearer which he makes them stand for in speaking, he does not speak intelligibly',[51] Locke should be concerned with the sameness of ideas if he is serious about communication and linguistic meaning. But on Hacking's view Locke is not concerned with the sameness of ideas, so Hacking concludes that Locke is not concerned with communication and linguistic meaning.

I will begin my response to this argument with some preliminary observations.

First, we need to distinguish clearly the epistemic issue of our *knowledge* of the sameness of our ideas from the metaphysical issue about the sameness of ideas. Although the question how we know we have the same ideas arises because Locke is a nominalist, and so ideas are particulars that are 'peculiar' to me,[52] it should not be assumed that this metaphysical position is sufficient to show that Locke cannot answer the epistemic

---

[48] Ian Hacking, *Why Does Language Matter to Philosophy?* (Cambridge, 1975), 44.

[49] Ibid. 52–3. Hacking has another argument based on a reading of Hobbes. He argues that for Hobbes signification is a theory about a relationship between signs: '*A* signifies *B* when *A* regularly follows or precedes thought,' and given this 'definition of "sign" it becomes very difficult to foist any theory of meaning on to Hobbes' (pp. 20 and 47). This seems to be a variant of the view I discussed above in Section III, namely that causal relations cannot be meaning relations.   [50] *Essay*, III. ii. 4, p. 407.

[51] Ibid. III. ii. 8, p. 408.   [52] Ibid. and III. iii. 1, p. 409.

question.[53] The peculiarity of my ideas does not preclude that you and I have the same *kind* of idea. What we need to find in Locke, if he is to have a theory of meaning, is (1) some account of when two ideas are of the same type or kind, and (2) how we come to know that we have the same kinds of ideas.

Second, the problem of whether or not Locke can account for the possibility of communication given that ideas are particulars is not tied to a representational interpretation of Locke's ideas, namely that ideas are veils between the mind and the rest of the world.[54] Suppose that Locke uses the term 'idea' very broadly and untechnically: it simply means 'to understand', 'believe', or 'think.'[55] The problem of the possibility of communication still remains. If the meaning of a term is a function of what I believe, understand, or think, and these states are peculiar to me, then Locke needs to worry about how I can communicate to others what I understand, believe, or think.

This worry remains even if we suppose that for Locke ideas give us *direct* access to external objects.[56] The source of Locke's problem of communication is that ideas are 'peculiar' to the person having those ideas and that we have immediate knowledge only of our own particular ideas, and this peculiarity is compatible with a non-representational theory of ideas. Even if external objects do literally appear to me in my mental states, how they appear to me is peculiar to me and only I have immediate knowledge of this state.[57] So if meaning is a function of my peculiar mental states, then we need an account of how the hearer can come to know what peculiar states I am in.[58]

[53] Apel assumes this at 'The Transcendental Conception of Language-Communication', 42.

[54] Ashworth, 'Locke on Language', 48; Bennett, *Locke, Berkeley, Hume*, 68–70; and Hacking, *Why Does Language Matter to Philosophy?*, 26–31 and 45, all attribute representationalism to Locke. Also see J. L. Mackie, *Problems from Locke* (Oxford, 1976), ch. 2.

[55] See D. Greenlee, 'Locke's Idea of "Idea" ', *Theoria*, 33 (1967), 98–106, and D. E. Soles, 'Locke on Ideas, Words, and Knowledge', *Revue Internationale de Philosophie*, 42 (1988), 156–7. According to Greenlee and Soles, human understanding, thoughts, and beliefs are the explananda for Locke's 'ideas'. This turns Locke on his head, for whom the human understanding is what is to be explained, and ideas are the explananda.

[56] See e.g. P. Alexander's *Ideas, Qualities and Corpuscles* (Cambridge, 1985), 92–3, 187–3, and 245–6; or C. Landesman, 'Locke's Theory of Meaning', *Journal of the History of Philosophy*, 24 (1976), 23–35, and John Yolton, *Locke and the Compass of Human Understanding* (Cambridge, 1970), 127–37 and 208–23.

[57] Even if the external object appears to me in the sense that it is a constituent of my perception, the external object is distinct from my perception and I need to decide how much of the external object appears to me (IV. iii. 23–4, pp. 553–5), and which aspect of the appearance is subjective and which is objective (IV. iv. 11–12, pp. 568–9).

[58] Soles, 'Locke on Ideas, Words, and Knowledge', 160, claims that for Locke communication requires only that the hearer have the thoughts or ideas the speaker has, not that the

Finally, we must be careful about our assumptions about the success or extent of communication. Philosophers can legitimately differ on how well human beings are capable of communicating with each other. Hacking and Locke differ about the extent to which communication is normal and can be successful. Locke was giving a theory of communication that captured his scepticism about communication, and if we do not share his scepticism, then we must attack his doubts, not his theory of signification.[59]

Locke explicitly states that language by its very nature is imperfect, and that the 'very nature of Words, makes it almost unavoidable, for many of them to be doubtful and uncertain in their significations'.[60] The source of '*the Imperfection of Words is the doubtfulness of their Signification*'.[61] This is not an idle observation on Locke's part. If we were more aware of the 'imperfections of Language . . . a great many of the Controversies that make such a noise in the World, would of themselves cease; and the way to Knowledge, and, perhaps, Peace too, lie a great deal opener than it does'.[62] So it is true that Locke's account limits communication, but this was an intended consequence of his theory of signification.

V. Communication and Rectification

Nevertheless, one may legitimately wonder if on Locke's account successful communication is *ever* possible. If it is never possible, perhaps a rereading of Locke on signification is warranted. But before we conclude that this is warranted, we should notice that Locke himself thought that communication is made possible not by signification alone, but also by rectification.[63] Rectification is the process of determining what 'secret reference' our words have in the minds of others, that is, whether speakers

hearer also know that the speaker has certain thoughts or ideas. This conflicts with Locke's claims that 'Man . . . [needs] external sensible Signs, whereby those invisible *Ideas*, which *his thoughts* are made up of, *might be made known to others* [my italics]' (III. ii. 1, pp. 404–5), and that the purpose of language is not only '*to convey* the *Knowledge* of Things', but also to '*make known* one Man's Thoughts or *Ideas* to another' (III. x. 23, p. 504). Moreover, successful communication requires conveying not only *what* the speaker had in mind, but *that* she had it in mind. In other words, a successful speech act requires a successful illocutionary act, namely that the hearer understands that I had something in mind with the words I used.

[59] For a related point see Ayers, *Locke*, i. 275.
[60] *Essay*, III. ix. 1, p. 476; also III. x. 1, p. 490.
[61] Ibid. III. ix. 4, p. 476.   [62] Ibid. III. ix. 21, p. 489.
[63] Hans Aarsleff, in 'Leibniz on Locke on Language', *American Philosophical Quarterly*, 1 (1964), 165–88, is to my knowledge the first in recent Locke scholarship to notice the importance of rectification in Locke's *Essay*.

and hearers have the same kinds of ideas. Rectification is similar in crucial respects to what we do in 'natural' and 'experimental' philosophy, where we try to find out what 'secret reference' our words have to '*the reality of Things*'.[64]

Before I turn to some of the details of Locke's theory of rectification, I want to discuss the passage that is often cited as the place where Locke discusses how we come to know if we have the same kinds of ideas, and that shows Locke was not interested in giving a theory of communication.[65] In this passage Locke wonders what if '*the same Object should produce in several Men's Minds different* Ideas at the same time', for example 'if the *Idea*, that a *Violet* produced in one Man's Mind by his Eyes, were the same that a *Marigold* produced in another Man's, and *vice versâ*'.[66] His response is that in fact people's sensible ideas produced by the same object 'in different Men's Minds, are most commonly very near and undiscernibly alike'. He writes that there are many reasons for believing this, but that he will not trouble us with them. If this were the place Locke discusses how we know that people have the same ideas, then indeed he has little to offer on this topic.

But this is not the place where *Locke* thinks he is discussing this issue. The topic here is not our knowledge of the sameness of sensible ideas, but whether our sense organs could be so different as to produce different kinds of ideas in different people in response to the same object. The hypothesis Locke does not bother to examine is that human beings have radically different sense organs. A discussion of this hypothesis would have required a discussion of contemporary physiology, which was indeed outside the *Essay*'s scope.[67]

Our knowledge of the sameness of ideas is discussed a few sections earlier, namely in a section where Locke addresses the 'double conformity' of our ideas.[68] We take our ideas to conform to external objects as well

---

[64] *Essay*, III. ii. 5, p. 407 and III. xi. 24, p. 521. In her essay 'Locke on Language' Ashworth does notice several crucial passages that belong to Locke's theory of rectification, but she sees them only as 'practical hints' (pp. 64–5).

[65] Hacking, *Why Does Language Matter to Philosophy?*, 44–5 and Bennett, *Locke, Berkeley, Hume*, 6.   [66] *Essay*, II. xxxii. 15, p. 389.

[67] However, we must keep in mind that for Locke we do not have certain and demonstrative knowledge that our sense organs are similar. For Locke there can be no demonstrative science of physical things (IV. iii. 26, p. 556). Our beliefs about nature, including all of '*experimental* Philosophy', were probabilistic. See J. Farr, 'Locke on Method', *Journal of the History of Ideas*, 48 (1987), 51–72, and B. Shapiro, *Probability and Certainty in Seventeenth-Century England* (Princeton, NJ, 1983), 41–4 and 58–60.

[68] Aarsleff's reading of Locke also emphasizes the 'double conformity' of language. For a critique, see Hacking, 'Locke, Leibniz, Language and Hans Aarsleff', *Synthese*, 75 (1988), 135–53.

as ideas that other people have, and the intelligibility of language depends on the latter conformity.[69] Can I ever know that my ideas conform to other people's ideas and vice versa? Locke's answer is emphatic: '*First* then, I say, That *when the Truth of our* Ideas *is judged of, by the Conformity they have to the* Ideas *which other Men have, and commonly signify by the same Name, they may be any of them false*.'[70] My judgement about the likeness my idea has to the idea of another person is fallible. Nevertheless, we can have good reasons for believing that they conform. In the case of simple ideas Locke thinks that we 'are *least* of all *liable to be so mistaken*' because 'every Day's Observation' gives us some reason to believe that you and I are seeing the same colour when looking at, say, a yellow marigold. If a person doubts this conformity 'he may easily rectify by the Objects they are to be found in'.[71] That is, we rectify the signification of a term by fixing it to an idea found in an object, e.g. the yellow of a marigold. That way we can try to make the ideas we signify conform to each other. In the case of complex ideas of mixed modes this is difficult to do because there is 'no settled Standard, any where in Nature existing, to rectify and adjust them by'.[72] The names that signify such ideas '*want Standards* in Nature, whereby Men may rectify and adjust their significations'.[73]

Rectification, then, involves fixing the signification of a term to a standard in nature, and for Locke a standard in nature is what is given to us passively without the contribution of our activity, as is the case with simple ideas.[74] In cases where we are passive with respect to a given idea, we can characterize its content in terms of its external causes.[75] Locke says as much when he writes:

our simple *Ideas*, being barely such Perceptions, as God has fitted us to receive, and given Power to external Objects to produce in us by established Laws, and Ways, . . . their Truth consists in nothing else, but in such Appearances, as are produced in us, and must be suitable to those Powers, he has placed in external Objects, or else they could not be produced in us: And thus answering to those Powers, they are what they should be, *true Ideas*.[76]

This causal account of content for simple ideas is suggested earlier in Locke's discussion of primary and secondary qualities. He writes that

---

[69] *Essay*, II. xxxii. 8, p. 386.   [70] Ibid. II. xxxii. 9, p. 386.   [71] Ibid. 387.
[72] Ibid. III. ix. 5, p. 477.   [73] Ibid. III. ix. 7, p. 478.
[74] For a possible exception to the passive nature of simple ideas, see Martha Brandt Bolton's discussion (Ch. 3 in this volume) of Locke's claim that ideas of shape are simple ideas of sight.
[75] Also see Ayers, *Locke*, i. 38 and 62–6, and his essay, Ch. 2 in this volume.
[76] *Essay*, II. xxxii. 14, p. 388.

since simple ideas of sensation are 'produced in us, only by different degrees and modes of Motion in our animal Spirits, variously agitated by external Objects, the abatement of any former motion, must as *necessarily* [my italics] produce a new sensation, as the variation or increase of it; and so introduce a new *Idea*, which depends only on a different motion of the animal Spirits in that Organ.'[77] Two people have the same kind of simple idea if their perceptions are brought about by the same causal powers, both the powers of the object as well as the powers of our sensory organs.

Since simple ideas are classified by their causes, Locke is not worried about the possibility that people have different sense organs and that simple ideas might actually appear differently to us. If all external objects 'that had the Texture of a *Violet*, produc[e] constantly the *Idea*, which he called *Blue*; and those which had the Texture of a *Marigold*, produc[e] constantly the *Idea*, which he as constantly called *Yellow*, whatever those Appearances were in his Mind; he would be able to regularly distinguish Things for his Use by those Appearances, and understand, and signify those distinctions, marked by the Names *Blue* and *Yellow*.'[78] If our sense organs are similar enough to produce distinct effects in response to distinct causes, we can say that our simple ideas are the same because they are produced by the same powers.[79]

So in the case of simple ideas of sensation I am justified in believing that your ideas conform to mine if I have reason to believe that our ideas causally co-vary with the same object. Hence the best way to 'mak[e] known the signification of the name of any simple *Idea*, is *by presenting to his Senses that Subject, which may produce it in his Mind*, and make him actually have the *Idea*, that Word stands for'.[80]

Complex ideas are more difficult to rectify because they are products of our voluntary activity.[81] Voluntary activity is not subject to lawlike regularities, and so we cannot rely on causality to classify our ideas.[82] As we have seen, for Locke this is especially true of names of mixed modes. The only way to rectify the names of mixed modes is to explicitly define the word in terms of the simple ideas that constitute the signified complex idea.

---

[77] Ibid. II. viii. 4, p. 133.   [78] Ibid. II. xxxii. 15, p. 389.

[79] Although Locke usually focuses only on the power in the objects (Locke's qualities), the importance of this passage is that here Locke explicitly recognizes that his account also requires that we include our sense organs among the powers that produce our ideas.

[80] Ibid. III. xi. 14, p. 515.   [81] Ibid. II. xxx. 3, p. 373 and III. ix. 7, p. 477.

[82] Jerry Fodor also claims in *Psychosemantics* (Cambridge, 1987), 99–100, that public language is not subject to nomological regularities because it is a voluntary act, while thoughts are involuntary and thus subject to laws.

However, substance or natural-kind terms do have standards in nature that can be used for rectification. These terms signify complex ideas that we have constructed on the basis of passively given patterns of simple ideas. We are not only given individual simple ideas; they are given to us in groups, and these given groups we form into complex ideas of substances.[83] For example, Locke claims that our 'simple ideas of Bright, Hot, Roundish, having a constant regular motion, at a certain distance from us, and, perhaps, some other' coexist in our experience.[84] Out of these coexisting ideas we construct a complex idea which we give a name.[85] Regularly coexisting simple ideas are the patterns or the archetypes we can use for the rectification of the signification of natural-kind terms.[86]

These patterns for natural-kind terms are not without their sources of uncertainty. For example, we cannot agree on the '*precise number of simple Ideas, or Qualities, belonging to any sort of Things, signified by its name*'.[87] There are too many simple ideas that are given to us coexisting for us to have exactly conforming ideas of substances, and consequently 'the complex *Ideas* of Substances . . . will be very various; and so the signification of [their] names, very uncertain'.[88]

Although we need to rectify our terms if we are to communicate, as a matter of fact people usually do not rectify the signification of their words. Instead, we usually just assume that we have the same kinds of ideas when we talk to each other:

Men stand not usually to examine, whether the *Idea* they, and those they discourse with have in their Minds, be the same: But think it enough, that they use the Word, as they imagine, in the common Acceptation of that Language; in which they suppose, that the *Idea*, they make it a Sign of, is precisely the same, to which the Understanding Men of that Country apply that Name.[89]

Although 'Common Use *regulates the meaning of Words* pretty well for Common Conversation'[90] and we should respect common use because the purpose of language is to communicate, common use is not sufficient to give us certainty about our communication. Locke writes: 'Indeed, the necessity of Communication by Language, brings Men to an agreement in the signification of common Words, within some tolerable latitude, that may serve for ordinary Conversation. . . . But common Use, being

---

[83] *Essay*, III. vi. 28, p. 456.   [84] Ibid. II. xxiii. 6, pp. 289–90.
[85] Ibid. III. vi. 28, p. 456.   [86] Ibid. III. xi. 13, p. 482.
[87] Ibid. III. vi. 30, p. 457.   [88] Ibid. III. ix. 13, p. 483.
[89] Ibid. III. ii. 4, p. 407. Compare my reading of this passage to Alexander, *Ideas, Qualities and Corpuscles*, 248. Alexander supposes that Locke's use of 'usually' in this passage is ironic, while I think he is being straightforward.   [90] *Essay*, III. ix. 8, p. 479.

but a very uncertain Rule, which reduces it self at last to the *Ideas* of particular Men, proves often but a variable Standard.'[91] Moreover, even when we use a word according to common use, we should not assume that the ideas its signifies are 'precisely the same'. The most we can strive for is that our words signify 'as *near as may be* [my italics] . . . *such* Ideas *as common use has annexed them to*'.[92]

It follows from Locke's account of common use that it cannot be the source of our knowledge of what kinds of ideas people have in mind.[93] In order to conform to common use, we already need to know what ideas people ordinarily signify with their words. Knowledge of what people have in mind when using words is arrived at by rectification: making and testing hypotheses about what people have in mind from their responses to objects and our beliefs about the structure of their perceptual apparatus. Without rectification, we can only 'suppose', 'think', and 'imagine', but never know, in any sense of the word, that in human discourse words signify the same ideas. In such a state of ignorance, it is not surprising that 'Men talk to one another, and dispute in Words, whose meaning is not agreed between them, out of a mistake, that the signification of common Words, are certainly established.'[94]

In sum, we communicate by making hypotheses about what other people signify with their words, and on the basis of these hypotheses we can enter into agreements about the signification of words. Although this does not yield certainty about the success of our communication, it does bring human beings 'to an agreement in the signification of common Words, within some tolerable latitude'. We can have probable opinion about the success of our communication, and in this respect communication is no worse off than the natural sciences. Moreover, given that our ideas are constantly changing as a result of new experiences, it follows that

---

[91] Ibid. III. xi. 25, p. 522.   [92] Ibid. III. xi. 11, p. 514.

[93] Alexander (ibid. 247–8) argues that for Locke common use can give us certainty about whether or not people have the same ideas. Alexander assumes that Locke 'is clearly giving part of what he takes to be a correct account of language and meaning' when Locke writes that people 'suppose, that the *Idea*, they make [a word] a Sign of, is precisely the same, to which the Understanding Men of that Country apply that Name' (III. ii. 4, p. 407). If Alexander is correct, then in this passage Locke is claiming that people are justified in assuming that we have exactly the same ideas, and that we can assume this without examining whether or not in fact those ideas are the same. If Locke is making this claim right at the beginning of book III, it is puzzling why he goes on to devote over 100 pages to an account of language according to which it is 'almost unavoidable' that the signification of language is 'doubtful and uncertain' (III. ix. 1, p. 476), and who in the end only gives some tentative rules that at best '*remedy the Defects of Speech* . . . to some degree' (III. xi. 8, p. 512).

[94] Ibid. III. xi. 25, p. 522.

linguistic meaning is also in constant flux, and consequently 'Languages constantly change.'[95]

VI. Conclusion

So Locke *does* have a theory of public discourse: his theory of signification together with his theory of rectification. An underlying constraint on Locke's account is his desire to take very seriously the failures of public discourse. Early modern thinking about language was driven by the fear of the failure to communicate. A recurring theme of seventeenth-century thinking about language was the 'Curse of Babel' [Gen. 11: 1 and 5–7].[96] Locke's *Essay* is no exception. He writes that when human beings 'speak of Things really existing, they must, in some degree, conform their *Ideas* to the Things they would speak of: Or else Men's Language will be like that of *Babel*; and every Man's Words, being intelligible only to himself, would no longer serve to Conversation'.[97]

The Curse of Babel is the failure of public discourse, and it is not surprising that in a period dominated by war and revolution seventeenth-century philosophy of language was more concerned with the failure than the success of communication. Locke's theory of language was only one of several responses to this perceived failure. Two other seventeenth-century responses to the Curse of Babel are represented in the so-called Webster–Ward Debate.[98] One was to search for the universal, prelapsarian language of nature that was destroyed by the Curse of Babel.[99] This was

---

[95] Ibid. II. xxii. 7, p. 291. See Locke's account of his own interpretative efforts in his preface to the *Paraphrase*. Locke's views on language and communication anticipate D. Davidson's views in 'A Nice Derangement of Epitaphs', in Ernest LePore (ed.), *Truth and Interpretation* (London, 1986), 433–46. According to Davidson's account, we communicate with a 'passing theory' that we develop and revise as we communicate. It should not come as a surprise that in 'A Parody of Conversation', ibid. 447–58, Hacking rejects Davidson's Lockean position. It is also noteworthy that Locke's own account contradicts R. Harris's contention in *The Language Myth* (New York, 1981) that Locke's view of communication ('the telementational model') imposes an 'invariance condition' on language, namely that 'Whatever may vary as between speaker and hearer, or between the conveyance of a given message on one occasion and conveyance of the same message on another occasion, cannot count as part of the language' (p. 88).

[96] See ch. 1 of R. Fraser's *The Language of Adam: On the Limits and Systems of Discourse* (New York, 1977), and Shapiro, *Probability and Certainty in Seventeenth-Century England*, 227–46.   [97] *Essay*, III. vi. 28, p. 456.

[98] A. G. Debus, *Science and Education in the Seventeenth Century: The Webster–Ward Debate* (New York, 1970).

[99] See A. Coudert, 'Some Theories of a Natural Language from the Renaissance to the Seventeenth Century', *Studia Leibnitiana: Sonderheft*, 7 (1978), 56–114.

the strategy of John Webster and other sixteenth- and seventeenth-century Neoplatonic hermeticists and alchemists. The other was to construct a universal philosophical language that would break the spell of confusion. This was the strategy of linguistic reformers Seth Ward and John Wilkins, among others.[100]

Locke rejects both of these responses to the failure of public discourse. He rejects the first because even Adam put together ideas 'only by his own Imagination'[101] and was at liberty to 'affix . . . any new name to any *Idea*'.[102] He rejects the second strategy because nobody 'can pretend to attempt the perfect *Reforming* the *Languages* of the world, no not so much as that of his own Country, without rendring himself ridiculous'.[103] Locke's own response, as we have seen, was to accept the curse as an unavoidable characteristic of human beings. Human beings cannot 'use their words constantly in the same sense' and only for 'determined and uniform *Ideas*'. All we can do is limit the 'Obscurity, Doubtfulness, or Equivocation, to which Men's Words are naturally liable'.[104]

In my view, a proper understanding of Locke's theory of signification must locate it in the context of this seventeenth-century debate about the possibility of public discourse, and this debate was alien to Scholastic philosophy. Therefore, even if Ashworth is right in that Scholastic theories of signification are not about meaning and Locke was familiar with Scholastic work on language, it does not follow that for Locke, writing in a revolutionary context, signification was not meaning. Ashworth ignores the seventeenth-century context of Locke's theory, and that is why she thinks that Locke is simply repeating or echoing commonplace Scholastic doctrines.[105] I think Locke would not repeat and dwell on what was for him an intellectual commonplace. Even if Scholastic signification were not linguistic meaning, for Locke and his contemporaries the debate had changed, and signification had turned into linguistic meaning.

---

[100] See J. Knowlson, *Universal Language Schemes in England and France 1600–1700* (Toronto, 1975). On Leibniz's attempts to synthesize these two strategies, see my 'Leibniz's Adamic Language of Thought', *Journal of the History of Philosophy*, 30 (1992), 523–43.

[101] *Essay*, III. vi. 46, p. 468.   [102] Ibid. III. vi. 51, p. 470.

[103] Ibid. III. xi. 2, p. 509.   [104] Ibid. III. xi. 3, p. 509.

[105] Ashworth, 'Do Words Signify Ideas or Things?', 307, 316, and 325.

6

Solidity and Elasticity in the Seventeenth Century

PETER ALEXANDER

I

Conventional atomism deriving from Epicurus took atoms to be absolutely solid and impenetrable and yet capable of rebounding from one another on direct impact. Observable physical and chemical changes were regarded as explicable in terms of the changes in motion of constituent atoms resulting from their impact. Atomism has been rejected for various reasons, among them the belief that absolutely solid atoms could not exist, or rebound on direct impact if they did. This controversy went on and on. I wish to consider some aspects of it.

My interest in this springs from Locke's discussion of solidity in his *Essay concerning Human Understanding*.[1] I interpret him as holding that the corpuscles of his favoured theory are absolutely solid and change one another's motions and arrangements by bouncing on impact, whether direct or oblique.[2] Nowadays it seems highly implausible that absolutely solid bodies could rebound on colliding directly, and yet Boyle, Descartes, Huygens, Wren, Gassendi, and others held that they could and did. I should like to try to understand what made the hard body view plausible to many distinguished natural and metaphysical philosophers.

I rely heavily on Wilson L. Scott's book *The Conflict between Atomism and Conservation Theory 1644–1860*.[3] He shows that the controversy was

---

[1] This occurs mainly in *Essay*, II. iv, but there are passages elsewhere in the *Essay* that have a bearing on his view of solidity.

[2] See my *Ideas, Qualities and Corpuscles: Locke and Boyle on the External World* (Cambridge, 1985) for a fuller account than I can give here.

[3] London, 1970. See ch. 1 for a summary. He sees the controversy as stemming from conflicting views held by Descartes and Newton.

still alive in the first half of the nineteenth century and involved distinguished and influential scientists and philosophers on both sides. This alone suggests that it was not simply absurd for Locke to hold in 1690 that absolutely hard bodies could rebound. There are good reasons on both sides why the controversy should have gone on for so long and they throw light on the relations between scientific theorizing, experimental results, conceptual development, and metaphysical beliefs. The controversy was complex. Centrally it concerned the questions: (1) Do absolutely solid bodies exist? and (2) Do they, or could they, rebound from one another on direct impact? It involved also the celebrated *vis viva* controversy and that concerning conservation laws. It was necesary to discover how to measure force if force was regarded as being conserved, and it was alleged that if hard bodies did not rebound from one another then conservation laws would be violated. This would militate against the uniformity of nature and the providence of a benevolent God.

I shall begin by briefly substantiating my view about Locke, then consider some of his contemporaries, and finally consider some features of the ensuing argument.

II

Locke begins his chapter 'Of Solidity' by saying that we get the idea of solidity originally by our sense of touch. It arises from the resistance we find in a body 'to the entrance of any other Body into the Place it possesses, till it has left it'. It is the idea we receive most often from our senses.[4] What hinders the approach of two bodies Locke calls 'solidity'. We may if we like, he says, call it 'impenetrability', although he prefers the more positive term and thinks that impenetrability is a consequence of solidity rather than identical with it. Although we come across solidity in sense experience, he says, 'Yet the Mind, having once got the *Idea* from such grosser sensible Bodies, traces it farther; and considers it, as well as Figure, in the minutest Particles of Matter, that can exist; and finds it inseparably inherent in Body, where-ever, or however modified.'[5] The 'minutest Particles of Matter' I take to be corpuscles.

In the next section Locke says 'This [sc. the idea of solidity] is the *Idea* which belongs to Body whereby we conceive it *to fill space*'; by virtue of

---

[4] See M. R. Ayers, *Locke*, 2 vols. (London, 1991) for a discussion of Locke's views on solidity, esp. i. 181–3 and ii. 149 ff.   [5] *Essay*, II. iv. 1, p. 123.

this a body prevents two other bodies from coming into contact if it is between them.[6]

On the corpuscular hypothesis all observable bodies are composed of corpuscles separated by empty spaces (pores). Such bodies are more or less hard as our sense of touch reveals. This empirical hardness is to be explained in terms of the sizes of the corpuscles and of the empty spaces between them. The larger the spaces in relation to the sizes of the corpuscles, the more mobile the corpuscles are and the softer the body is. Individual corpuscles have no empty spaces in their constitution; matter completely fills their boundaries. They are therefore absolutely solid. Absolute solidity is an idea we reach from the ideas of increasing empirical hardness as the corpuscles of bodies are more and more tightly packed. It is *approximated* by the most tightly packed collection of corpuscles, but never reached by such a collection. It is, in its inception, *theoretical*, suggested by observation but never observed, and designed for use in explanation. But it is not an ideal, in the sense of something non-existent, a fiction. It exists, but in individual, unobservable corpuscles only. If it did not the world would not appear to us as it does.

The resistance whereby a body (here, any body, simple or complex) keeps other bodies out of the space it occupies 'is so great, That no force, how great soever, can surmount it'.[7] Locke instances a drop of water, which, of course, is a composite body, and says that 'All the Bodies in the World' pressing it on all sides 'will never be able to overcome the Resistance, which it will make, as soft as it is, to their approaching one another, till it be removed out of their way.'[8]

That is, complex bodies, whether hard or soft, are ultimately impenetrable. They are compressible, normally, up to a certain limit. That limit is reached if the corpuscles are of such shapes and sizes that they can be made to occupy all the previously empty spaces or of such shapes and sizes that they reach a point at which, although there is still some empty space, no further movement is geometrically possible. That there is such a limit confirms that two bodies cannot occupy the same space at the same time. It is explained if the corpuscles are absolutely solid and cannot be penetrated under any conditions. That this is Locke's view is supported by his statement that the parts of a diamond are no more solid than the parts of a drop of water; what makes the water softer than the diamond is the greater ease with which those parts of the water will move relatively to one another.[9]

[6] Ibid. II. iv. 2, p. 123.   [7] Ibid. II. iv. 3, p. 124.
[8] Ibid.   [9] Ibid. II. iv. 4, p. 125.

We must be careful about impenetrability. In vulgar speech we may say that a nail driven into a piece of wood penetrates it. According to the corpuscular theory it does so by entering the empty spaces between the corpuscles of the wood, pushing the corpuscles apart where necessary. Strictly here no body penetrates another in the sense of coming to occupy exactly the same place at the same time as it or any part of it. Because a single corpuscle has no empty spaces and no movable parts, nothing can penetrate it even in the vulgar sense. That is why impenetrability is a consequence of solidity rather than solidity itself. In distinguishing solidity from empirical hardness, Locke says that solidity consists in repletion and so 'the utter Exclusion of other Bodies out of the Space it possesses' whereas hardness consists in 'firm Cohesion of the parts of Matter making up masses of a sensible bulk, so that the whole does not *easily* change its Figure'.[10] So hardness is a quality of complex, observable bodies only; felt hardness is the idea we get of this and it admits of degrees. Solidity belongs to single corpuscles only and does not admit of degrees.

Locke now implicitly attacks Descartes by distinguishing the 'Extension of Body' from the 'Extension of Space'. However, he agrees that absolutely hard bodies bounce. He says '*Upon the Solidity of Bodies* also *depends their mutual Impulse, Resistance, and Protrusion.*'[11] This strongly suggests that individual corpuscles, which are absolutely solid, cause changes in one another's motions by impact. One meaning given for 'protrude' in the *Oxford English Dictionary* is 'to push or thrust into any position'.

In case this passage is thought to refer only to the actions of complex bodies, there is further evidence when Locke says that bodies produce ideas in us by impulse, 'the only way we can conceive Bodies operate in'. When we perceive the qualities of external bodies at a distance by sight 'some singly imperceptible Bodies must come to them from the Eyes and thereby convey to the Brain some Motion' which produces ideas of them.[12] These 'singly imperceptible Bodies' must be light corpuscles, a collection of which does not constitute a body. They form a stream of separate corpuscles which can take on different patterns depending upon the ways in which they originate and are reflected or refracted. These patterns are communicated to the corpuscles of the eyes, the nerves, and the brain to rearrange them. So they must be capable of moving these corpuscles by impact. When in later editions of the *Essay* Locke made concessions to Newton's view about action at a distance he never removed his statement that 'the only way we can conceive Bodies operate in' is 'by impulse'.

---

[10] Ibid.   [11] Ibid. II. iv. 5, p. 126.   [12] Ibid. II. viii. 12, p. 136.

Descartes had in 1644 rejected both indivisible atoms and the void, but held that there were some perfectly hard material particles or 'globules' in the universe.[13] They were not indestructible, but could be worn away into finer particles because all their parts were at rest and not bound by any forces.[14]

However, he firmly accepted a principle of conservation: God always maintains the same quantity of motion in the universe. Descartes says

As far as the general and first cause [of motion] is concerned, it seems obvious to me that this is none other than God Himself, who being all-powerful in the beginning created matter with both movement and rest; and now maintains in the sum total of matter, by His normal participation, the same quantity of motion and rest He placed in it at that time.[15]

The conservation principle appears to rest on a theological belief rather than empirical findings. Descartes of course meant by 'quantity of motion' the product of size and speed although it is usually represented by MV.[16]

As a consequence of this conservation law, Descartes held, hard bodies must rebound on collision. His Third Law of Nature is 'that a body, upon coming in contact with a stronger one, loses none of its motion; but that, upon coming in contact with a weaker one, it loses as much as it transfers to that weaker body'.[17] The 'strength' of a body appears to depend upon its size and its speed.[18]

Commenting on this Law of Nature Descartes says 'Thus we know from experience that when any hard bodies which have been set in motion strike an unyielding body, they do not on that account cease moving, but are driven back in the opposite direction; on the other hand, however, when they strike a yielding body to which they can easily transfer all their motion, they immediately come to rest.'[19] This is a little mysterious. Was Descartes talking of perfectly hard bodies, in view of his claim to know about them from experience? On the other hand, if hard bodies do exist then it would seem to follow from his conservation law that they will rebound on colliding. Moreover, in the next two sections Descartes gives 'proofs' of his Third Law which are not based on experiments or observations.

[13] René Descartes, *Principles of Philosophy* (1644), trans. and ed. V. R. Miller and R. P. Miller (Dordrecht, 1983–4), III. cxxii–cxxiii, pp. 153–4.
[14] Ibid. II. liii–lix, pp. 69–70.   [15] Ibid. II. xxxvi, pp. 57–8.
[16] Ibid., ed.'s n. 31 to II. xxxvi, p. 58.   [17] Ibid. II. xl, pp. 61–2.
[18] Ibid. II. xlvii–lii, pp. 65–9.   [19] Ibid. II. xl, pp. 61–2.

The proof of the first part, about hard bodies colliding, depends upon the distinction between quantity of motion and direction of motion. In hard body collision there is a cause that prevents the striking body from proceeding in the same direction, but there is no cause which would change the motion itself, 'since movement is not contrary to movement'. So the quantity is conserved but the direction is reversed.[20] It seems that the 'unyielding' body is not only absolutely solid but also fixed.

The proof of the second part, that a hard body transfers its motion to a yielding one and itself comes to rest, depends upon the 'immutability of God's manner of working in uninterruptedly maintaining the world by the same action by which he created it'.

It is worth noting that, in discussing the globules of his second element which surround the stars, Descartes says that they 'in proportion to their size, are as solid as any body can be, because we understand that they contain no pores filled with other . . . matter'.[21] This is very similar to Locke's definition of solidity as repletion.

Descartes's view about the bouncing of hard particles on account of the law of conservation of the quantity of motion was taken up by various natural philosophers in opposition to Newton. According to Scott, the view was not directly challenged until 1673 when Edmé Mariotte published his treatise on percussion.[22] It appears to have been fairly generally accepted by mathematicians until the Royal Society invited papers on impact in 1668.

While Locke was putting the finishing touches on his *Essay*, Leibniz was developing a view about hard bodies that was radically at variance with conventional atomism and Locke's view. Leibniz's relevant works were published from about 1686 onwards, so it is not surprising that they appear to have had no effect on the first edition of the *Essay*.

Round about 1686 Leibniz introduced two far-reaching considerations into the discussion of hard bodies and their impact. They were universal elasticity and the law of continuity. In a letter of 1687 aimed at Malebranche, Leibniz enunciated a 'principle of general order' and claimed that both Descartes and Malebranche had violated it in their laws of motion. It is valid in both geometry and physics because 'the sovereign wisdom, the source of all things, acts as a perfect geometrician, observing

---

[20] Ibid. II. xli, p. 62.   [21] Ibid. III. cxxiii, p. 153.

[22] E. Mariotte, *Traité de la percussion ou choc des corps* (1673), in *Œuvres* (Leiden, 1717), i. 28. See Scott, *The Conflict between Atomism and Conservation Theory*, 6.

a harmony to which nothing can be added'.[23] For our purpose it is the physical applications that matter. In *Primary Truths*, usually dated about 1686 but now thought to be of 1692 or later, he says that he has shown that 'from the notion of each and everything follows all of its future states' and that this in turn follows from the nature of truth, that the predicate is always in the subject. Then he says, 'This is also illustrated in our experience of nature. For bodies really rebound from others through the force of their own elasticity, and not through the force of other things, even if another body is required in order for the elasticity (which arises from something intrinsic to the body itself) to be able to act.'[24] He continues by arguing against the vacuum and indivisible atoms. Extension and motion are mere phenomena, like rainbows, and are not sufficient to constitute bodies. 'Something lacking in extension is required for the *substance* of bodies, otherwise there would be no source for the reality of phenomena or for true unity.'[25] These are arguments we are familiar with from the *New System* of 1695–6 where Leibniz talks of the necessity for the notion of *force* 'which is very intelligible, despite the fact that it belongs in the domain of metaphysics'.[26]

In his *Critical Thoughts on the General Part of the Principles of Descartes* (1692) Leibniz calls his principle 'the law of continuity' and says of it,

If Descartes had taken into consideration that every body that collides with another must, before it is repelled, first reduce its advance, then come to a stop, and only then be turned back, and must thus pass from one direction to the opposite, not by a leap but by degrees, he would have set up other rules of motion for us. We must recognize that no matter how hard, every body is thus flexible and elastic to some degree.[27]

Leibniz frequently repeats this point, for example in *On Body and Force* (1702)[28] and *A Specimen of Dynamics* (1695)[29] where he says that 'no change happens through a leap' and that 'all rebound arises from elasticity'. He

---

[23] Gottfried Leibniz, *Letter of Mr Leibniz on a General Principle Useful in Explaining the Laws of Nature through a Consideration of the Divine Wisdom* (1687), in *Philosophical Papers and Letters*, ed. L. E. Loemker, 2 vols. (Chicago, 1956), i. 539.
[24] Gottfried Leibniz, *Primary Truths* (probably after 1692), in *Philosophical Essays*, ed. R. Ariew and D. Garber (Indianapolis, 1989), 33.   [25] Ibid. 34.
[26] Leibniz, *A New System of the Nature and Communication of Substances, and of the Union of the Soul and Body* (1695), in *Philosophical Essays*, 139.
[27] Leibniz, *Critical Thoughts on the General Part of the Principles of Descartes* (1692), in *Philosophical Papers*, ii. 655.
[28] Leibniz, *On Body and Force, Against the Cartesians* (1702), in *Philosophical Essays*, 252–4.   [29] Leibniz, *A Specimen of Dynamics* (1695), in *Philosophical Essays*, 132.

here refers to the elegant experiments of Edmé Mariotte to show that
'a body is deformed before it is impelled'.[30]

All this provides Leibniz with arguments against atoms, supplement-
ing those based on infinite divisibility in the *New System* and elsewhere.
Presumably the thought is that indivisible hard material atoms are inconceivable not only because anything with dimensions is divisible, at least in
thought, but also because hard atoms could neither rebound nor not
rebound from one another. Their rebounding is impossible because, as
they are not deformable, there can be no new cause of their moving in the
opposite direction; and their not rebounding would involve an instantan-
eous change from motion to rest, which is impossible.

Mariotte's experiments (1673) were indeed elegant, and they bring out
a general problem involved in the ensuing controversy.[31] Using simple
pendulums with soft clay bobs he measured the force of impact when
they collided by the extent of the flattening of the clay. He thus set up
some laws of inelastic impact. He then linked these with the laws governing elastic collision via the principle that a perfectly elastic body deformed
by the impact of a hard inelastic one regains its original shape and, in
doing so, imparts to the impacting body its original speed. He confirmed
this by bouncing a hard pendulum bob off a stretched string. He then
showed that apparently hard bodies in fact deform on impact. He dropped
glass and ivory balls from varying heights on to a steel anvil lightly coated
with dust; circles in the dust of various sizes enabled him, he claimed, to
measure the degree of flattening of the balls. This turned out to be
directly proportional to the speed of impact. The bouncing of the balls to
the height from which they were dropped confirmed the full restoration
of the shape and size of the balls.

These experiments do not, of course, establish that all bodies are
elastic or that perfectly hard bodies do not rebound. For the atomist who
accepted perfect hardness, it was impossible *ex hypothesi* to experiment
with perfectly hard bodies individually. He would be happy to admit that
the hardest bodies available for experimentation were in fact elastic and
he would be ready with an explanation.

Leibniz does not say that Mariotte's experiments establish either universal elasticity or the failure of perfectly hard bodies to rebound. What
he does say is that his own view, involving universal elasticity and his
principle of continuity, *enables him to explain* Mariotte's results. Mariotte
himself says that if hard bodies are inflexible then it is *impossible to explain*

---

[30] Ibid.   [31] Mariotte, *Traité de la percussion*, in *Œuvres*, i. 3–57.

their moving after impact, that it is elasticity alone that produces reflected movement and that when an inflexible body collides with an inflexible and immovable one it will not move 'even slightly backwards because there would be no new cause of movement in that direction'.[32] This appears to be a direct criticism of Descartes.

These conclusions come not from Mariotte's experiments alone but from them together with the necessities of explanation and the equivalence of cause and effect. Nothing in the experimental results rules out the possibility that perfectly hard bodies bounce and, indeed, it is difficult to see how any direct experiment could do that.

In *On Body and Force, Against the Cartesians* of 1702 Leibniz says that if a body in motion could come to rest instantaneously, if elastic forces were lacking, then 'What I call the law of continuity, through which leaps are avoided, would not be observed in things, nor would the law of equivalences by which absolute forces are conserved, nor would there be place for other excellent contrivances of the Architect of Nature . . .'.[33] Here what happens appears to be inferred from the law of continuity rather than discovered purely experimentally.

It is unfortunate that Locke appears to have had no direct contact with Leibniz, even in correspondence. In about 1695 Leibniz sent a short paper on Locke's *Essay* to Sir Thomas Burnet of Kemney. Locke did not receive it until 1697. In a letter to William Molyneux in that year Locke says that he has read this and a paper by Leibniz referred to in it.[34] These two papers did not mention the matter of hard bodies and their impact. They repeated some of his criticisms of the Cartesians and sketched some of his own views about topics discussed in Locke's *Essay* but without going into his logical and metaphysical reasons for holding them. Since Locke was clearly unfamiliar with Leibniz's central doctrines he was doubtless in no position to appreciate Leibniz's objections. It seems likely that Locke read little, if anything, else by Leibniz.

Leibniz was by no means wholly critical of Locke, and he indicated considerable admiration for and agreement with him. Locke's response was churlish. He refused to be drawn into correspondence with Leibniz and wrote slightingly to Molyneux about his two papers.[35] He showed no

---

[32] Ibid. 28.   [33] Leibniz, *On Body and Force*, in *Philosophical Essays*, 255–6.

[34] Leibniz, *Reflexions de M. L——— sur l'essai de l'entendement humain de Monsieur Locke* (*c.*1695), in Locke, *Works*, 3 vols. (London, 1727). The other paper referred to is Leibniz, *Meditations on Knowledge, Truth and Ideas* (1684), in *Philosophical Papers*. See also Nicholas Jolley, *Leibniz and Locke: A Study of the 'New Essays on Human Understanding'* (Oxford, 1984), 36–8.   [35] Locke, Letter to William Molyneux, 3 May 1697.

inclination to learn more about Leibniz's philosophy, and it is not surprising that I have found no evidence of his having any later contact with his writings. Lady Masham corresponded with Leibniz but only after Locke's death.[36]

This episode serves to suggest that Locke's ignorance of Leibniz's views was large at least up to 1697 and probably later. He had no relevant works of Leibniz in his library. On the other hand, he was familiar with the works of Descartes and Gassendi, some of which he did possess. It seems likely then that at this stage Locke had come across no serious discussion of the view that elasticity was always involved in the rebounding of bodies from one another and was not even aware of a serious problem.

Newton in writing the *Principia* appears to have been uncertain whether absolutely hard bodies could rebound from one another.[37] In his Scholium to the Laws of Motion, having described Wren's pendulum experiments to verify the Third Law ('To every action there is an equal and opposite reaction'), Newton says that Wren, Wallis, and Huygens 'did severally determine the rules of the impact and reflection of hard bodies'. However, he says, it must not be thought that the Third Law supposes bodies to be 'either absolutely hard or at least perfectly elastic'; this is a canard put about by those who object to the law on the ground that no such bodies exist in nature. In fact, the experiments 'succeed as well in soft as in hard bodies'. He continues, 'By the theory of Wren and Huygens, bodies absolutely hard return from one another with the same velocity with which they meet. But this may be affirmed *with more certainty* of bodies perfectly elastic. In bodies imperfectly elastic the velocity of the return is to be diminished together with the elastic force. . .'.[38] This passage leaves the position of absolutely hard bodies still in doubt. If rebound 'with the same velocity with which they meet' may be affirmed '*with more certainty*' of perfectly elastic bodies than of absolutely hard ones, then it is left open that absolutely hard bodies *may* rebound.

There were some, among them perhaps Wren and Huygens, who identified perfect elasticity and perfect hardness, and Maupertuis in 1751 accused many mathematicians of confusing them.[39]

[36] Cranston, 416–17.

[37] I. Newton, *Principia Mathematica* (1687), trans. A. Motte (1729), rev. F. Cajori (5th imp. Berkeley, Calif., 1962), 22–5.   [38] Ibid. 25, my italics.

[39] P. L. M. de Maupertuis, *Essai de Cosmologie* (1750), in *Œuvres* (Lyons, 1756), i. 37–9. See Scott, *The Conflict between Atomism and Conservation Theory*, 75–6.

In the *Opticks* Newton clearly accepted the atomic constitution of material substances, basing this on indirect evidence from observable phenomena which he regards as explicable if substances are composed of atoms that attract and repel one another. Then he comes to the conclusion that the atoms must be hard, impenetrable, and indestructible. Thus

All these things being consider'd, it seems probable to me, that God in the Beginning formed Matter in solid, massy, hard, impenetrable, moveable Particles, of such Sizes and Figures, and with such other Properties, and in such Proportion to Space, as most conduced to the End for which he form'd them; and that these primitive Particles being Solids, are incomparably harder than any porous Bodies compounded of them; even so very hard, as never to wear or break in pieces; no ordinary Power being able to divide what God made one in the first Creation.[40]

The hardness and indestructibility of the atoms are required to explain the existence of uniform and enduring substances. If the atoms were to break up then 'the Nature of Things depending on them would be changed'. He says

Water and Earth composed of old worn Particles and Fragments of Particles, would not be of the same Nature and Texture now, with Water and Earth composed of entire Particles in the Beginning. And therefore, that Nature may be lasting, the Changes of corporeal Things are to be placed only in the various Separations and new Associations and Motions of these permanent Particles . . .[41]

However, motion is not conserved and is 'much more apt to be lost than got, and is always in Decay', for, he says,

Bodies which are either absolutely hard, or so soft as to be void of Elasticity, will not rebound from one another. Impenetrability makes them only stop. If two equal Bodies meet directly *in vacuo*, they will by the Laws of Motion stop where they meet, and lose all their Motion, and remain in Rest, unless they be elastick, and receive new Motion from their Spring.[42]

It is worth noting that Newton defined 'absolutely hard bodies' in a way familiar to atomists when he referred to particles 'whose Parts touch in all the Space between them without any Pores or Interstices to weaken their Cohesion'.[43]

Even elastic bodies lose some proportion of their motion on collision; they lose all but what they recover from their elasticity. Clearly Newton is rejecting Leibniz's law of continuity, since hard bodies, he holds,

---

[40] I. Newton, *Opticks* (repr. based on 4th edn. of 1730, New York, 1952), 400.
[41] Ibid. [42] Ibid. 398. [43] Ibid. 390.

come to an instant stop on colliding. Nor is it possible for Newton that, as Leibniz held, motion or force apparently lost on collision is in fact conserved because it is transferred to the inner parts of the bodies. For Newton the atom has no separately movable parts.

However, in the universe as a whole motion is conserved for Newton, Since motion is lost in the collision of hard bodies, the physical world would, if left to itself, run down. However, 'Seeing therefore the variety of Motion which we find in the World is always decreasing, there is a necessity of conserving and recruiting it by active Principles, such as are the cause of Gravity . . . and the cause of fermentation'.[44] Similarly, the causes of the heating of the inner parts of the earth and the heating of the earth by the sun must be active principles, for it becomes him who created the world to keep it going. 'Such a wonderful Uniformity as we find in the Planetary System must be allowed the effect of Choice.' He continues by listing various enduring uniformities in the natural world, and says that they 'can be the effect of nothing else than the Wisdom and Skill of a powerful ever-living Agent'. It appears that God directly intervenes to sustain the uniformity in the world and to counteract its decay.[45]

Locke may have noted Newton's reference to the views of Wren and Huygens in the Scholium to the Laws of Motion quoted above even if he did not already know those views. They held according to Newton that 'bodies absolutely hard return one from another with the same velocity with which they meet'. This would have supported Locke in the view that I believe he held. He would also have seen Newton's remarks about elastic bodies that follow, but they were hardly strong enough to deflect Locke. They can be read as indicating that Newton was merely contemplating the possible existence of a problem. Even if Locke grasped this possibility there appears to be nothing in his writings to suggest that he was seriously worried by it. The edition of the *Opticks* in which Newton indicated clearly that he had concluded that absolutely hard bodies would stop on collision was not published until 1706, two years after Locke's death.

Newton's atomism is of a new kind. Direct collisions between atoms do nothing but produce rest and work against conservation. Oblique collisions can still change the direction of the motion of atoms. These two features can figure in the explanation of changes, especially chemical changes. Perhaps more important for the explanation of changes in general are the attractive and repulsive forces between atoms. This is what

---

[44] Ibid. 399.   [45] Ibid. 402–3.

differentiates Newtonian atomism most sharply from Epicurean atomism and Boyle's corpuscularianism. It is *dynamic* in contrast to the kinematic systems of conventional atomism.

I have argued elsewhere that Locke followed Boyle in favouring a corpuscularianism that avoided the use of forces on the ground that they are occult and not useful for explanation. His acknowledgement of Newton's use of forces acting at a distance and his consequent changes in later editions of the *Essay* were half-hearted and incomplete; he was clearly unable to bring himself to abandon his view that all action between bodies was by impact.[46] This enhanced the value, for explanation, of the postulation of absolutely solid bodies. There is evidence that Locke was hampered in his understanding of Newton by his lack of mathematical knowledge, and this may be relevant to his doubts about action at a distance.[47]

So by the beginning of the eighteenth century we find at least four kinds of view about hard bodies. There is conventional atomism and the related corpuscularianism, in which atoms are conceived as absolutely solid and capable of rebounding on direct collision; the anti-atomism of Descartes, some of whose particles are perfectly hard, not indestructible and capable of rebounding; the anti-atomism of Leibniz, whose smallest physical particles are theoretically divisible and rebound because they are deformable and elastic; and the atomism of Newton, whose perfectly hard atoms do not rebound on direct collision and exert forces of attraction on one another.

Among the arguments involved were: that something enduring must underlie change, that the rebounding of absolutely hard bodies avoids an explanatory regress and is required because forces are occult, that body consists in extension, and that quantity of motion is conserved. There were arguments based on the analyticity of true statements, the infinite divisibility of dimensions, the law of continuity, the uniformity of nature, and Newton's Laws of Motion. Underlying many of the arguments was a belief in the wisdom and goodness of God and his concern to prevent the universe from running down, a belief that could lead in either direction.

It is interesting to note that although both Descartes and Newton called in God to ensure conservation, they did so in rather different ways. Descartes's God arranged the laws governing the behaviour of bodies

---

[46] Alexander, *Ideas, Qualities and Corpuscles*, 163–5; Jolley, *Leibniz and Locke*, ch. 4.
[47] Cranston, 337.

in such a way that the conservation of the quantity of motion was ensured by, as it were, natural processes. Thus his Third Law says that
hard bodies rebound to achieve that end. Newton's God arranged the
laws of the behaviour of bodies in such a way that conservation of motion
was not ensured in the natural course of things. So God has to intervene
to ensure overall conservation. The alleged rationalist Descartes chooses
what we might call a theological–scientific course, while the alleged empiricist Newton chooses what we might call a theological–metaphysical
course.

III

Wilson L. Scott has shown how the controversy about hard bodies
continued for a century to have its effect on scientific experimentation
and theorizing. He sees it as essentially a struggle between Cartesians and
Newtonians stemming from Descartes's statement in *Principles of Philosophy* at Part II, section 40 that hard bodies rebound on direct collision
and Newton's statement in query 31 of *Opticks* that, on the contrary, they
come to a stop. I have quoted both these in Section II. He sees it also as
part of a wider conflict between atomism and conservation theories, involving the *vis viva* controversy. He makes it clear that although the hard
body view was eventually and rather mysteriously abandoned in the first
half of the nineteenth century, its proponents made enormous contributions to the development of the physical sciences. The view provided, he
says, the conceptual background for d'Alembert's principle, the principle
of least action, the Carnot cycle, the chemical atomic theory, the law of
Dulong and Petit, the ideal gas law, the kinetic theory of gases, and,
indirectly, the law of conservation of energy.[48]
    The story of the development of these connected problems is so
complex that I can do no more than indicate a few of its features that I
take to reveal something of the nature of the controversy and to help
to explain its endurance. Up to the end of the seventeenth century the
arguments on both sides were largely a priori; they were conceptual or
mathematical or metaphysical or theological. At that stage they doubtless
had to be because of the impossibility of direct experiments on individual
atoms, corpuscles, or globules, the only bodies conceived of as absolutely
solid.

---

[48] Scott, *The Conflict between Atomism and Conservation Theory*, 275–6.

It is striking that in spite of a wealth of experimental investigation of impact during the eighteenth and early nineteenth centuries the arguments that kept the controversy alive were largely the old a priori ones. The names of Boyle, Leibniz, Descartes, and Newton kept cropping up. Much was contributed by chemists, engineers, and others with practical interests, but the arguments against hard bodies were, even in the end, inconclusive. There was a fading of interest in hard bodies rather than an outright rejection of them, and a strong tendency to keep them but give them a position in which the problems they raised could do no harm, although their presence appears to have given some comfort.

The seeds of progress were contained in Leibniz's law of continuity and his belief in the conservation of *vis viva*. The proportionality of force to the square of the velocity foreshadows the concept of kinetic energy ($\frac{1}{2}MV^2$). His view that force apparently lost in the collision of soft inelastic bodies was transformed into the motion of the inner parts of those bodies foreshadowed the law of the conservation of energy.[49] The growth of these seeds needed the concepts of work and energy and more knowledge of, for example, heat, which led to the idea that the motions of the inner parts of colliding bodies constituted heat, that is, the idea of the reciprocal conversion of mechanical energy into other forms of energy.

Papers on the hard body problem were invited by the Royal Society in 1668 and the French Académie des Sciences in 1724 and 1726. Wallis, Wren, and Huygens responded to the Royal Society and Jean Bernoulli and Colin Maclaurin to the Académie. Maclaurin accepted Newtonian hard atoms while Bernoulli rejected them on Leibnizian grounds of continuity, arguing that an absolutely hard body would be compressible by an infinite force. He appears also to have believed in perpetual motion.[50]

In 1743 Jean d'Alembert argued that the debate about whether force was to be measured by MV or MV^2 was empirically undecidable and a mere dispute about words.[51] He claimed that the effects of force could be measured in various ways, so conservation of MV and MV^2 could be used in the same system. Many historians have thought that this settled the dispute, but Laudan has shown that it did not and that the controversy continued until at least the 1790s.[52] Between 1743 and 1790 many thought that the dispute was settled, not for d'Alembert's reasons but because the

---

[49] Leibniz, *Discourse on Metaphysics*, in *Philosophical Essays*, 49–50; also *Leibniz–Clarke Correspondence* (1717), ed. H. G. Alexander (Manchester, 1956), 87–8.

[50] Scott, *The Conflict between Atomism and Conservation Theory*, 39.

[51] J. d'Alembert, *Traité de dynamique* (Paris, 1743), p. xxi.

[52] L. Laudan, 'The *Vis Viva* Controversy: A Post-Mortem', *Isis*, 59 (1968), 131–43.

champions of MV had triumphed. Thomas Reid in his *Essay on Quantity* put forward a view similar to d'Alembert's.[53]

The main problem was that different phenomena suggested that neither MV nor MV^2 was a universally applicable measure of force. It looked as if MV^2 was appropriate for falling bodies, as Leibniz claimed in *Discourse on Metaphysics*, section 17, while MV was appropriate for the impact of both elastic and inelastic bodies, as Maclaurin claimed.[54] This cast doubt on the idea that any universal conservation law had been found. The trouble was that Maclaurin based his view on the existence of Newtonian hard bodies but Leibniz rejected them.

In 1805 William Hyde Wollaston argued before the Royal Society that further direct experimention on impact was useless for settling the *vis viva* controversy because the controversy depended on different interpretations of the same experimental results.[55] This was surely an important insight because it suggests that the real disagreement was not about the phenomena but about fundamental and general principles in the light of which the phenomena were interpreted. As I have suggested, I think this can be seen operating both before and after Wollaston, and it no doubt accounts for the endurance of the controversy and its eventual petering out through neglect.

Wollaston gives some particular examples in support of his view. I shall not go into them because we have seen in general how plausible it is. If, like Newton, we are not worried by loss of motion or force in each particular collision we will be content to hold that perfectly hard bodies stop on impact. If, like Descartes, we attach great importance to laws of motion that ensure the conservation of motion we will think it obvious that perfectly hard bodies bounce. If, like Leibniz, we attach central importance to continuity we will regard both these views as showing the impossibility of hard bodies. So much for theory, but basic attitudes will have their effect on the interpretation of experimental results and the construction of further detailed theories. Our interpretation of experiments will depend importantly on whether we take as fundamental some conservation law, a law of continuity, certain principles of mechanical explanation, the 'equality' of cause and effect, the possibility of infinite forces or perpetual motion, or the wisdom of God, who tends to be made in our own image.

---

[53] T. Reid, *An Essay on Quantity* (1748), in *Essays on the Powers of the Human Mind* (Edinburgh, 1812), vol. i, pp. i–xviii.

[54] Scott, *The Conflict between Atomism and Conservation Theory*, 25 ff.

[55] W. H. Wollaston, 'On the Force of Percussion', *Philosophical Transactions*, 96 (1806), 13–22.

Wollaston, in consequence of his reconsideration of experiments with pendulums with bobs of various materials, made an important conceptual advance by distinguishing between *force acting through space* (FS = MV^2) and *force acting through time* (FT = MV). He thus introduced the ideas of *energy* and *work* and paved the way for the law of conservation of energy.

During the second half of the eighteenth century there had been contributions to the controversy from engineers and practical men working on hydrodynamics. Hard bodies that did not rebound figured in explanations of the incompressibility of water, and Jean Charles de Borda in 1769 held that there were losses of *vis viva* in agitated water owing to the impact of these particles.[56] Later came the vital work of Count Rumford (1798) and Davy (1800) on the production of heat by friction.[57] Then in 1845 James Joule accounted for the apparent loss of *vis viva* in agitated water by conversion to heat; and by his famous paddle-wheel experiment showed that mechanical energy was convertible into exactly equivalent quantities of heat energy.[58] In 1804 Peter Ewart, rejecting hard bodies for Leibniz's reasons and accepting the conservation of *vis viva*, had arrived at a position that can be summed up in the slogan 'No conservation without conversion'.[59] This avoided having to rely on infinite forces in nature. Interestingly, Ewart held that for practical purposes bodies become more elastic as they become harder.

Early in the nineteenth century Leibniz's law of continuity came under attack from the direction of chemistry. It was argued by Louis Proust, Gay-Lussac, and others round about that time that chemical combination occurs in jumps. It had been thought that when oxygen combined with hydrogen to form water it did so gradually. It was now shown that no combination took place until the correct proportion of oxygen to hydrogen was reached, when it happened all at once. Proust showed that in metallic oxides 'not only were the proportions between the metals and oxygen . . . constant in the individual compounds, but also that the combining proportions increased by leaps, and not gradually, when two

---

[56] Scott, *The Conflict between Atomism and Conservation Theory*, 106.

[57] Benjamin Thompson, Count Rumford, 'An Experimental Inquiry concerning the Source of Heat which is Excited by Friction', *Philosophical Transactions*, 88 (1798), 80–102; H. Davy, *Elements of Chemical Philosophy* (London, 1812), 94 ff.

[58] J. P. Joule, 'On the Existence of an Equivalent Relation between Heat and the Ordinary Forms of Mechanical Power', *Philosophical Magazine*, ser. 3, 27 (1845), 205 ff.

[59] P. Ewart, *On the Measure of Moving Force* (1808), in *Memoirs of the Literary and Philosophical Society of Manchester* (Manchester, 1813), 105–258; Scott, *The Conflict between Atomism and Conservation Theory*, 143–6.

elements unite to form more than one compound'.[60] Thus there are just three oxides of iron with no intermediate ones: ferric oxide (FeO), ferrous oxide (Fe_2O_3), and ferroso-ferric oxide (Fe_3O_4). Proust's view was later confirmed experimentally by Dalton.

In setting out his chemical atomic theory in his *New System of Chemical Philosophy* (1808) John Dalton showed a considerable reluctance to reject hard atoms altogether, although elastic interactions at the atomic level were central in his explanations of chemical phenomena. Following Lavoisier he accepted caloric as a subtle elastic fluid 'the particles of which repel one another, but are attracted by all other bodies'. Dalton held that observable bodies are composed of extremely small hard atoms, each surrounded by caloric, which prevents their actual contact with one another. The caloric makes the individual atoms interact as if they were elastic.[61] So his explanations could use the elastic rebound of caloric-wrapped atoms. Dalton's reasons for retaining hard atoms appears to be that, in deference to Newton, he believed that ultimately there must be only one species of matter.

John Herepath, an early exponent of the kinetic theory of gases, in 1847 still adhered to hard atoms, and even hard molecules, that bounce, at least under certain conditions. He acknowledged a debt to Wren and Huygens.[62] Maxwell at first accepted hard molecules but later criticized Herepath's use of them and in 1871 made it clear that he now accepted the elastic impact of molecules. However, his reason was to preserve the conservation of energy, although this principle was by no means beyond doubt.[63] As Scott points out, 'the corpuscular theory of matter has been reconciled with the law of conservation of energy on the hypothesis of elastic molecules', which, however, solves the central problem by avoiding it: 'If molecules can be elastic, it matters not if the atoms are hard.' Kelvin in 1871 also abandoned hard bodies on the ground that they would violate the law of conservation of energy. He never gave a stronger reason.[64] There was still no direct evidence for the elasticity or inelasticity of the ultimate particles. Maxwell had a better reason for abandoning

---

[60] Quoted from E. von Meyer, *A History of Chemistry* (London, 1898), by Scott, *The Conflict between Atomism and Conservation Theory*, 199.

[61] J. Dalton, *New System of Chemical Philosophy* (London, 1808), 141 ff.

[62] J. Herepath, *Mathematical Physics* (London, 1847), vol. i, pp. xvii, 102, 112.

[63] J. C. Maxwell, *Theory of Heat*, 9th edn. (London, 1888), 307–8; Scott, *The Conflict between Atomism and Conservation Theory*, 280.

[64] William Thomson, Baron Kelvin, *Mathematical and Physical Papers* (Cambridge, 1910), v. 72–3.

hard bodies, but, interestingly, in the very act of doing so he stressed the point of talking of hard atoms in the first place. He said

The small hard body imagined by Lucretius, and adopted by Newton, was invented for the express purpose of *accounting for the permanence of bodies*. But it fails to account for the vibrations of a molecule as revealed by the spectroscope. We may indeed suppose the atom elastic, but this is to endow it with the very property for the explanation of which, as exhibited in aggregate bodies, the atomic constitution was originally assumed.[65]

Does this passage remind you of anything? It reminds me of Locke's saying that of course Mr Newton must be right about bodies acting at a distance and yet continuing to say that the only way we can conceive bodies to act is by impulse. In each case a fundamental principle thought to govern intelligibility is being put up against a new idea doing greater justice to the phenomena but of doubtful intelligibility at first sight, in Maxwell's case the vortex atom. It appears to be touch and go which wins: 'The question is . . . which is to be master, that's all.'

IV

I should now like to imagine myself thinking about atoms, as Locke was, in the 1660s. The virtuosi are all talking about *The Sceptical Chymist* this year; some have even read it. I have never heard of force or work or energy as technical terms. Newton's laws of motion and his idea of the attraction and repulsion of atoms have not yet arrived. I am aware of striking regularities in the world, but I have only vague ideas about elasticity or the conservation of anything. I am not a mathematician, and, besides, the mathematicians have not much applied themselves to these matters. I find Boyle's chemical experiments and Harvey's observations more accessible and interesting than Galileo's games with marbles, inclined planes, and pendulums.

I am impressed by the apparent explanatory power of atomism and I wonder what properties to attribute to the atoms. The explanations of the relative hardnesses and of the rebounding of observable bodies are plausible. The smaller the spaces between the atoms in relation to the sizes of the atoms, the harder the body. Such objects are relatively hard or soft because their atoms can move closer to one another and slide past

[65] J. C. Maxwell, *Scientific Papers of J. Clerk Maxwell* (Cambridge, 1890), ii. 445–84, quoted from 470–1.

one another depending on their spatial arrangements. They can approach absolute hardness if subjected to pressure in all directions at the same time; but only *approach* it because no pressing body or containing vessel is absolutely hard and because the atoms would have to have very special shapes and sizes for all spaces between them to be eliminated. So if a body contained no empty spaces or movable parts wouldn't it be absolutely hard, or solid as we might say? So if a single atom is like this we avoid an explanatory regress. However, many possible explanations of phenomena appear to require the bouncing of atoms if explanations in terms of forces are unavailable or thought to be unacceptable because forces are occult and action at a distance is taken to be inconceivable.

But would absolutely hard atoms bounce on direct impact? Why not? A soft ball of clay dropped on to a hard surface does not bounce, but if it is baked in the sun it bounces a little. A wooden ball bounces better still, an ivory or glass ball better than that, and an iron ball best of all those I have available. I am not very good at controlled experiments; these are more or less careful qualitative observations. They appear to support the idea that the harder the body, the better the bounce, and that an absolutely hard ball would be a perfect bouncer. So the atom should bounce. This indeed appears to be the view of those natural philosophers with whom I have had any contact.

Unfortunately this must be a matter of speculation because I cannot get at individual atoms in order to experiment with them. However, perhaps I can reassure the doubter by using the hypothesis that atoms are absolutely hard and perfect bouncers to provide explanations of the phenomena that are more successful than explanations based on the other available hypotheses.

If we are thinking empirically we might think of absolute hardness as a limiting concept derived from the sorts of observation I have described; but it must not be thought to lie at the end of a series of relative hardnesses. No matter how far you go along that series, the hardness of a body is due to the tightness of the packing of its atoms. But the absolutely hard body has no inner parts to be more or less tightly packed. Absolute hardness is not a kind of relative hardness, so it is not a kind of empirical hardness either.

There is an atomistic explanation of the bouncing of relatively hard bodies. It is easy to see how a collection of atoms can be compressed because of its 'pores', although it is not so easy to see theoretically why it should recover its original shape and size. However, I know from experience that many bodies do recover, more or less completely, from being compressed. People are just beginning to call this 'elasticity'. It seems plausible that elasticity varies with hardness: the harder a body is to compress, the more it tends, while you are trying to compress it, to spring back. I now see that observed bouncing probably depends on elasticity in an obvious way; two colliding bodies are compressed and tend to recover and push each other away.

Now, of course, I am faced with a problem. The atom is not deformable and so not elastic. How could it bounce? Consider again relatively hard bodies. All but the very best bouncers, perhaps, are deformed on colliding because the atoms are pushed closer together but never touch. Perhaps in the very best bouncers, short of perfection, some of the atoms do touch. Atoms, being perfectly hard, are perfect bouncers, so their touching reinforces the bounce due to deformation alone. Bouncing by deformation is imperfect bouncing, as relative hardness is imperfect hardness.

The atom is the perfect bouncer because it does not have to overcome the disadvantage of having empty spaces in its constitution. It just bounces straight away without having to deform another or recover from its own deformation. Just as perfect hardness is quite unlike imperfect hardness, so perfect bouncing is quite unlike imperfect bouncing and is not to be explained in the same way. Perhaps it is not to be explained at all, but just taken as primitive; perfect bouncing goes with absolute hardness, as heads goes with tails or inside with outside.

I am now at the most fundamental level of my theorizing where not everything can be proved or empirically confirmed. Assumptions are in order, but I still have the urge to provide reasons of some sort for them. So I may give reasons of a kind that will no longer figure once I start proving or confirming detailed statements about the phenomena. I refer to God's wisdom, power, or pleasure, or I say that the contrary is inconceivable, or that my hypothesis gives the best or the only hope of explaining the phenomena, or . . . At this stage we must not confuse elasticity with bounceability. If later we were to come to think of bouncing as *always* explained in terms of elasticity that is a view that would have to be worked for. It would have to be discovered that the hardest bodies available for experiment were deformed on collision. Then it would be a hypothesis that it was the recovery from this deformation that provided a new cause of backward motion, and that in turn would need confimation. Even then it would have to be accepted that one universal explanation of bouncing was a desideratum, but what would be the grounds for that? It would also be necessary to find explanations for the phenomena that did not depend on the absolute hardness of the atoms.

It seems to me that it was reasonable for a philosopher at the end of the seventeenth century who was interested in general theories for the explanation of physical phenomena to embrace a theory based on absolutely hard, rebounding atoms. Whichever currently available theory was chosen for serious consideration, it would give rise to problems that looked, to someone at the time, insuperable. However, since these problems usually arose as a result of the acceptance of fundamental principles of explanation or intelligibility or metaphysical or theological propriety about which different views could be held, there was always hope that the insuperability was illusory. Moreover, we can now see that, whatever choice our philosopher made, he would not have been mistaken in supposing that the investigation and defence of it would last him a lifetime.

7

Rediscovering America: The Two Treatises *and Aboriginal Rights*

JAMES TULLY

Three hundred years after its publication Locke's *Two Treatises of Government* continues to present one of the major political philosophies of the modern world. By this I mean it provides a set of concepts we standardly use to represent and reflect on contemporary politics. This arrangement of concepts is not the only form of reflection on modern politics, not our 'horizon' so to speak, but it is a familiar and customary one.

At the centre of Locke's political philosophy is a theory that accounts for much of its appeal. This is a delegation theory of popular sovereignty built out of two concepts: political society and property. First, political societies are said to be derived from the delegated political powers of the individual members. The members always retain the right to regain these powers when their governors act contrary to their trust, overthrow them by means of revolution, and set up new governors as they think good. Second, the productive powers of any political society are said to be derived from the labour powers, the property, of the individual members. These powers also are, as Locke puts it, 'given up' in establishing political societies so they may be 'regulated' by government for the public good. Again, if labour power is regulated contrary to the trust the members have the right to overthrow their governors and set up new ones.

Many of the leading problems of the modern world, as well as the diverse solutions to them, can be and have been posed in the terms of this theory of popular sovereignty. Locke's concept of political society provides the foundation for questions of political legitimacy: What constitutes consent to delegate political power? How much power should be

First pub. in James Tully, *An Approach to Political Philosophy: Locke in Contexts* (Cambridge: Cambridge University Press, 1993).

delegated and for what ends? What levels of participation and representation are appropriate? When is revolt justifiable? His concept of property
provides the foundation for questions of economic justice: To what
extent should labour power be regulated? Can it be organized without
exploitation? What is a just distribution of the products of labour? These
great questions of political and economic justice, from the Scottish Enlightenment through Wollstonecraft, Marx, and Mill to Rawls and
Dworkin, have been asked and answered to a remarkable degree within
the problem space opened up by Locke's concepts of political society and
property.[1]

In this chapter I do not wish to deny that these two concepts provide
an appropriate and useful representation of many aspects of modern
politics. Rather, I would like to argue that the concepts of political society
and property are inappropriate to and misrepresent two specific political
problems: the problems of aboriginal self-government and ecology. These
two problems are closely related. The struggle of aboriginal peoples for
recognition as self-governing 'First Nations' is not only a struggle to right
an injustice that dates from the era of European expansion: the denial of
their status as distinct political societies with title to their traditional
lands. It is also a struggle to reclaim their traditional lands and to practise
their customary forms of land use. This has brought them into direct
conflict with the modern forms of land use that pose the greatest threat
to the environment. Whether they are the Maori of New Zealand, the
aboriginal peoples of the Amazon rainforests, or the Haida of the Queen
Charlotte Islands, the 250 million aboriginal peoples are at the forefront
of the ecological movement. The ecologically benign forms of land use,
attitudes to nature, and property relations they seek to preserve seem to
offer an alternative to the ecologically destructive forms of property and
attitudes to nature that have gradually elbowed theirs aside over the last
400 years. I mean that aboriginal land use and property relations offer an
alternative, not in the sense of a solution, but in the sense of a contrasting
concept of property that is different enough from our own to give us the
much-needed critical distance from the basic assumptions that continue
to inform our debates about property and ecology.[2]

The reason why Locke's concepts of political society and property
are inadequate to represent these two problems clearly is that Locke

---

[1] See e.g. Ian Shapiro, 'Resources, Capacities and Ownership: The Workmanship Ideal
and Distributive Justice', *Political Theory*, 19/1 (Feb. 1991), 47–73.

[2] For an introduction, see Julian Burger, *First Peoples: A Future for the Indigenous World*
(New York, 1990).

constructed them in contrast to Amerindian forms of nationhood and property in such a way that they obscure and downgrade the distinctive features of Amerindian polity and property. Let me state this thesis in two parts. First, Locke defines political society in such a way that Amerindian government does not qualify as a legitimate form of political society. Rather, it is construed as a historically less developed form of European political organization located in the later stages of the 'state of nature' and thus not on a par with modern European political formations. Second, Locke defines property in such a way that Amerindian customary land use is not a legitimate type of property. Rather, it is construed as individual labour-based possession and assimilated to an earlier stage of European development in the state of nature, and thus not on equal footing with European property. Amerindian political formations and property are thereby subjected to the sovereignty of European concepts of politics and property. Furthermore, these concepts serve to justify the dispossession of Amerindians of their political organizations and territories, and to vindicate the superiority of European, and specifically English, forms of political society and property established in the New World. In using these concepts in this way Locke was intervening in one of the major political and ideological contests of the seventeenth century.

What were the long-term consequences? Locke's theory of political society and property was widely disseminated in the eighteenth century and woven into theories of progress, development, and statehood. Debates—between jurists and humanists, free traders and mercantilists, and capitalists and socialists—over the great questions of political and economic justice have thus tended, as we have seen, to work within this basic conceptual framework. Consequently, in interpreting the *Two Treatises* there is a similar tendency to overlook the European–Amerindian context and to ask questions which take the concepts for granted.[3] Indeed, the very manner in which Locke arranged these concepts causes a reader to overlook the way European concepts of political society and property are imposed over and subsume Amerindian nations and property (thus foreshadowing what was to occur to a large extent in practice in the following

[3] There are notable exceptions to this tendency to ignore the American context. See Richard Ashcraft, 'Political Theory and Political Reform: John Locke's Essay on Virginia', *Western Political Quarterly*, 22/4 (Dec. 1969), 742–58; John Dunn, 'The Politics of Locke in England and America in the Eighteenth Century', in John Yolton (ed.), *John Locke: Problems and Perspectives* (Cambridge, 1969), 45–80; Peter Laslett, 'John Locke, the Great Recoinage, and the Origins of the Board of Trade 1695–1698', in Yolton, *John Locke*, 137–65; Herman Lebovics, 'The Uses of America in Locke's *Second Treatise of Government*', *Journal of the History of Ideas*, 47 (1986), 567–81.

centuries). One misses the philosophical and ideological contest in the text between European and Amerindian sovereignty and property (for a reader sees only the result of the contest) and misunderstands some of the basic arguments of the text. Moreover, in so far as these concepts of political society and property continue to be taken for granted, aboriginal claims to self-government are misunderstood. And, the critical perspective on the ecological crisis that their systems of property and resource use could provide is correspondingly lost.

Accordingly, my aim in this chapter is to recover the context in which Locke presented the concepts of political society and property in contrast with Amerindian forms of government and property, and to show how this increases and alters our understanding of the *Two Treatises*. By setting out a clear view of how these four concepts were arranged, I also hope to loosen their continuing hold on political thought today.[4] The chapter consists in three sections. The first two are on the role of the state of nature and the account of state formation in the *Two Treatises* in the light of the Amerindian context. A brief section on the dissemination of Locke's arguments in the eighteenth century rounds off the argument.

I. Dispossession: The Role of the State of Nature

Locke had extensive knowledge of and interest in European contact with aboriginal peoples. A large number of books in his library are accounts of European exploration, colonization, and of aboriginal peoples, especially Amerindians and their ways. As secretary to Lord Shaftesbury, secretary of the Lords Proprietors of Carolina (1668–71), secretary to the Council of Trade and Plantations (1673–4), and member of the Board of Trade (1696–1700), Locke was one of the six or eight men who closely invigilated and helped to shape the old colonial system during the Restoration. He invested in the slave-trading Royal Africa Company (1671) and the Company of Merchant Adventurers to trade with the Bahamas (1672), and he was a Landgrave of the proprietary government of Carolina. His theoretical and policy-making writings on colonial affairs include the *Fundamental Constitutions of Carolina* (1669), Carolina's agrarian laws (1671–2), a reform proposal for Virginia (1696), memoranda and policy recommendations for the boards of trade, covering all the colonies,

---

[4] For this type of approach, see James Tully (ed.), *Meaning and Context: Quentin Skinner and his Critics* (Princeton, NJ, 1988).

histories of European exploration and settlement, and manuscripts on a wide range of topics concerning government and property in America.[5]

In the *Two Treatises* America is immediately identified as one example of the 'state of nature' and then classified as the earliest 'age' in a world-wide historical development. '[I]n the beginning all the World was *America*', Locke asserts in the *Second Treatise*.[6] America is 'still a Pattern of the first Ages in *Asia* and *Europe*',[7] and Amerindians and Europeans who make contact with them 'are perfectly in a State of Nature'.[8]

The two basic elements of his theory of popular sovereignty in a state of nature are illustrated by examples of life in native America. First, the inhabitants exercise what has come to be called 'individual popular sovereignty' or 'individual self-government'. That is, 'the *Execution* of the Law of Nature is in that State, put into every Mans hands'.[9] This individual and natural exercise of political power comprises the abilities to know and to interpret standards of right (natural laws), to judge controversies concerning oneself and others in accordance with these laws, and to execute such judgements by punishments proportionate to the transgression and appropriate for purposes of restraint and reparation.[10] Individuals are free to order their actions within the bounds of natural laws and are equal in the 'Power and Jurisdiction' to govern the actions of those who transgress these bounds.[11] This system of individual self-government is illustrated with examples from America.[12] Political society is then defined in explicit contrast to this natural mode of individual self-government: namely, where individuals have given their 'natural power' to the community and set up 'a common establish'd Law and Judicature to appeal to, with Authority to decide Controversies between them, and punish Offenders'.[13]

The second aspect of life in America that is definitive of the state of nature is individual and exclusive rights over one's labour and its products. Everyone is free to exercise their labour in accordance with natural

---

[5] There is no collection of Locke's colonial writings, nor even a bibliography of them. See John Locke, *The Fundamental Constitutions of Carolina*, in *Works*, x. This volume also contains 'The Whole History of Navigation from its Original to this Time' (1704), 358–511, sometimes attributed to Locke. John Locke, 'Some Chief Grievances of the Present Constitution of Virginia . . .', Bodl. MS Locke e.9. Bodl. MS Locke c.30 is on colonial affairs. See also W. Noel Sainsbury (ed.), *Calendar of State Papers, Colonial Series, America and the West Indies*, 43 vols. (London, 1862), esp. ix–xi; *Records in the British Public Record Office relating to South Carolina 1663–1710*, 5 vols. (Cambridge, 1928–47); Langdon Cheves (ed.), *The Shaftesbury Papers and Other Records relating to Carolina . . . to 1676*, South Carolina Historical Society Collections, v (London, 1897).

[6] Laslett, II. 49.   [7] Ibid. II. 108.   [8] Ibid. II. 14; cf. II. 109.
[9] Ibid. II. 7.   [10] Ibid. II. 7–12, 136.   [11] Ibid. II. 4, 6.
[12] Ibid. II. 9, 14, 107.   [13] Ibid. II. 87.

law for the sake of preservation and without the consent of others. Appropriation without consent is illustrated with examples of Amerindians acquiring fruit and venison, hunting deer, growing corn,[14] and so on. Property in political society is then defined in explicit contrast to this natural mode of labour-based property: namely, where labour, appropriation, and its products are regulated by government and positive laws.[15]

Two major conclusions follow from the premiss that America is a state of nature. First, Locke claims in the *First Treatise* that no one doubts that European planters have a right to wage war 'against the *Indians*, [and] to seek Reparation upon any injury received from them', and this without authorization from a constituted political authority.[16] In this case, a European planter in the West Indies is exercising his right to execute the law of nature and seek reparations as explained in the *Second Treatise*. Although Locke calls this a 'strange Doctrine',[17] there is one sense in which it is commonplace.

Within the long reflection on European contact with America from 1492 to 1690, a number of justifications were advanced for the assertion of European sovereignty over the New World. Papal grants, royal charters, symbolic acts, such as the planting of crosses, discovery and occupation, the right to trade, and the duty to spread Christianity to non-Christians were the most common. Objections were raised to each of these justifications by writers such as Francisco de Vitoria (1480–1552), Alonso de la Vera Cruz (1507–84), and Bartholomé de Las Casas (1484–1566).[18] After advancing a number of objections to the standard justifications, Vitoria concluded his long discussion with a justification of conquest he believed to be invulnerable. Since both Spaniards and Amerindians are in the state of nature, if the Spaniards conduct themselves in accordance with the law of nature, then they have the right to defend themselves against any

---

[14] Ibid. II. 26, 30, 48.   [15] Ibid. II. 30, 38, 50, 129.
[16] Ibid. I. 130; cf. I. 131.   [17] Ibid. II. 9.
[18] For surveys of European justifications for sovereignty in America see Delia Opekokew, *The First Nations: Indian Government and the Canadian Confederation* (Saskatoon, 1980); Brian Slattery, *Ancestral Lands, Alien Laws: Judicial Perspectives on Aboriginal Title* (Saskatoon, 1983); Wilcomb E. Washburn, 'The Moral and Legal Justifications for Dispossessing the Indians', in James M. Smith (ed.), *Seventeenth-Century America: Essays in Colonial History* (Chapel Hill, UNC, 1959), 15–32; Ruth Barnes Moynihan, 'The Patent and the Indians: The Problem of Jurisdiction in Seventeenth Century New England', *American Indian Culture and Research*, 2/1 (1977), 8–18; Chester Eisenger, 'The Puritan Justification for Taking the Land', *Essex Institute Historical Collections*, 84 (1948), 131–43; Maureen Davies, 'Aspects of Aboriginal Rights in International Law', in Bradford Morse (ed.), *Aboriginal Peoples and the Law* (Ottawa, 1985), 16–47; James Muldoon, *Popes, Lawyers, and Infidels* (Liverpool, 1979); L. C. Green and Olive P. Dickason, *The Law of Nations and the New World* (Calgary, 1988); Robert A. Williams Jr., *The American Indian in Western Legal Thought: The Discourse of Conquest* (Oxford, 1991).

wrong committed by the Amerindians 'and to avail themselves of the rights of War'.[19] The natural right of self-defence to proceed with force against the violators of natural law was adapted by Francisco Suarez (1548–1617), Hugo Grotius (1583–1645), and Samuel Pufendorf (1632–94). Locke's 'strange Doctrine', although it differs in some respects from the arguments of his predecessors, is a reassertion of this conventional justification of war and, as we have seen, Locke uses it in this context.

When a person violates natural law he loses his natural rights and may be enslaved or killed.[20] Scholars who work on this part of Locke's theory assume that it refers to black slavery.[21] Notwithstanding, it may also refer to Amerindian slavery. Of all the English colonies, Carolina had the largest slave-trade. In 1663 eight proprietors were granted full title to the area that covers most of present-day North Carolina, all of South Carolina, and almost all of Georgia. The proprietors established government and a system of property in order to recruit settlers to engage in agriculture, initially drawing surplus planters from Barbados. Lord Shaftesbury and Locke assumed leadership of the project in 1669. Their plan was to make a profit from land-rent and the trade of agricultural products. The colonists turned instead to the more lucrative fur- and slave-trade with the Amerindians, even though this was expressly forbidden in Article 112 of the Constitution. Agriculture failed, the settlers became heavily indebted to the proprietors, little profit accrued to the proprietors, and the trade with the coastal native nations, the Cusabos and Coosas, led to conflict. Locke introduced a temporary law in 1672 forbidding Amerindian slavery and offering the native peoples individual plots of land under proprietary government. The colonists ignored the law and, after the 1674 peace treaty with the powerful Westos nation against the Spanish to the south, they expanded their trade. The Lords Proprietor responded with an unsuccessful proposal to settle a new group of planters at Locke's Island and with an attempt to control the Indian trade themselves, declaring a monopoly in 1677. By 1680 the fur-trade and the sale of Indian slaves to the West Indies were the staples of Carolina's economy.[22]

---

[19] Francisco de Vitoria, *De Indis et de Jure Belli Relectiones*, Classics of International Law (Oxford, 1917), sect. ii (p. 153e).   [20] Laslett, II. 16–24.

[21] This scholarship is reviewed in Wayne Glausser, 'Three Approaches to Locke and the Slave Trade', *Journal of the History of Ideas*, 51/2 (Apr.–June 1990), 199–216.

[22] Bodl. MSS Locke c.6, fos. 213, 216, and c.30; *Records in the British Public Record Office relating to South Carolina*, ii. 200; Cheves, *The Shaftesbury Papers*, 171–3, 193, 266–7, 311, 352, 381–2, 400, 432. The Agrarian Law of 21 June 1672 is in William J. Rivers, *A Sketch of the History of South Carolina to the Close of the Proprietary Government by the Revolution of 1719* (Charleston, sc, 1856), 358. See Herbert R. Paschal, *Proprietary North Carolina: A Study in Colonial* Government (Ph.D. dissertation, University of North Carolina, 1961).

When either slavery failed or all other means of dealing with the Amerindians proved ineffective, the practice in the colonies was to make war against the local tribes in a piecemeal fashion. For example, the colonists in Carolina revolted against the proprietors' monopoly on Indian trade, declared war on the Westos in 1679, and killed those they were unable to enslave. The usual justification for wars of this type was that the Indians had resisted the settlers in some way or stolen something, and so violated natural law, activating the settlers' right to defend themselves and avail themselves of the rights of war.[23]

Locke underscores in no uncertain terms the right in natural law to punish theft and violence with death, and these passages in chapters ii and iii of the *Second Treatise* are standardly interpreted as references to the right to punish Charles II in an armed revolt. Be this as it may, the very terms Locke uses to describe the offenders who may be 'destroyed' are the terms used to describe, and so dehumanize, Amerindians in the books in Locke's library.[24] Offenders are characterized as 'wild Savage Beasts' who 'may be destroyed as a *Lyon or a Tyger*'.[25] The natural right of the governments of England, France, and Holland to punish or put to death 'an Indian' who violates natural law is put forward as the proof and illustration of this violent doctrine.[26]

The second major conclusion Locke draws from the premiss that America is a state of nature is that appropriation of land may take place without consent. Appropriation without consent is the main argument of chapter v of the *Second Treatise*. The sections are carefully organized to prove and substantiate it. Nor is it surprising that Locke took such care in presenting his argument, for it is a departure from his earlier views, from the views of earlier natural law writers, and from the fundamental principle of Western law: *Quod omnes tangit ab omnibus tractari et approbari debet* (What touches all must be approved by all).[27]

Appropriation without consent has given rise to more commentary than any other argument in Locke's political philosophy. The problem is

---

[23] For the war of 1679, see M. Eugene Sirmans, *Colonial South Carolina* (Chapel Hill, UNC, 1966), 3–75. For the use of just war arguments, see Francis Jennings, *The Invasion of America: Indians, Colonialism and the Cant of Conquest* (New York, 1975), 105–28.

[24] e.g. John Smith, *A Description of New England* (London, 1616). See, in general, Robert F. Berkhofer, *The White Man's Indian: Images of the American Indian from Columbus to the Present* (New York, 1978).

[25] Laslett, II. 11, 16.   [26] Ibid. II. 10.

[27] For Locke's earlier view that property must be based on consent, see 'Morality', Bodl. MS Locke c.28, fos. 13–40. For his predecessors, see James Tully, *A Discourse on Property: John Locke and his Adversaries* (Cambridge, 1980).

to show how appropriation can take place given the background premiss that everyone has a natural right to the means of preservation.[28] This is a problem generated in part and in theory by Filmer's criticism of the role of consent to property in Grotius' theory, but in some of the secondary literature the background premiss is overlooked and it is then mistaken as solely a problem of justifying the division of English and European societies into propertied and propertyless classes.[29] The fact that the chapter is organized around a contrast between Europe, where appropriation without consent is not permitted because political societies exist, and America, where appropriation without consent is permitted because it is a state of nature, is rarely mentioned. That the argument justifies European settlement in America without the consent of the native people, one of the most contentious and important events of the seventeenth century and one of the formative events of the modern world, is normally passed over in silence. On the other hand, among scholars who specialize in the European dispossession of Amerindians reference to Locke's argument is commonplace.[30]

In the first section of chapter v of the *Second Treatise* Locke introduces appropriation without consent as the problem he endeavours to solve in the chapter,[31] and he says he has solved it in the middle and final sections.[32] The appropriation of common fruits and nuts, fish and game, and vacant land by means of individual labour is legitimate and creates a property right in the products as long as they do not spoil and there is enough and as good left in common for others. No other forms of exclusive property are recognized and all land that is not actively under cultivation is said to be vacant. Appropriation without consent continues until money is introduced, land becomes scarce, and there is no longer enough and as good for others. Until then, 'there could be no doubt of Right, no room for quarrel',[33] and 'no reason of quarrelling about Title, nor any

---

[28] For the background premiss and the full theoretical framework of Locke's argument, see Tully, *A Discourse on Property*, 53–95; Richard Ashcraft, *Locke's 'Two Treatises of Government'* (London, 1987), 81–150; Gopal Sreenivasan, *The Limits of Lockean Rights in Property* (Oxford, 1994); Stephen Buckle, *The Natural History of Property* (Oxford, 1991).

[29] For typical misinterpretations along these lines, see Jeremy Waldron, *The Right of Private Property* (Oxford, 1989); G. A. Cohen, 'Marx and Locke on Land and Labour', *Proceedings of the British Academy*, 71 (1985), 357–89; Neal Wood, *John Locke and Agrarian Capitalism* (Berkeley, Calif., 1984). For refutation, see ch. 3 above, and Ashcraft, *Locke's 'Two Treatises'*; and Sreenivasan, *The Lockean Limits*, for a detailed refutation of Cohen and Waldron.

[30] See William Cronon, *Changes in the Land: Indians, Colonists and the Ecology of New England* (New York, 1983); and n. 18 above.

[31] Laslett, II. 25, lines 16–19.   [32] Ibid. II. 39, 51.   [33] Ibid. II. 39.

doubt about the largeness of Possession it gave'.[34] Illustrating his solution throughout with examples drawn from America, Locke confidently concludes that any person could appropriate inland vacant land in America without consent: 'let him plant in some in-land, vacant places of *America*, we shall find that the *Possessions* he could make himself upon the *measures* we have given, would not be very large, nor, even to this day, prejudice the rest of Mankind, or give them reason to complain, or think themselves injured by this Man's Incroachment.'[35] The 'Controversie about . . . Title' and the 'Incroachment on the Right of Others',[36] by the 'Quarrelsom and Contentious', driven by 'Covetousness',[37] which Locke constantly refers to and claims to settle, raged across Europe and America from the early sixteenth century to well after 1690. These were controversies over title in the New World among competing European powers, jurisdictional disputes among the colonies, between colonists and their royal or proprietary governors, traders versus planters, and all of these against the aboriginal peoples who had been there for over 12,000 years. Much of Locke's work for the boards of trade and Carolina concerned these disputes.

By the early seventeenth century the accepted justification for the assertion of sovereignty in European international law was the discovery, occupation, and defence of any part of America not already occupied by a Christian ruler, as long as the settlement was warranted by a charter or grant. Settlement and defence were said to constitute occupation and long usage, the oldest and most widely recognized principle of legal title in the world.[38] This served as a justification relative to other European nations, establishing the monopoly right of a particular European nation to treaty with the native nations within its sphere of influence to the exclusion of other European nations. It did not justify the assertion of sovereignty over the native nations or even the claim to establish co-sovereignty or trading arrangements with them. These relations with the ancient nations of America require a second step.[39] One answer to this further justificatory step was to ignore the Amerindians and to characterize America as *terra nullius*, a vacant land (a condition the principle of occupation and long usage requires). Another strategy was to downgrade the status of the aboriginal peoples to that of beasts or savages so no juridical recognition was required. Often a royal grant would simply grant explorers and invaders the right 'to subdue, occupy and possesse' the

---

[34] Ibid. II. 51.   [35] Ibid. II. 36.   [36] Ibid. II. 51.
[37] Ibid. II. 34.   [38] See n. 18 above.   [39] Slattery, *Ancestral Lands*, 26.

inhabitants, 'getting into us the rule, title, and jurisdiction', as Henry VII unsuccessfully commissioned John Cabot.[40]

The rationalizations in royal charters and inter-European agreements were out of touch with the real world of seventeenth-century America. The European newcomers were outnumbered by the natives and dependent upon them for food, trade, and survival. Under these conditions some form of recognition of and accommodation to aboriginal title was required. The natives understood themselves to be self-governing nations exercising sovereign authority over their people and territory, and with a far better claim to occupancy and long usage than any recent European settlement huddled on the coastline could muster. Accordingly, the indigenous nations signed numerous international peace and friendship treaties with European nations, in which they granted rights of trade and use over some of their territory and agreed to co-existing or parallel sovereignty in other areas, and asserted, time after time, their inalienable sovereignty. The classic presentation of this view informs many of the treaties between the Haudenosaunee (Iroquois) Confederacy and the Dutch, English, and French nations. The First Nations represent it by a belt of two parallel rows of wampum:

These two rows will symbolise two paths or vessels, travelling down the same river together. One, a birch bark canoe, will be for the Indian people, their laws, their customs and their ways. The other, a ship, will be for the white people and their laws, their customs, and their ways. We shall travel together, side by side, but in our own boat. Neither of us will try to steer the other's vessel.[41]

This view is the basis of all treaties the First Nations made with European governments and their descendants.

A prevalent rival view was that sovereignty resides wholly in a European Crown to which Amerindians are subject. Amerindians have natural rights only to their goods and the small amounts of land they had under active cultivation at the time of contact, and these rights are subject to European law. As the English began to settle and plant, and not just trade, they began to argue that the Amerindians neither occupied and used in the appropriate manner the lands they claimed, nor did they live in political or civil societies. Hence, most of the land was vacant, no

---

[40] In Richard Hakylut, *Voyages Touching the Discovery of America* (London, 1850), 21–2.

[41] Grand Chief Michael Mitchell of the Mohawk Council of Akwesasne, 'An Unbroken Assertion of Sovereignty', in Bryce Richardson (ed.), *Drumbeat: Anger and Renewal in Indian Country* (Toronto, 1989), 105–37. For the treaties of the Haudenosaunee Confederacy and the recognition of native sovereignty, see Francis Jennings (ed.), *The History and Culture of Iroquois Diplomacy* (Syracuse, NY, 1985), pp. xiv–xv.

consent was required for its use, and the colonists claimed they signed formal treaties, not out of recognition of aboriginal rights, but only when necessity demanded it to mollify the wild and threatening natives.

The proponents of these rival views came into conflict in the 1630s. The first major quarrel began in 1633 as a jurisdictional dispute between Boston, led by John Winthrop, and Plymouth, led by Roger Williams. Williams argued that the royal patent did not convey title to Indian land and that the only legitimate means of possession was by treaty with Amerindian nations in order to acquire rights of usufruct on their property, as he did in Rhode Island and the Dutch in New York. Governor Winthrop replied that the Indians possessed only what they cultivated; the rest was open for appropriation without consent. The second major contention was the claim brought against the colony of Connecticut by the Mohegan Indians for sovereignty over their traditional lands. It began in the 1670s, appeals were made to the Privy Council in London, and litigation continued for 100 years. What was at stake in these celebrated cases was nothing less than the legitimacy of English settlement in America. They, in turn, were surrounded by innumerable other land disputes throughout the colonies between 1630 and 1690. In addition, two devastating wars against the Indians were connected to these disputes: against the Pequot, 1636–7, and against the Narragansett, 1674–5 (King Philip's War).[42]

In this contentious context appropriation by cultivation and without consent began to be employed to justify the dispossession of Amerindians of their traditional hunting and gathering territories. Some of the major authors are Samuel Purchas, the editor of Hakylut's *Travels* (1629), John White in Virginia (1630), Robert Cushman and Francis Higginson in New England, and John Cotton, who replied point-by-point to Roger Williams, Governor Winthrop, and the lawyers for Connecticut in the Mohegan appeals to the Privy Council.[43] The arguments and the very

---

[42] For Roger Williams and John Winthrop, see Moynihan, 'The Patent and the Indians', and Jennings, *The Invasion of America*, 128–46. For the Mohegan nation v. the Colony of Connecticut, see J. H. Smith, *Appeals to the Privy Council from the American Plantations* (New York, 1950), 417–42. For the wars against the Pequot and Narrangansett nations, see Jennings, *The Invasion of America*, 177–326.

[43] Samuel Purchas, *Hakluytus Posthumus, or; Purchas his Pilgrimes* (London, 1625), vol. iv, book 9, ch. 20; John White, *The Planters Plea* (London, 1630), Robert Cushman, 'Reasons and Considerations Touching the Lawfulness of Removing out of England into Parts of America' (1621), in Alexander Young (ed.), *Chronicles of the Pilgrim Fathers of the Colony of Plymouth* (Boston, 1844), 239–53; Francis Higginson, *New Englands Plantation* (London, 1631), *Proceedings of the Massachusetts Historical Society*, 62 (1929); John Cotton, 'John Cotton's Answer to Roger Williams', in *The Complete Writings of Roger Williams*, 7 vols. (New York,

terms used in the pamphlets are strikingly similar to chapter v of the *Second Treatise*. No author put forth an account that is as theoretically sophisticated as Locke's, but the basic terminology, premises, and conclusions for such a theory are present. Locke added his own knowledge of colonial affairs and of the sophisticated analyses of money, labour, and productivity by the mercantile writers of the Restoration to create the powerful theory in chapter v.[44]

Let me now illustrate this with a number of quotations that are similar to the more familiar arguments of chapter v. Replying directly to the argument that it is illegitimate to 'enter upon the land which hath beene soe longe possessed by others [Indians]', Winthrop writes, 'that which lies common, and that has neuer been replenished or subdued is free to any that possesse and improue it'. This is a 'natural right' that holds 'when men held the earth in common[,] every man sowing and feeding where he pleased'. He illustrates this with the same biblical reference Locke uses.[45] In contrast, a 'civil right' to jurisdiction over a whole territory only comes into existence after population increase and the enclosure of land make unused land scarce.[46]

Roger Williams argued that hunting and land-clearing certainly constitute use and occupation and, therefore, Amerindians have title to their traditional lands: they 'hunted all the Countrey over', he wrote, 'and for the expedition of their hunting voyages, they burnt up all the underwoods in the countrey, once or twice a yeare'.[47] To circumvent this defence, Williams's opponents deployed the argument that only sedentary agriculture and improvement constitute the kind of use that gives rise to property rights and, therefore, hunting and gathering lands may be looked on as vacant wasteland.

'We did not conceive that it is a just Title to so vast a continent, to make no other improvement of millions of acres in it, but onely to burne it up for a pastime,' Cotton rejoined.[48] 'As for the Natiues in New England,' Winthrop explained, 'they inclose noe Land, neither have any setled habytation, nor any tame cattle to improue the Land by, and soe

1963), ii; John Winthrop, 'Reasons to be Considered, and Objections with Answers', in *Winthrop Papers*, 2 vols. (Boston, 1931) ii. 138–45; *Winthrop's Journal*, ed. J. K. Hosmer (New York, 1908), 293–5.

[44] As I have sought to show in *An Approach to Political Philosophy* (Cambridge, 1993), esp. chs. 2–4, Locke in addition addressed other problems and contexts in ch. v of the *Second Treatise*.   [45] Laslett, II. 38; Genesis 13: 5.

[46] Winthrop, *Winthrop Papers*, 140–1.

[47] Cited by John Cotton, 'John Cotton's Answer', in *The Complete Writings of Roger Williams*, ii. 46–7.   [48] Ibid. 47.

have no other but a Naturall Right [i.e. in the products of their labour].'[49]
'The Indians', Higginson concurs, have no right to their traditional lands
because they 'are not able to make use of the one-fourth part of the Land,
neither have they any settled places . . . nor any ground as they challenge
for their owne possession, but change their habitation from place to
place.' Since they possess very little land, America is *vacuum domicilium*,
a 'vacant' or 'waste' land, and so *Vacuum Domicilium cedit occupanti*.[50] 'In
a vacant soyle', Cotton points out to Williams, 'he that taketh possession
of it, and bestoweth culture and husbandry upon it, his right it is.'[51]
Enunciating a principle similar to Locke's famous proviso in section 27 of
the *Second Treatise*, Winthrop concludes, 'soe . . . if we leave them [the
Amerindians] sufficient for their use, we may lawfully take the rest, there
being more than enough for them and us'.[52]

It is clear, therefore, that two functions are served by situating America
in a state of nature. First, Amerindian political organization is disregarded and replaced by a so-called natural system of individual self-
government, thereby dispossessing Amerindian governments of their
authority and nationhood and permitting Europeans to deal with them
and punish them on an individual basis. Second, the Amerindian system
of property over their traditional territory is denied and it is replaced by
a so-called natural system of individual, labour-based property, thereby
dispossessing Amerindians of their traditional lands and positing a va-
cancy which Europeans could and should use without the consent of the
First Nations. As we have seen, this 'agricultural' dispossession argument
was usually advanced with the qualification that, from the colonists' perspective, at the time of first European appropriation there was enough
and as good land left for the aboriginal peoples.

Locke was aware that the native peoples did not govern themselves in
the wholly individual and independent manner laid out in his description
of the state of nature, but were organized politically into nations. However, he describes their national forms of government in such a way that
they are not full 'political societies' and thus native Americans can be
dealt with as if they are in a late stage of the state of nature. In chapter
viii of the *Second Treatise* he asserts that, although Amerindians are called
'nations'[53] and are ruled by elected 'Kings',[54] they fail to meet the criteria
of a distinct political society. The reason for this is that their kings 'are

---

[49] Winthrop, *Winthrop Papers*, 141.
[50] Higginson, *New Englands Plantations*, 316.
[51] Cotton, 'John Cotton's Answer', in *The Complete Writings of Roger Williams*, ii. 47.
[52] Winthrop, *Winthrop Papers*, 141.   [53] Laslett, II. 41.   [54] Ibid. II. 108.

little more than *Generals of their Armies'*, who, although 'they command absolutely in War', in peacetime and in internal affairs 'they exercise very little Dominion, and have but a very moderate Sovereignty, the Resolution of Peace and War, being ordinarily either in the People, or in a Council'.[55] They lack the European institutions that, according to Locke, constitute the universal criteria of political society: subjection to majority rule rather than consensus,[56] an institutionalized legal system, institutionalized judiciary, legislature, and executive,[57] and the sovereign right to declare war and peace removed from popular control and lodged exclusively in the hands of the king or 'federative' authority.[58]

The reason Amerindians do not have these institutions is that they have no need of them. They have 'few Trespasses, and few Offenders', 'few controversies' over property, and therefore 'no need of many laws to decide them'.[59] As a result, they settle the few disputes they have on an ad-hoc, consensual, and individual basis, as in the state of nature.[60] They have few disputes because they have limited and moderate amounts of property. In turn, the explanation for this, which explains their whole system, is that they have limited and fixed desires: 'confineing their desires within the narrow bounds of each mans smal propertie made few controversies'.[61] Their desires are limited and they have 'no Temptation to enlarge their Possessions of Land, or contest for wider extent of Ground' because they lack money and large population which activate the desire to possess more than one needs.[62] That is, they lack the acquisitive desire to enlarge their possessions that leads to disputes over property and thus to the need for a distinct political society with an established system of property law to settle them. Locke sums this up in *The Third Letter concerning Toleration*:

Let me ask you, Whether it be not possible that men, to whom the rivers and woods afforded the spontaneous provisions of life, and so with no private possessions of land, had no inlarged desires after riches or power, should live in one society, make one people of one language under one Chieftain, who shall have no other power to command them in time of common war against their common enemies, without any municipal laws, judges, or any person with superiority established amongst them, but ended all their private differences, if any arose, by the extemporary determination of their neighbours, or of arbitrators chosen by the parties.[63]

---

[55] Ibid.; cf. I. 131. [56] Ibid. II. 86–7. [57] Ibid. II. 87.
[58] Ibid. II. 144–8. [59] Ibid. II. 107. [60] Ibid.
[61] Ibid. [62] Ibid. II. 108. [63] Cited ibid. II. 108 n.

The typical form of Amerindian government encountered by Europeans was a confederation of nations presided over by an assembly of the national chiefs.[64] A nation was governed by a council or longhouse of chiefs (*sachems*) from the internal clans. Each nation had a clearly demarcated and defended territory, a decision-making body, a consensus-based decision-making procedure, and a system of customary laws and kinship relations. There were few religious sanctions (in marked contrast to New England), no standing army, bureaucracy, police force, or written laws. They lacked the state-centred European features Locke lays down as essential to any political society, yet they performed the functions of government, as many Europeans observed. '[T]he wildest Indians in America', Roger Williams noted, 'agree upon some forms of Government . . . [and] their civil and earthly governments be as lawfull and true as any Governments in the World.'[65]

Hence, like many European writers, Locke highlights three features of Amerindian political organization to the neglect of the customary system of government that underlies them. He interprets the war-chief from an European perspective as a kind of primitive and proto-European sovereign, and he stipulates that native popular (non-delegated) government over matters of war and peace is by definition not a political society. But the war-chief was, and still is, a temporary military commander with no political authority and who can be, and often is, talked down by a political authority, such as a clan mother. Of course, Europeans often took the war-chief as the sole leader in order to undermine the authority of the traditional councils (and perhaps because they were accustomed to the fusion of military and political rule in one person in the colonial lieutenant-governors and governors-general). Second, the chiefs and the council often appointed ad-hoc arbitrators of justice. The ad-hoc procedure may be a source of Locke's concept of individual self-government, but he overlooks the appointment procedure and the unwritten yet orally transmitted system of customary law and sanctions that govern it. Third, he emphasizes the lack of crime and litigation in Amerindian communities, and he explains this by reference to their limited material possessions and their limited desires, as did many observers. Yet, he disregards the national, clan, and family systems of community property and distribution that underpin these features.

[64] This is a simplification of a complex range of political organizations. For an introduction, see Anthony F. Wallace, 'Political Organisation and Land Tenure among Northeastern Indians 1600–1830', *Southwestern Journal of Anthropology*, 13 (1957), 301–21.

[65] Williams, 'The Bloody Tenant . . .', in *The Complete Writings of Roger Williams*, iii. 250.

With respect to property, the territory as a whole belongs to the nation, often the women are custodians, and jurisdiction over it is held in trust by the chiefs.[66] It is inalienable, and the identity of a nation as a distinct people is inseparable from their relation to and use of the land, animals, and entire ecosystem. Although the land belongs to them, it is more accurate to say, as the Inuit stress, that they belong to the land. Clans and families have a bundle of matrilineal rights and responsibilities of use and usufruct over land for various uses. That is, property rights and duties inhere in the clans and apply to activities and to the geographical location in which the activities take place, not, in the first instance, to the products of the activities. The activities include hunting, trapping, gathering berries, non-sedentary agriculture, clam bed cultivation, fishing, and so on. The distribution and trade of the products is governed by custom and kinship tradition. When the coastal Indians made property agreements with the settlers, as Williams explained to Winthrop, they were granting them rights of co-use of the land, not rights to the land itself (which was inalienable).[67] Finally, families and individual family members own their goods, yet there is a casual attitude towards possessions and an overriding custom of sharing and gift-giving. From the Amerindian point of view, therefore, appropriation without consent is expropriation without consent.

In his depiction of Amerindian property, Locke highlights one specific form of activity—industrious labour and the products of industrious labour—and does not recognize the native system of national territories, the bundle of property rights and responsibilities in activities and their locales, and the customs governing distribution. If he had recognized these forms of property, as Roger Williams and many others who signed treaties did, European settlement in America without consent would have been illegitimate by his own criteria of enough and as good. In addition, Locke has a further reason not to recognize the traditional property of the Amerindians. The argument for dispossession by agricultural improvement was often supplemented by the natural law argument for just conquest if the native people resisted.[68] But, in Locke's theory of conquest (written for another purpose) the conqueror has no title to the property of the vanquished.[69] The conqueror has no right 'to dispossess the

---

[66] See Wallace, 'Political Organisation and Land Tenure'; Tim Ingold, D. Riches, and J. Woodburn (eds.), *Hunters and Gatherers: Property, Power and Ideology*, 2 vols. (New York, 1988).   [67] Cronon, *Changes in the Land*, 61.

[68] The conquest justification of European sovereignty is spurious because the Amerindians did not surrender and the European–Indian wars do not meet the criteria of conquest in international law (Davis, 'Aspects of Aboriginal Rights in International Law', 37–40).

[69] Laslett, II. 180, 184.

Posterity of the Vanquished, and turn them out of their Inheritance, which ought to be the Possession of them and their Descendants to all Generations'. Therefore, if the Amerindians had property in their traditional land conquest would not confer title over it. However, as Locke repeats twice in section 184 of the *Second Treatise*, in the case of conquest over a people in the state of nature, 'where there . . . [is] more *Land*, than the Inhabitants possess, and make use of', the conqueror, like 'any one[,] has liberty to make use of the waste'; thereby bringing his theories of conquest and appropriation into harmony.

In the second half of chapter v of the *Second Treatise* the concepts of property and political organization in the state of nature are shown to play a further and equally important role. Because the Amerindian political and property system is tied to a world of limited desires and possessions it is unsuited to the development of modern states and systems of property that Locke unfolds in the second half of the chapter. The dynamic development unleashed by the expansion of human desire for possessions after the introduction of money leads to interminable property disputes and so to the need to set up modern states to regulate and govern property relations. From this perspective, Amerindian societies are, as we have seen, defined by the specifically European institutions they lack and by superimposing on them the rudiments of individual, labour-based property, which plays such a prominent role in Locke's theory of historical development. To this we now turn.

II. World Reversal: Property and Political Society in a Civilization of Commerce and Improvement

Locke's theory of the historical development of politics and property comprises the following stages: different degrees of industry among individuals account for differences in possessions in the pre-monetary stage of nature. Money and trade are gradually introduced, spurring the growth of population and the applied arts. An elastic desire for more than one needs comes into being, uprooting for ever the pre-monetary economy of limited desires and needs. People seek to enlarge their possessions, either by honest industry or by preying on the honest industry of others, in order to sell the surplus in the market for a profit. All available land becomes occupied and put to use. To solve the quarrels and insecurities that inevitably follow people set up political societies with institutionalized legal and political systems to regulate and protect property.

Each stage in the development of a modern system of what is now
called surplus production and accumulation is defined by contrast to the
Amerindian system of 'underproduction' and 'replacement consumption'.[70]
First, the ethic of 'industriousness' that drives and legitimizes the process
is defined contrastively as superior to Amerindian land use. Although
God gave the 'World to men in Common', he did not mean that they
should leave it 'common and uncultivated', but rather that they should
'draw from it' the 'greatest conveniences of life'. Accordingly, he 'gave it
to the Industrious and Rational, (and *Labour* was to be his *Title* to it;)'.[71]
Amerindians are then said to draw less than one-hundredth of the number
of conveniences from the land that the English are able to produce.[72]
Second, Locke sets up cultivation as the standard of industrious and
rational use, in contrast to the 'waste ' and lack of cultivation in Amerindian hunting and gathering, thus eliminating any title they might claim.[73]
The planning, co-ordination, skills, and activities involved in native hunting, gathering, trapping, fishing, and non-sedentary agriculture, which
took thousands of years to develop and take a lifetime for each generation
to acquire and pass on, are not counted as labour at all, except for the
very last individual step (such as picking or killing), but are glossed as
'unassisted nature' and 'spontaneous provisions' when Locke makes his
comparisons;[74] whereas European activities, such as manufacturing bread,
are described in depth.[75] Moreover, the 'industrious' use or labour that
gives rise to property rights is equated with European agriculture, based
on pasturage and tillage,[76] thereby eliminating Amerindian non-sedentary
agriculture as a type of use and subverting any title that might have been
derived from it.

The coastal Indians lived in villages and engaged in non-sedentary
agriculture. Several of the English settlers sought to expropriate the
agricultural lands of the natives, for this eliminated the hard labour of
clearing land themselves.[77] To justify expropriation, they argued that the
Indians, who left their cornfields for the clam beds each year, neither
tilled nor fenced, and who let the fields rot and compost every three
years, for purposes of soil enrichment, did not cultivate the land in the

---

[70] For these concepts, see Marshall Sahlins, *Stone Age Economics* (Chicago, 1972).
[71] Laslett, II. 34.   [72] Ibid. II. 41.   [73] Ibid. II. 37, 41–3, 45, 48.
[74] Ibid. II. 37, 42, 108 n.   [75] Ibid. II. 42–3.   [76] Ibid. II. 42.
[77] See Washburn, 'The Moral and Legal Justifications for Dispossessing', 23–5; Jennings,
The Invasion of America, 58–84; James P. Ronda, 'Red and White at the Bench: Indians and
the Law in Plymouth Colony 1620–1691', *Essex Institute Historical Collections*, 110 (1974),
200–15; and Peter Thomas, 'Contrastive Subsistence Strategies and Land Use as Factors
for Understanding Indian–White Relations in New England', *Ethnohistory*, 23 (1976), 1–18.

proper fashion, and, therefore the land was open for use by others. 'They [the Indians] are not industrious,' Robert Cushman explained, 'neither have they art, science, skill or faculty to use either the land or the commodities of it; but all spoils, rots, and is marred from want of manuring, gathering and ordering.'[78] Locke elevates this justification of expropriation to the status of a law of nature: 'if either the Grass or his Inclosure rotted on the Ground, or the Fruit of his planting perished without gathering, and laying up, this part of the Earth, notwithstanding his Inclosure, was still to be looked on as Waste, and might be the Possession of any other'.[79]

The second contrast is between the limited desires of Amerindians and the unlimited desire of the English to accumulate possessions. When this is not mistaken for a contrast between bourgeois and proletarian motivation in the secondary literature it is often taken to be an astute observation on the difference in motivation of individuals in non-market and market societies—an anticipation of Adam Smith.[80] It is now possible to define Locke's contrast more specifically.

In section 37 of the *Second Treatise* the desire for more than one needs is said to follow from the introduction of money and population increase. This acquisitive motivation is contrasted with the pre-monetary motivation of Amerindians.[81] As he famously writes in section 48 of the *Second Treatise*, without money and a world trading system that develops with it, and so the hope of selling one's surplus on the market for money, no one would have the reason or motivation to enlarge his possessions:

Where there is not something both lasting and scarce, and so valuable to be hoarded up, there Men will not be apt to enlarge their *Possessions of Land*, were it never so rich, never so free for them to take. For I ask, What would a Man value Ten Thousand, or an Hundred Thousand Acres of excellent *Land*, ready cultivated, and well stocked too with Cattle, in the middle of in-land Parts of *America*, where he had no hopes of Commerce with other Parts of the World, to draw *Money* to him by the Sale of the Product? It would not be worth the inclosing.[82]

On the other hand, once money and world commerce are introduced, the motivation of the same person will be transformed and they too will seek to enlarge their possessions: 'Find out something that hath the *Use and*

---

[78] Cushman, 'Reasons and Considerations Touching the Lawfulness of Removing out of England', 243.   [79] Laslett, II. 38.
[80] e.g. in the fine article by John Dunn, 'Bright Enough for All Our Purposes: John Locke's Conception of a Civilized Society', *Notes and Records of the Royal Society of London* 43 (1989), 133–53.   [81] Cf. Laslett, II. 108.
[82] Ibid. II. 48.

Value of Money amongst his Neighbours, you shall see the same Man will begin presently to *enlarge* his *Possessions*.'[83]

Locke's argument comprises three claims: Amerindians have limited desires and so no motivation to acquire more than they need; the introduction of a world commercial market ushers in the desire and reason to acquire more than one needs; and this new acquisitive rationality shows itself in the acquisition of land in order to sell the products for money. Leaving aside Amerindian pre-monetary motivation for the moment, the latter two claims need to be qualified. First, it is not true that the introduction of money and world commerce invariably leads to the desire for enlarged possessions of land. The Amerindians had been trading with Europeans for over 100 years when Locke wrote the *Two Treatises*. Certainly this gave them the incentive to increase their fur-trapping and to kill animals beyond the limits their replacement needs had previously set. There is no evidence, however, that they desired to turn to private property in land and market-oriented agriculture. Quite the contrary. They were quite satisfied to trade with the Europeans and to preserve their traditional ways.[84] Furthermore, after 300 years of coercion, not only by market forces but also by missionaries and successive governments to destroy their traditional way of life and to assimilate them to a system of private property, market agriculture, and acquisition, they show few signs of motivational transformation.[85]

Second, it is not an accurate generalization even for all Europeans. The French *Canadiens* in New France traded with the Indians in a world market for at least as long as the English. Yet they did not develop a desire to enlarge their possessions of land and turn to agriculture. They preferred to engage in the fur-trade and adapt to native ways.

None the less, from Locke's perspective that the Amerindians had no property in their traditional lands, Amerindian claims to land and their contention that colonists must purchase land from them would appear to be proof that they had acquired the desire to enlarge their possessions, not by honesty industry, but by illegitimate means. They would appear to be 'Quarrelsom and Contentious', driven by 'covetousness'[86] to engross more than they could use.[87] Many of the colonists argued in exactly this

---

[83] Ibid. II. 49.

[84] See A. J. Ray, *Indians in the Fur Trade: Their Role as Hunters, Trappers and Middlemen in the Lands Southwest of Hudson Bay 1660–1870* (Toronto, 1974), 68–9; Cronon, *Changes in the Land*, 97–9; Bruce Trigger, *Natives and Newcomers: Canada's Heroic Age Reconsidered* (Montreal, 1985), 164–225.

[85] J. R. Miller, *Skyscrapers Hide the Heavens: A History of Indian–White Relations in Canada* (Toronto, 1989).   [86] Laslett, II. 34.   [87] Ibid. II. 31.

way, claiming that the Indians had no desire for land until they learned
they could make a profit by selling it to the newcomers. Then the Indians
invented fictitious land deeds and sold them many times over to the
unsuspecting settlers. Since the Indians had no records of fixed property
in land, the conflicting claims were shrouded in mystery and this led to
endless disputes over title. So, the colonists continued, even if they wished
to recognize Amerindian title, it turned out to be impossible in practice.
The colonists concluded that the only sure and indisputable title was thus
occupation and cultivation.[88]

Locke's analysis of motivation should also be seen as an observation on
the disputes which arose among the English settlers themselves over their
insatiable desire to enlarge their possessions. There were two ways to act
on the acquisitive desire to enlarge one's possessions of land in the colonies: by agricultural production for the market or by turning to trade with
the Indians and to various 'deed-games' in order to avoid the work of
agricultural production and the high rents the proprietors levied, and to
reap the benefits of acquiring land which was valuable due to its growing
scarcity. The latter type of land acquisition was a major cause of contention among the colonists, not only in New England but also in Carolina
and Virginia.[89] The colonists of Carolina were so outraged by the system
of absentee landlords and high rents that Shaftesbury and Locke had
established by the Constitution of 1669 they finally revolted and over-
threw the Constitution in 1719. When John Norris wrote a justification of
this revolt against the Constitution Locke had helped to design and establish he cleverly based his argument on the *Two Treatises of Government*.[90]

The introduction of money and commerce leads to the situation where
all available land is under cultivation.[91] People are thus no longer free to
hunt, gather, and cultivate as they please, but are compelled to live in the
system of surplus production and accumulation.[92] Locke presents two
arguments to justify the extinguishment of the Amerindian system of
limited production and replacement consumption. First, money is said to

---

[88] This is the view presented by John Bulkley, *An Inquiry into the Right of the Aboriginal
Natives to Land in America* (1725), pp. xvi, xli, discussed below, Sect. III. For a different
view of the 'deed games' over Indian land, see Jennings, *The Invasion of America*, 128–46.

[89] See Bodl. MS Locke c.6, fos. 215–16; Cheves, *The Shaftesbury Papers*, 13–32, 195, 248,
284, 466–8.

[90] John Norris, *The Liberty and Property of British Subjects Asserted in a Letter from an
Assembly Man in Carolina to his Friend in London* (London, 1726). See Sirmans, *Colonial South
Carolina*, 29–31. For the extent of Locke's authorship of *The Constitution of Carolina*, see
J. R. Milton, 'John Locke and the Fundamental Constitution of Carolina' (unpub. MS).

[91] Laslett, II. 40.   [92] Ibid. II. 36.

be introduced by 'mutual consent' into a system of pre-monetary trade of perishables for durables such as shells (i.e. wampum), pebbles, metal, or diamonds.[93] This hypothesis seems to be based on his knowledge of trade with Amerindians and it is fairly accurate. Amerindians adapted remarkably quickly to trade with the Europeans, often to their advantage, well into the nineteenth century in some cases.[94]

Locke sometimes presents the mutual consent to money as the sole justification required for the putting of all land under commercial cultivation and the extinguishment of the freedom people originally had to hunt, gather, and cultivate as they pleased, on the assumption that agreement to money entails agreement to the consequences.[95] However, his major justification is that the market system produces a greater quantity of conveniences (the standard laid out in *Second Treatise*, section 34). The presentation of this justification takes up the central sections of the chapter.[96]

In his first comparison, enclosure and agriculture are said to require one-tenth of the amount of land as hunting and gathering to produce the same quantity of conveniences.[97] Locke then revises the ratio to one-hundredth: 'For I aske whether in the wild woods and uncultivated wast of America left to Nature, without any improvement, tillage or husbandry, a thousand acres will yield the needy and wretched inhabitants as many conveniences of life as ten acres of equally fertile land doe in Devonshire where they are well cultivated?'

It can be seen from the quotation that the comparison is made from the perspective of the system of commercial agriculture, not from an impartial standpoint. The quantity of conveniences each system produces is an irrelevant standard to measure the Amerindian system, since, as Locke knows, the system is designed to produce limited (replacement) conveniences.[98] Also, Amerindian cultivation is overlooked. In addition, the inhabitants are said to be 'needy' and 'wretched', but this would only be the case if they had acquired a desire for more than they need. Finally, he claims that an English farmer in effect leaves 90 acres to mankind in common, relative to the hunter and gatherer who uses 100 acres, because he cultivates only 10 acres.[99] This is slightly disingenuous because he later points out[100] that the same person will be motivated to enlarge his

---

[93] Ibid. II. 46–7.

[94] See James Axtell, *The Invasion Within: The Contest of Cultures in Colonial North America* (Oxford, 1981), and references as nn. 84–5.   [95] Laslett, II. 36, 50.

[96] Ibid. 37–44.   [97] Ibid. II. 37.   [98] Ibid. II. 36, 48.

[99] Ibid. II. 37. See Winthrop, *Winthrop Papers*, 139, for a similar comparison. Thomas, 'Contrastive Subsistence Strategies', figures that natives and newcomers used about the same amount of land.   [100] Laslett, II. 49.

possessions. Hence, it appears that Locke is comparing the two systems either without regard to the standard of replacement, which he knows governs the Amerindian system,[101] or on the assumption that the native peoples acquired the post-monetary desire for more than one needs.

The sustained argument for the superiority of commercial agriculture begins at section 40. 'Nor is it so strange', he opens, 'that the *Property of labour* should be able to over-ballance the Community of Land.' The reason is that '*Labour . . . puts the difference of value* on every thing.' He states that nine-tenths of the conveniences that are useful to 'the Life of Man', and therefore of value, are the effect of the improvement of labour whereas only one-tenth is due to unimproved nature. This ratio is then adjusted up to 99 parts out of 100 and illustrated with a questionable comparison of the American Indians, who, 'for want of improving it [the soil] by labour, have not one hundredth part of the Conveniences we enjoy: And a King of a large and fruitful Territory there feeds, lodges, and is clad worse than a day labourer in *England*'.[102] Again, the argument presupposes a universal desire to acquire conveniences, since people would not value conveniences above all else, nor perhaps even possess this concept, and thus not use up all the land in labouring to produce them, unless they possessed an elastic desire for them.

The thesis that labour creates conveniences of value and benefit to mankind is illustrated in the next section with a contrast between the products of hunting, trapping, and gathering and the labour-intensive products of a commercial society.[103] He then rounds his argument off with another comparison with American Indians. Here value and benefit are defined even more explicitly and narrowly as how much a 'convenience' will fetch on the market as a commodity:

An Acre of Land that bears here Twenty Bushels of Wheat, and another in *America*, which, with the same Husbandry, would do the like, are, without doubt, of the same natural, intrinsick Value. But yet the Benefit Mankind receives from the one, in a Year, is worth 5l and from the other possibly not worth a Penny, if all the Profit an *Indian* received from it were to be valued, and sold here; at least, I may truly say, not $\frac{1}{1000}$.[104]

It seems clear, therefore, that the central sections on labour, value, and commodities are designed to legitimize and to celebrate the superiority of English colonial market agriculture over the Amerindian hunting, gathering, and replacement agriculture that it forcibly displaced. The

---

[101] Ibid. II. 36, 48, 107–8.   [102] Ibid. II. 41.
[103] Ibid. II. 42.   [104] Ibid. II. 43.

destruction of centuries-old native American socio-economic organizations and the imperial imposition of commercial agriculture is made to appear as an inevitable and justifiable historical development. It is justified, according to Locke, because native Americans had no rights in the land, consented to the market system in agreeing to the use of money, and desired the change because the use of money changed their motivation. Furthermore, they are better off because the European market system produces 'more conveniences'—a manifestly partial standard that continues to be used down to this day to measure and legitimize the non-native socio-economic systems of North America.

The question-begging standard of 'more conveniences' is also common in the pamphlet literature of the early seventeenth century.[105] For all the confidence these writings convey, they were written against a backdrop of considerable doubt. Long before Marshall Sahlins pointed out the bias in the standard employed, some colonists were raising the same sort of doubts and objections.[106] In the *New English Canaan* (1632), Thomas Morton, like Locke, observed that Amerindians had few needs and these they were able to satisfy with a minimum of work, leaving them with more leisure time than the colonists. When the colonists alleged that the Indians were therefore poorly clothed, needy, and lazy, Morton replied that perhaps they should be seen as rich and the colonists as poor: 'Now since it is but foode and rayment that we that live needeth . . . why should not the Natives of New England be said to live richly, having no want of either.'[107] Pierre Biard, a Jesuit of New France, compared the limited desires of Amerindians with the insatiable desires of settlers, as did Locke, and concluded: 'their [the Amerindians'] days are all nothing but pastime. They are never in a hurry. Quite different from us, who can never do anything without hurry and worry; worry, I say, because our desire tyrannizes over us and banishes peace from our actions.'[108]

The normative difference that Locke draws between the two systems is defined further by his contrast between 'improvement' and 'waste'. 'Land that is left wholly to Nature, that hath no improvement of Pasturage, Tillage, or Planting, is called, as indeed it is, *wast*; and we shall find the benefit of it amount to little more than nothing'.[109] Similar contrasts run

---

[105] See references at n. 43 above.   [106] Cronon, *Changes in the Land*, 78–81.

[107] Thomas Morton, *New English Canaan* (1632), in Charles F. Adams (ed.), *Publications of the Prince Society*, xiv (Boston, 1883), 175–7. For reactions to Morton, see Richard Drinnon, *Facing West: The Metaphysics of Indian Hating and Empire Building* (Minneapolis, 1980).

[108] Pierre Biard, SJ, 'Relation', in *The Jesuit Relations and Allied Documents . . . 1610–1791*, 73 vols., ed. Reuben G. Thwaites (Cleveland, Oh., 1896–1901), iii. 135.

[109] Laslett, II. 42.

throughout the colonial literature.[110] The juxtaposition gives the impression that land which is not put under labour-intensive cultivation for the market is wasted or is not used beneficially. Those who fail to improve the land and take this attitude towards it are looked upon as neither rational nor industrious, and sinful in not heeding God's injunction to appropriate and improve.[111]

The impression is false. Amerindians did not 'waste' the land; they used it in different and, in a number of respects, more ecologically benign ways.[112] According to their religious beliefs, all of nature is a world infused with spiritual power and humans are one family of spirits among many with no superior status. Consequently, they tend to seek adjustment to a natural world that is alive and of infinite value independent of human labour. The idea that nature is a wasteland of no value until it is 'improved' by commercial agriculture is sacrilegious for them. The New Englanders, on the other hand, with their Christian voluntarism, saw themselves above the rest of nature and under an injunction to subdue and improve it for human purposes.[113] The ethic of improvement underwrites an exploitive stance towards nature in the name of 'greater conveniences for mankind' and stigmatizes any other stance as wasteful.[114]

The dynamic process that is set in motion by the introduction of money and world trade leads to the expansion of private property and surplus production until available land is under production. The disputes over property that follow cannot be solved by the ad-hoc and individual forms of adjudication available in the state of nature. At this historical juncture people agree to establish political societies in order to regulate and protect their property.[115] Thus, by definition, a political society only comes into being on the basis of, and to govern, a regime of private property created by expanding needs and intensive agricultural production for the market: '(where the Increase of People and Stock, with the *Use of Money*) had made Land scarce, and so of some Value, the several *Communities* settled the Bounds of their distinct Territories, and by Laws within themselves, regulated the Properties of the private Men of their Society, and so, *by*

---

[110] See references at n. 43 above.

[111] Laslett II. 34–5. Roger Williams reversed this, arguing that the colonists were sinful in appropriating without consent (*The Complete Works of Roger Williams*, ii. 40).

[112] Cronon, *Changes in the Land*.   [113] Axtell, *The Invasion Within*, 15–19, 131–78.

[114] See Carolyn Merchant, *Ecological Revolutions: Nature, Gender and Science in New England* (Chapel Hill, NC, 1989) for a somewhat similar argument.

[115] Laslett, II. 123–6.

Compact, and Agreement, *settled the property* which Labour and Industry began'.[116]

The formation of 'states and Kingdoms' is defined by a series of contrasts to Amerindian society.[117] Since American Indians lack the dynamic system of market-oriented property, they have no need for the institutions of a political society to regulate it, and therefore they do not have governments; 'For in Governments the Laws regulate the right of property, and the possession of land is determined by positive constitutions.'[118] In an even more ethnocentric conclusion, the system of modern states and commercial property is identified with civilization itself—'those who are counted the Civiliz'd part of Mankind, who have made and multiplied positive Laws to determine Property'—in explicit contrast to American Indians.[119]

In addition to conferring greater conveniences on the members of society, the system of political society and property is said to increase the power or hardness of that society *vis-à-vis* its neighbours. Locke introduces this mercantile theme at the end of his demonstration of the superiority of agriculture and industry over hunting, trapping, and gathering:

This shews, how much numbers of men are to be preferd to the largenesse of dominions, and that the increase of lands and the right imploying of them is the great art of government. And that Prince who shall be so wise and godlike as by established laws of liberty to secure protection and incouragement to the honest industry of Mankind against the oppression of power and narrowness of Party will quickly be too hard for his neighbours.[120]

If we read this brief and incomplete remark in the light of Locke's supervision of the old colonial system and his other writings on colonial policy and the art of government, I believe it is possible to locate chapter v of the *Second Treatise* in a larger context than I have done thus far. After 1674 England's chief rival was France. Shaftesbury and Locke turned their attention to how England and the Protestant states could contain and win out against this powerful competitor for hegemony over the resources of the non-European world. In 1689, with the English throne securely in the hands of a Protestant prince who shared this vision and led England into the Nine Years War, Locke insisted that the contest with France must be the first concern of policy.[121] The centre of gravity

[116] Ibid. II. 45.   [117] Ibid. II. 38, 45.   [118] Ibid. II. 50.
[119] Ibid. II. 30.   [120] Ibid. II. 42.
[121] James Farr, 'John Locke on the Glorious Revolution: A Rediscovered Document', *Historical Journal*, 28/2 (1985), 385–98, 395–8.

of the struggle with France was America, where the English colonies were surrounded by the French fur-trading routes and military alliances with the Indian nations to the east and north.

There were two major differences between the French and the English in America. France had a small population spread over a large area, whereas England had a larger population concentrated along the coast. Second, France established a non-agriculture, fur-trading empire in America and conformed, to a large extent, to Amerindian hunting, trapping, and gathering customs. The English in the colonies brought their agricultural system with them. I conjecture that Locke refers to these two differences in section 42: 'This shews, how much numbers of men are to be preferd to largenesse of dominions, and that the increase [in the productivity] of lands and the right of imploying of them is the great art of government.'

Therefore, I would like to suggest tentatively that in arguing for the superiority of commercial agriculture over Amerindian hunting, trapping, and gathering Locke may also be arguing for the superiority of English colonization over the French fur-trading empire. The recommendation of the chapter as a whole may be the following. Not only do the English colonists have every right to settle there, but also, if they settle down to agricultural surplus production, and if the king regulates, encourages, and employs them properly, imperial England 'will quickly be too hard' for the French Empire, based as it is on what Locke has argued to be the comparatively inefficient, underproductive, wasteful, and outmoded fur-trapping system of the Amerindians. More research on the colonial documents is needed to test this hypothesis.

III. Dissemination

We have seen how Locke's concepts of political society and property are, among other things, a sophisticated theoretical expression of the basic arguments of early colonial writers. Let us now ask if the colonists in turn employed Locke's arguments in their continuing struggle to justify English settlement in native America.

The litigation, mentioned above, between the colony of Connecticut and the Mohegan Indians continued into the eighteenth century and it was considered to be 'the greatest cause that ever was heard at the [Privy] Council Board'.[122] The Mohegans claimed to be a distinct political society

[122] Smith, *Appeals to the Privy Council*, 418.

with sovereignty over their traditional lands. Hence the Royal Charter could not confer sovereignty over their land to the colony of Connecticut. The only way the colony could gain legitimacy would be for the English nation to negotiate an international agreement with the Mohegan nation in accord with international law. The Privy Council ruled in favour of Mohegan sovereignty in 1705 and again in 1743.[123]

In 1725 the Reverend John Bulkley of Colchester, Connecticut published a book by Roger Wolcott, the late Governor of Connecticut, entitled *Poetical Meditations*, and included an article he wrote entitled 'An Inquiry into the Right of the Aboriginal Natives to the Land in America'. It is a refutation of the Mohegan's claim to political society and property in their traditional lands based in its entirety on Locke's *Two Treatises*. He brings out and presses into service exactly those contrasts I have sought to bring to light in this paper, illustrating each step in the argument with a quotation from Locke.[124]

Everyone agrees, Bulkley begins, that the natives have some property rights. The great question is how extensive they are. The defenders of the Mohegans claim that they have a right to all the land and that Europeans must acquire it by compact. But this is false.[125] The Amerindians are either in a state of nature or in political society. If they are in a state of nature, then the only property they have is that acquired by labour, improvement, and rudimentary exchange. Labour starts and limits property.[126] Since the Amerindians had plenty and no motive to acquire more than they needed, they did not cultivate or till.[127] It is thus knavish and ignorant to assume they had large tracts of land. They had only a few spots of enclosed and cultivated land.

Furthermore, he continues, the Indians did not have civil societies: they lack laws, established judges, and a legislature.[128] Their chiefs are simply generals of their armies. None the less, he takes up the counter-factual hypothesis that the Indians did form political societies.[129] If they set up political societies by compact, then either they went on to settle

---

[123] Ibid. 434.

[124] John Bulkley, 'An Inquiry into the Right of the Aboriginal Natives to the Land in America', in Roger Wolcott (ed.), *Poetical Meditations* (New London, 1726), pp. i–lvi. Bulkley's essay was published separately later in the century. For Bulkley and the rivalry among colonists for Mohegan land, see Richard Bushman, *From Puritan to Yankee: Character and Social Order in Connecticut 1690–1765* (Cambridge, Mass., 1967). For the Mohegan's long struggle, see John DeForest, *History of the Indians of Connecticut from the Earliest Known Period to 1850* (Hartford, Conn., 1853). Since Bulkley's argument follows the sections of the *Two Treatises* discussed above I have given only a brief recapitulation of it below.   [125] Bulkley, 'An Inquiry', p. xvi.

[126] Ibid., p. xxiv.   [127] Ibid., p. xxviii.
[128] Ibid., p. xxx.   [129] Ibid., p. xxxv.

property among themselves or they did not. Since they lacked commerce and money, they had no incentive to depart from their natural property of catching and gathering. What inducement or motive was there, he asks, to fix a property in land when they had such a 'rude, mean, inartful way of living'?[130] Others argue on the contrary that they did have settled property. But this happened only after the English arrived when the Indians saw the advantages of claiming large tracts of land for the purpose of sale.[131] To settle these later claims we would need clear records of fixed property, but none exist. Native claims, such as the Mohegan claims, are shrouded in darkness and lead to disputations.[132] On the other hand, he roundly concludes, the English had an 'undoubted right to enter upon and impropriate all such parts as lay waste or unimproved'.[133]

When the Mohegan dispute was heard again in 1743 commissioners Horsmanden and Morris restated the case for Mohegan sovereignty. In an acidic commentary William Samuel Johnson employed the Locke–Bulkley Eurocentric concept of political society to undermine their claim:

When the English treated with them [the Amerindians] it was not with Independent States (for they had no such thing as a Civil Polity, nor hardly any one circumstance essential to the existence of a state) but as with savages, whom they were to quiet and manage as well as they could, sometimes by flattery; but oftener by force. Who would not Treat if he saw himself surrounded by the Company of Lyons, Wolves or Beasts whom the Indians but too nearly resembled . . . but you would not immediately call them an independent State (though independent enough God knows) . . . This notion of their being free States is perfectly ridiculous and absurd. Without Polity, Laws, etc. there can be no such thing as a State. The Indians had neither in any proper sense of the words.[134]

Fifteen years later in Europe the same kind of argument was written into the law of nations. In 1758 Emeric de Vattel (1714–67) stipulated that agricultural improvement and a political society with established laws are necessary conditions for the recognition of sovereignty and nationhood in international law. Accordingly, the Indians of North America not only lacked sovereignty but they also failed in their natural duty to cultivate the soil. Employing these familiar Lockean concepts he concluded that the establishment of 'various colonies upon the continent of North America' has been 'entirely lawful':

The cultivation of the soil . . . is . . . an obligation imposed upon man by nature . . . Every Nation is therefore bound by the law of nature to cultivate the

---

[130] Ibid., p. xl. [131] Ibid., p. xli. [132] Ibid., p. xliii. [133] Ibid., p. liii.
[134] Smith, *Appeals from the Privy Council*, 434–5 n. 109.

land which has fallen to its share. There are others who, in order to avoid labour, seek to live upon their flocks and the fruits of the chase . . . Now that the human race has multiplied so greatly, it could not subsist if every people wished to live after that fashion. Those who still pursue this idle mode of life occupy more land than they would have need of under a system of honest labour, and they may not complain if other more industrious nations, too confined at home, should come and occupy part of their lands . . . The peoples of those vast tracts of land roamed over them rather than inhabited them . . . when the Nations of Europe, which are too confined at home, come upon lands which the savages have no special need of and are making no present and continuous use of, they may lawfully take possession of them and establish colonies in them.[135]

The 'agricultural' or 'improvement' justifications presented by Locke and Vattel were widely cited throughout the eighteenth and nineteenth centuries to legitimize settlement without consent, the removal of centuries-old aboriginal nations, and war if the native peoples defended their property. Vattel's *The Law of Nations* was selected as a classic of international law in 1902 and thereby became an authoritative source of international law for the modern world. The arguments that the aboriginal peoples are not self-governing nations and have property only in the products of their labour, and that the 'civilised part of mankind' have the right to appropriate and 'improve' their territories in the name of 'greater conveniences', continue to be used in the courts, legislatures, and public opinion.[136]

In conclusion, Locke's concepts of land use, property, and political society are set in a Eurocentric theory of historical development which serves to subordinate and to legitimize the dispossession of Amerindian forms of land use, property, and political organizations. A number of Amerindian and Euro-American writers, including John Marshall, Chief Justice of the US Supreme Court, went on to dismiss the Eurocentric bias in the theory and to argue, as Roger Williams had done, that Amerindian forms of use, property, and polity are different from European forms yet equal in juristic status in international law. These writings have provided the

---

[135] Emeric de Vattel, *Le Droit des gens; ou, Principes de la loi naturelle* (1758), trans. Charles G. Fenwick as *The Law of Nations, or; the Principles of Natural Law* (Washington, 1902), I. viii. 81, I. xviii. 207–10.

[136] See James Tully, 'Placing the *Two Treatises*', in Nicholas Philipson and Quentin Skinner (eds.), *Political Discourse in Early Modern Britain: Essays in Honour of John Pocock* (Cambridge, 1993). For a recent example, see Hamar Foster, 'The Saanichton Bay Marina Case: Imperial Law, Colonial History and Competing Theories of Aboriginal Title', *UBC Law Review*, 23/3 (1989), 629–50, 642–7.

justification of the struggle of the aboriginal peoples of North America to retain or reclaim their traditional territories and self-government.[137] Unfortunately, Western political theory has not undergone the analogous process of decolonization. Many theories of property and political society continue to take Locke's premises for granted.

If the bias in Locke's theory is removed, and the land use, property, and governments of the aboriginal peoples are seen as different yet equal in juristic status, then all the settlement in America that is not based on treaties of nation-to-nation consent is 'conquest' as Locke defines it in chapter xvi of the *Second Treatise*, as we saw in Section I. In this case, according to Locke's argument, Amerindians today have the right to reclaim their lands and re-establish their own governments. As Locke puts it:

The *Inhabitants* of any Country, who are descended, and derive a Title to their Estates from those, who are subdued, and had a Government forced upon them against their free consents, *retain a Right to the Possessions of their Ancestors*, though they consent not freely to the Government, whose hard Conditions were by force imposed on the Possessors of that Country. For the first *Conqueror never* having *had a Title to the Land* of that Country, the People who are the Descendants of, or claim under those, who were forced to submit to the Yoke of a Government by constraint, have always a Right to shake it off, and free themselves from the Usurpation, or Tyranny, which the Sword hath brought it upon them, till their Rulers put them under such a Frame of Government, as they willingly, and of choice consent to.[138]

What better use could there be of the *Two Treatises* at its tercentenary than to expose and redress this monumental injustice which it once served to legitimize?

---

[137] See James Tully, *An Approach to Political Philosophy: Locke in Contexts* (Cambridge, 1993), 169–76, where this article is reprinted and continued; 'Multirow Federalism and the Charter', in Phil Bryden, Stephen Davis, and John Russell (eds.), *Protecting Rights and Freedoms* (Toronto, 1994); and Tully, 'Placing the *Two Treatises*'.

[138] Laslett, II. 192.

8

The Politics of Christianity

IAN HARRIS

Historians are not sufficiently interested in sin. The subject, intriguing at any time, is especially important in connection with John Locke. It links two of his significant interests, Christianity and politics, and links them in an unexpected way. For *Two Treatises of Government* is a significant point in the *history* of Locke's opinions about Christianity. It has been clear for twenty years past that one of the conditions of understanding Locke and his works lies with his Christianity.[1] But if his theology helps us to understand other parts of his thought, it too is explained by them. This chapter considers how the demands of political theory affected what Locke understood by Christianity.

To be specific: Christianity does not involve the same ideas for Filmer and for Locke. The reason for the difference is that Filmer's account of political power employs the logic of one Christian view of the Fall of Man. Locke, as we know, wished to overturn Filmer's political theory. In order to dispose of it he had to distance himself from the Christian motif that Filmer had employed. But he did more and his *Treatises* used a method of interpreting Scripture which ruled out that motif. Indeed Locke went further. He wished to substitute another political theory. His explanation of human conduct, in his writings on education as much as those on politics, is silent about an idea which is related to, if distinct from, the motif Filmer had used. Not least, the account of personal identity presented in Locke's *Essay* is incompatible with the motif in question.

It was not merely in presenting these alternative positions that Locke differed. The account of Christianity which he himself eventually developed is constructed on explicitly different lines. Locke's view of the Fall and its consequences rejected the theological motif that was implicit in Filmer's politics. So with Locke we have a case which is not simply one

[1] John Dunn, *The Political Thought of John Locke* (Cambridge, 1969).

of theology moulding the general assumptions of his politics: but more particularly one in which his political commitments affected what he understood by Christianity.

I

In the beginning it was a question of representation. As every schoolboy knows (if he is sufficiently erudite) Filmer argued that kings enjoyed a power derived from Adam, a power political in its reference and absolute in its extent. In order to make good this case, Filmer had to show *how* Adam's political power devolved to subsequent monarchs. This was partly a matter of adducing descent, though Filmer was rather chary of producing specific family trees.[2] But it was also a matter of representation. 'What was given unto Adam', Filmer assumed, 'was given in his person to his posterity.'[3]

How can we make sense of this proposition, 'given in his person to his posterity'? The task would not be easy from the text alone, for Filmer was at no pains to explain it. But that untroubled reticence suggests that he was using a common assumption. Filmer *was* deploying an idea familiar to his readers. This notion of representation is one from a certain sort of Christian theology.

It figures in one account of the Fall. In this account Adam was the representative of mankind. When Adam sinned by eating the forbidden fruit he was erring not only on his own account but also on behalf of everyone else. In that sense he was the representative of mankind. Perhaps this notion sounds somewhat odd to modern ears, so a little historical explanation is in order.

How did the doctrine arise? Here, as in so many places, it is best to begin with St Augustine. Augustine put a peculiar construction on Scripture. At Romans 5: 12 Paul stated that sin exists, as the Authorized Version puts it, 'for that all have sinned'. Augustine understood the phrase ἐφ' ᾧ πάντες ἥμαρτον ('because all have sinned') to refer to Adam and to mean *in quo omnes peccaverunt* ('in whom all have sinned').[4] This

---

[2] e.g. Robert Filmer, *Patriarcha*, in Filmer, *Patriarcha and Other Writings*, ed. J. P. Somerville (Cambridge, 1991), ch. 1.8, pp. 10–11.

[3] Robert Filmer, *The Anarchy of a Limited or Mixed Monarchy*, in *Patriarcha and Other Writings*, 138.

[4] Augustine, *De Peccatorum Meritis et Remissione*, I. ii, in J. P. Migne (ed.), *Patrologia Latina* (Paris, 1843–66), xl. 116.

reflects an insecure grasp of the Greek language; but if an error it is historically important, for it was general amongst the Reformers.[5]

How can we make sense of the doctrine? How had all sinned with Adam? Augustine himself had no particularly clear answer to the conundrum[6] and declared frankly that nothing was more difficult to understand than the consequences of Adam's Fall.[7] But you can always rely on Calvin to be outstandingly resourceful. He declared that mankind was derived from Adam, as he put it, not only 'seminally' but also 'federally'.[8] This 'federally' may seem *obscurum per obscurius*. Yet what it means is fairly straightforward.

'Federally' affords an explanation of how Adam was mankind's representative at the Fall. Clearly it was not enough to suggest that Adam was representative merely because he was the first man or a parent of mankind (to which Calvin's 'seminally' alluded delicately). Something besides is needed, which might make use of Adam's priority. 'There is a further step,' remarked Gilbert Burnet—and who more alive to transitional manoeuvres than a Scotsman who had become an English bishop?— 'made by all the disciples of St Austin, who believe that a covenant was made with all mankind in Adam, as their first parent: that he was a person constituted by God to represent them all.'[9] Burnet's testimony is borne out by William Perkins, who had stated without argument that 'Adam was not . . . a private man, but represented all mankind.'[10] What covenant was made? It was suggested that Adam was party to an agreement in which obedience to a law of conduct would be rewarded with felicity and deviation from it punished with misery. If we assume—as evidently it was assumed—that mankind needed representation whilst Adam was the only person in the world, God would not have far to look for a type of mankind. So, as Edward Reynolds wrote, 'we were in him parties of that covena[n]t, had interest in the mercy, & were liable to the curse which belonged to the breach of that covenant'.[11] Adam figured as not just mankind's ancestor but also its representative.

---

[5] H. Heppe, *Reformed Dogmatics*, trans. G. T. Thomson (Edinburgh, 1950), 347–8.

[6] Augustine, *De Civitate Dei*, XIII. 14, in Migne, *Patrologia Latina*, xli. 386, says that all are justly damned as his progeny.

[7] Augustine, *De Moribus Ecclesiae Catholicae*, I. 40, in Migne, *Patrologia Latina*, xxxii. 1328.

[8] John Calvin, *Institutes of the Christian Religion*, II. i. 4–6, 8; II. v. 19; cf. I. xv. 4, and see esp. II. i. 5 for Calvin consciously improving on Augustine's explanation.

[9] Gilbert Burnet, *An Exposition of the Thirty-Nine Articles of the Church of England* (1699; Oxford, 1845), sub. art. ix, p. 128.

[10] William Perkins, *A Golden Chain, or the Description of Theology*, ch. xi, in *The Works of William Perkins*, ed. Ian Breward (Abingdon, 1970), 191.

[11] Edward Reynolds, *Three Treatises* (London, 1631), 134.

Of course his natural role of ancestor was important. For the function for which the the device of representation was needed involved descent too. Augustine had wished to explain how the sin of Adam was visited on his descendants. This account of representation fitted part of that bill. It showed how mankind would be liable for whatever punishment Adam incurred in breaking God's law: people would be liable for what their representative did. If, as Gabriel Towerson put it, a law were 'given to *Adam*, not only in his personal capacity, but as he was the Representative of Mankind,' then 'this Law must be consequently supposed to have been obligatory to us, as well as to him to whom it was immediately given'.[12] But it remained to show how punishment was transmitted. The answer was that, because Adam was the ancestor of all mankind, whatever punishment marked him would be passed on to them quite unavoidably as an inherited characteristic. To put the matter shortly, the entire human race would be liable for punishment, and it was certain that everyone in fact was punished. 'Wee all are sharers,' Reynolds concluded, 'because *Adams* person was the Fountaine of ours, and *Adams* Will the Representative of ours.'[13] Because of Adam's capacity his sin could be imputed justly to mankind as a whole.[14]

On what assumption does the whole theory turn? It involves thinking that the human race was inextricably one with Adam. As we might say, in the eyes of God they made but one person with Adam; as a seventeenth-century writer in fact put it, 'we are some ways, one person with him, either by Nature, or Law, or both, and God did so account of us'. We can hardly do better than summarize the theory in the words of George Lawson:

By Nature, for he was the Root, and all men the Branches. By Law, for . . . God did account *Adam*, and all Mankind as one. And so far as God judged him one, and made *Adam* the Head and Representative of all: so far in *Adam* all men might be bound to obedience or penalty . . . And if God had not considered *Adam*, and all his posterity as one person, By one man sin could not have entered into the World . . . so as to pass upon all men.

Mankind was represented in Adam and the punishment of his transgression fell upon all, for they were 'one person with him'.[15]

---

[12] Gabriel Towerson, *An Explication of the Decalogue*, 3rd edn. (London, 1685), 8.

[13] Reynolds, *Three Treatises*, 135.

[14] For this reason the terms 'representative' and 'imputationist' will be used interchangeably.

[15] George Lawson, *Theo-Politica: or, a body of Divinity* (London, 1659), I. xv. 5, p. 74.

It is in this light that Filmer's statement is explicable. He had written that 'what was given unto Adam, was given in his person to his posterity'. This makes sense if we understand mankind as 'one person' with Adam. He represented his posterity: so whatever referred to him referred just as much to them: as another writer observed, 'Whatsoeuer he receiued of God, he receiued for himselfe and for them all.'[16] The theory besides helps us to understand Filmer's reasoning. With the representative theory Adam receives and transmits punishment for sin. With Filmer he obtains, and transmits, political power. The logic is the same: what Adam obtains he receives as a representative figure and transmits as a natural ancestor.

Filmer's political theory assumes the type of reasoning employed in the Augustinian view of the Fall of Man. Let us turn to see how Locke came across that reasoning and how he treated it.

II

The motif of Adam's representation appears in the *First Treatise*. To be specific, it figures in at least two contexts. The first is in the discussion of Eve's subordination to Adam. The second is when Locke discussed Filmer's explanation of how Adam's regal power passed to his descendants.[17]

In whatever context the supposition was vital to Filmer. The mere fact of descent from Adam was inadequate to his purpose. If one were dealing with a kingdom which had standing laws of succession, one could locate an adequate title to the throne simply by finding the line of descent specified by legislation. But this could not apply to descent from Adam, certainly not in the first instance, for there were no positive laws in being. The function of explaining that regal power was inheritable was fulfilled by our motif: what was given to Adam was given to his posterity in his person.

Locke had little difficulty in dealing with *this* use of the motif. In the second of his two discussions he simply pointed out that Adam's posterity comprised the whole human race. Let him speak for himself, in his inimitable, knowing style: 'Here again our *A.* informs us, that the *Divine Ordinance* hath limited the descent of *Adam's* Monarchical Power. To whom? *To* Adam's *Line and Posterity*, say our *A.* A notable *Limitation*, a

[16] Thomas Tuke, *The High-uuay to Heaven* (London, 1609), 56–7.
[17] Laslett, I. xi. 111, p. 239–40; I. v. 45–7, pp. 190–2.

Limitation to all Mankind.'[18] But if this particular employment of the motif could be dispatched with ease, the motif itself was more significant. We should turn to Locke's first context.

The motif was significant, because if conceded to Filmer, a large part of Locke's case in both *Treatises* went with it. The principles on which Locke constructed both his attack on Filmer's theory and his alternative to it involve the exclusion of Adam's representative quality.

In the first and most important place Locke's method of interpreting Scripture is incompatible with Filmer's use of Adam's person. Filmer's case depended at many points on scriptural interpretation. Locke responded by showing that his adversary's citations did not agree with the literal sense of the text. In other words he treated a literal interpretation as the standard of canon.

For example, let us turn to one of Filmer's key assertions and to Locke's treatment of it. If Adam's transmission was going to be valuable for Filmer, he had to posit a grant to the father of mankind from God. Specifically, Filmer supposed that God gave Adam an exclusive dominion over 'all creatures', 'being commanded to multiply, and people the earth, and to subdue it'.[19] Locke observed that the literal sense of the texts adduced would not support Filmer's contentions: there was no grant to Adam *alone*, and the grant made was not actually political,

'Tis nothing but the giving to Man, the whole Species of Man . . . the Dominion over the other Creatures. This lies so obvious in the plain words, that any one but our *A.* would have thought it necessary to have shewn, how these words that seem's to say the quite contrary, gave *Adam Monarchical Absolute Power* over other Men, or the *Sole Property* in all the Creatures.[20]

When Filmer claimed that the donation is addressed to Adam alone, Locke suggested that Scripture spoke in the plural.

Locke's choice of a literal interpretation against Filmer's looser one was dictated, doubtless, by polemical convenience. But it involved a choice between scriptural methods. One might take the line that Scripture presented a repertory of types or patterns for interpreting future cases, as John Pearson in *The Patriarchal Funeral* (which likens Joseph the son of Jacob to Christ) or John Dryden in *To His Sacred Majesty, a Panegyrick on His Coronation* (which likens Charles II returning to England to Noah landing on Mount Ararat).[21] Locke himself used typology to

---

[18] Ibid. i. xi. 111, pp. 239–40.

[19] Robert Filmer, *Observations upon Aristotles Politiques*, preface in *Patriarcha and Other Writings*, 236. [20] Laslett, i. iv. 40, pp. 186–7.

[21] John Pearson, *The Patriarchal Funeral* (London, 1658); John Dryden, *To his Sacred Majesty, a Panegyrick on his Coronation* (London, 1661), esp. lines 1–10.

the end of his life, describing Adam as 'the figure and type of Christ who was to come'.[22] This, however, was not the chief emphasis of his *Treatises*. There he preferred a more literal interpretation. John Worthington's verdict that 'we are not to value' the work of interpreters 'if they speak what is plainly cross to the unforced and easy meaning of the text'[23] parallels John Locke's view that our prepossessions 'cannot Authorize us to understand Scripture contrary to the direct and plain meaning of the Words'.[24]

It was in this frame of reference that Locke raised the matter of representation. In chapter v of his *First Treatise* he argued the case that Genesis 3: 16 referred not, as Filmer had argued, to sovereignty, but merely to conjugal authority. In particular he considered the condemnation of Adam to labour: this he said was not a time 'when *Adam* could expect any Favours, any grant of Priviledges, from his offended Maker'. But what if the text were taken more generally? 'It will perhaps be answered again', wrote Locke, 'that these words are not spoken Personally to *Adam*, but in him, as their Representative, to all Mankind.'[25] What was the Lockean response?

Locke could not admit that the God was addressing 'all Mankind'. It would have upset his attack on Filmer's view of Adam's political authority. Locke had just asserted in chapter iv that Genesis 1: 28 was addressed to mankind in general and not Adam alone. His case depended on taking the text literally—on referring the text's 'them' to the plural number and not to a singular. Locke, in consistency, could not admit that the singular address of the passage in hand, its 'thou', was meant for mankind in general.

The wider implication of this rejection was that Locke could not easily admit Adam's representative capacity at all. For Genesis 3 was the text by which that role was traditionally warranted. For instance, Henry Ainsworth's popular *Annotations upon the First Book of Moses, Called Genesis* commented at this place that 'neither was it his owne sinne onely, but the common sinne of us all his posterity'.[26] This note is silent in Locke's *Treatises*. The theory, it is true, is considered, but at that merely hypothetically and in relation to woman only, not the human race as a whole: if indeed, Locke queried, any command were properly present at all.

Certainly the view implied, that a representative is appointed by God

---

[22] *Paraphrase*, ii. 525 and note on Romans 5: 14.

[23] *The Diaries and Correspondence of John Worthington*, ed. R. Crossley and R. C. Christie, 3 vols. in 2 (Manchester, 1847–86), II. i. 7.

[24] Laslett, I. iv. 36, p. 183; on obscure writers, also *Essay*, III. ix. 10, p. 481.

[25] Laslett, I. v. 45, p. 191.

[26] Henry Ainsworth, *Annotations upon the First Book of Moses, Called Genesis* (London, 1639), 15.

immediately, is dissonant with the doctrine of the *Second Treatise*. For the people that are free and equal must be supposed, in one sense or another, to choose their representatives for themselves: having, as Locke said, 'reserved to themselves the Choice of their *Representatives*'.[27] So the view of representation implied in Filmer and the Augustinians was incompatible with Locke's politics.

Of course one could say that political representation is an idea distinct from what is involved in the Fall of Man: and so it is. Yet they involve that same *sort* of reasoning: and the seventeenth century did not overlook the analogy. It applied the theological idea to political representation. We find Thomas Tuke declaring that '*Adam* was no priuate person, but represented all mankinde,' and reasoning that

> therefore we stood and fell with him. For hee was the root, and we are his branches: he was the spring, and we are the streams: he was the head, and wee are as the members. As the King, his Nobles, Knights and Burgesses doe represent the whole realme in the Parliament: euen so did *Adam* represent the person of his whole posteritie.[28]

So that to allow Adam's representative position in theological discourse involved the corresponding admission in political theory.

The political implications of the Augustinian view, indeed, disagreed with Locke's politics. His chapter on conquest in the *Second Treatise* argued, amongst other things, that even the conqueror with a just cause had at his mercy only the person of the vanquished. The latter's goods and his posterity could not be touched legitimately. Quite another view follows if we apply to politics Adam's representative capacity, under which all mankind suffered punishment for one man's error. We can see as much in the way Samuel Parker interpreted the law of treason. 'If any Person be convicted of Treason against the Crown, he is thereupon attainted,' he wrote, 'and not only his Estate escheats to the King as Supream Lord, but his Blood too is corrupted, so that his Posterity are not capable of Inheritance.' On what assumption did Parker base this account? 'And thus,' he continued, 'that Entaill of Priviledges, which God of his free goodnesse had settled upon *Adam* and his Heirs forever, upon Condition of their Obedience . . . was by the disobedience of *Adam* cut off from himself and his Posterity.'[29] This thinking had further

---

[27] Laslett, II. xix. 222, p. 431.   [28] Tuke, *High-uuay*, 56–7.
[29] Laslett, II. xvi. 182–3, pp. 407–9; Samuel Parker, *An Account of the Nature and Extent of the Divine Dominion and Goodnesse* (1667), in *A Free and Impartial Censure of the Platonick Philosophie*, 2nd edn. (Oxford, 1667), 137–8.

applications. Whilst Locke was keen to deny that slavery could pass from parent to child, the Adamic model could suggest that the descendants of slaves must have servile status. 'As poison is carried from the fountain to the cisterne,' wrote Edward Reynolds, 'as the children of traytors have their blood tainted with their Fathers treason, and the children of bondslaves are under their parents condition,' just so 'We were *all one in Adam*. and *with him*.'[30] The Lockean view of politics was incompatible with Adam being mankind's representative.

Locke's political position was at odds with the motif to which Filmer had alluded. The view of the Bible which his treatment of Filmer deployed, the premisses of his *Second Treatise*, and some of its details did not agree with Adam's representative quality and the political inferences which could be drawn from it. Filmer's assumption of a certain kind of Christianity did not accord with Locke's politics.

III

If the imputationist theory is incompatible with Locke's politics, how does Locke's view of human nature stand? The answer would appear to be that Locke's works can be related to some version of the Fall: but at first the Fall was described indistinctly, and latterly it assumed a somewhat attenuated character.

Where did Locke stand on original sin before and after the *Treatises*? First, what is original sin? Original sin usually has a reference wider than the first man. It can be taken to mean the sin Adam committed at the original point in human history. But more frequently it refers to the involvement of mankind, without exception, in the consequences of Adam's action.

How is the latter doctrine intelligible? It can make sense as part of the story of the Fall of Adam, told in a certain way. Mankind would be diminished in some way by his defection. The matter can be illustrated in several ways. The Fall might involve the loss of some amenity, like Eden, or of some feature intrinsic to human nature. For instance, there might be some loss of moral perception or self-control, or, again, mankind might lose the immortality which it had possessed by nature. At any rate, whatever the specific nature and extent of the loss, loss there was supposed to be.

---

[30] Laslett, II. xvi. 189, p. 411; Reynolds, *Two Treatises*, 134.

This notion is distinct from imputation. Imputation suggests that through Adam's representative character mankind as a whole was *guilty* of his sin. For mankind's liability to original sin can be explained merely through descent from Adam without supposing that there was any juridical liability to suffer a penalty. Adam, for instance, might be supposed to be punished by being deprived of certain powers to perceive or do good. This deficit would be passed on in an entirely natural manner to the children he fathered after his loss and so to all mankind. In other words it is not necessary to espouse imputation in order to explain original sin.

It is important to recognize two aspects to original sin, one fixed, the other variable. The former is that original sin must be universal in its operation. It would affect all of Adam's descendants, which would be the whole of mankind. The variable point was the *degree* and *kind* of loss to which people would be liable. Suppose we were considering moral loss. The human race might be thought to suffer a total obliteration of their powers for good or perhaps merely a more limited kind of damage. The degree and kind were variable, for no warranted explanation could be given on the basis of Genesis for what mankind's affliction was, save ejection from Eden and certain other physical incoveniences. Indeed, it is hardly out of the question that some of the consequences of Adam's sin could be escaped by natural means if one supposed that the Fall involved only a mild degree of damage.

At any rate, because original sin lacked a biblical specification a variety of opinions about its extent were expressed. If the account of Genesis is silent, so too is the Judaic literature of apocalypse, and, for that matter, the rabbis too. The spokesmen for the Eastern Church on the whole and Jerome in the West did not believe in a hereditary propensity towards sin. The Western Church and Gregory of Nyssa in the East attributed a limited weakness to Adam's descendants.[31] Stronger lines were possible.

One could take a high line, as Augustine and Calvin did, which suggested that every human power was turned to evil. The view finds a full-blooded expression in the work of William Whately, who informed the world in 1619 that

A man in the state of corrupt nature, is nothing else but a filthy dunghill of all abominable vices: hee is a stinking rotten carrion, become altogether vnprofitable and good for nothing: his heart is the diuels store-house, an heape of odious lusts; his tongue is a fountaine of cursing and bitternesse, and rotten communication; his hand is a mischieuous instrument of filthinesse, deceit, and violence; his eyes

---

[31] C. A. Patrides, *Milton and the Christian Tradition* (Oxford, 1966), 98.

great thorowfares of lust, pride, and vanity; his feet are swift engins, mouing strongly to reuenge, wantonesse and lucre; his life a long chaine of sinfull actions, euery later linke being more wicked than the former: yea it is but (as it were) one continued web of wickednesse, spun out, and made vp, by the hands of the diuell and the flesh, an euill spinner, and a worse weauer.[32]

This particular view lies at an unambiguous point on a spectrum.

A diversity of opinions was current in seventeenth-century England. Gilbert Burnet's *Exposition of the Thrity-Nine Articles of the Church of England*, published almost at the end of the century, mentioned several views. One was that mankind suffered nothing at Adam's Fall. Another, 'in opposition to this', suggested that Adam forfeited the tree of life and so his descendants were born mortal. A third maintained that 'there is a corruption spread through the whole race of mankind, which is born with every man'. This view, the Augustinian interpretation, suggested that corruption was thoroughgoing. Or one might suppose that there was a damage to man's nature, but that it was of a less grievous degree. Specifically, that there was a 'great disposition' in man 'to appetite and passion', so that 'pains' were needed to attain 'an ordinary measure of virtue': in other words, virtue would not be easy for post-lapsarian beings, yet effort might bring them to it.[33]

In the face of this baffling diversity of explanation—and, really, only a tithe of the views possible have been presented—it was natural enough for the layman not to commit himself very definitely. That in fact was very much the position on the moral consequences of the Fall with the young Locke. For instance, in his *English Tract*, we have a graphic statement about human conduct but no distinct explanation of it. 'We cannot doubt', he declared, 'there can be anything so good or innocent which the frail nature or improved corruption of man may not make use of to harm himself or his neighbour,' and added that 'Ever since man first threw himself into the pollution of sin, he sullies whatever he takes into his hand, and he that at first could make the best and prefectest nature degenerate cannot fail now to make other things so too.'[34] The point is clear enough: man is entirely capable of sin. But we are left at a loss for

---

[32] William Whately, *The Neuu Birth* (London, 1618), 7–8.

[33] Burnet, *An Exposition of the Thirty-Nine Articles*, 122, 123, 128. For a very general survey of opinion, see W. M. Spellman, *John Locke and the Problem of Depravity* (Oxford, 1988). For an important survey of Christian institutions and thought in Restoration England, see John Spurr, *The Restoration Church of England* (New Haven, Conn., 1991).

[34] John Locke, *English Tract* [19], in *Two Tracts*, 155. For related statements, see pp. 124, 133, 142.

an explanation. Locke's second sentence suggests the view that the Fall had utterly destroyed man's capacity for good: but, read again, it is seen to assert a temporal rather than a causal sequence. The first sentence, with its reference to 'frail nature' bespeaks a milder view. As, indeed, does the reference to 'improved corruption', for you cannot improve a corruption which is complete and ineffaceable, even if you mean the word 'improve' in an ironic way.

Locke's *Essays on the Law of Nature* tell a similar story. Whilst there was less sense of a complete corruption of human faculties, it is hard to see any particular explanation for the characteristics people actually have. There was an insistence that everyone acknowledges that good and evil are distinguishable by nature, that the law of nature was knowable by their natural faculties, and indeed that a knowledge of it could be kept only from those who preferred to cast off nature. This assertiveness, however, was coupled with a silence about original sin as an explanation of moral or immoral conduct. Locke's sole mention of it is to remark on its irrelevance to his purpose: it would not affect what one was describing.[35] Evidently Locke had no particular desire to declare himself about original sin at this point.

The *Two Treatises* are more definite. They were not only incompatible with imputation but also with an extreme view of man's moral debility on account of the Fall. Certainly man is viewed as a creature liable, indeed likely, to commit sins. Yet the propensity to do wrong is not explained through original sin. For instance, let us turn to concupiscence.

Concupiscence is interesting because central to the Augustinian assessment of post-lapsarian man. Augustine understood it as an incontinent desire, significant because in its sexual manifestation it explained at once the propagation of the species and the sinful nature of its continuance. This generous treatment was founded on the notion that children begotten by parents in a state of concupiscence would partake of it themselves. Adam and Eve were in that state when they fell, since at 'enmitie' to God, and so, as universal parents, transmitted it to the world: Samuel Crooke, the minister who baptized Locke, described humanity's corruption as 'an hereditary disease'.[36] As such, because of the Fall sin was unavoidable for everyone.

Locke had quite a different view. For instance, a sexual instinct was

---

[35] *Law of Nature*, no. 1, p. 114; no. 2, title, p. 122; no. 6, p. 188 (cf. no. 4, p. 154, and no. 7, p. 200); no. 3, p. 138.

[36] Samuel Crooke, *Briefe Direction to True Happinesse* (London, 1613), sect. 8, p. 8; τα Διαφέροντα, *or; Divine characters* (London, 1658), pt. ii, ch. 2, p. 586.

the deliberate handiwork of the deity, for 'God in his infinite Wisdom has put strong desires of Copulation into the Constitution of Men.'[37] This in itself indicates merely that Locke did not share Augustine's assessment of the *extent* of man's punishment for the Fall. If we read further in the *Treatises* we shall find that human concupiscence could hardly be attributable to the Fall of Adam at all.

For Locke mentioned concupiscence in the eighth chapter of his *Second Treatise*. He discussed its prevalence in terms which suggested that there was a time when it had not been manifest, an age 'before vain Ambition, and *amor sceleratus habendi*, evil Concupiscence, had corrupted Mens minds'. The time is plainly post-lapsarian, for Locke suggests that government existed. And as well as being post-lapsarian it was a 'Golden Age'.[38] But if concupiscence came upon the scene some time after the Fall, indeed after a golden age, it must be true that not everyone was inescapably liable to it. Some people, those living after the Fall but before vain ambition did its work, were presumably exempt from its operation. Indeed if we follow the phrase *amor sceleratus habendi* to its source, we find Ovid's *Metamorphoses* describing quite a late stage in the development of society.[39]

Would it be right to think that Locke considered that the Fall did not affect nature at all? The *Treatises* are inexplicit. What we have just seen is compatible with an interpretation of the Fall which does not allude to concupiscence. But, if damage there was to human nature, it was evidently limited. It is virtually needless to remark that the God of *Two Treatises* had 'given Man an Understanding to direct his Actions, has allowed him a freedom of Will, and liberty of Acting, as properly belonging thereunto, within the bounds of the Law he is under'.[40] In other words, whatever difficulties people laboured under were sufficiently limited for them to be able to conduct themselves rationally: which was quite enough for Locke's ends.

Of course Lockean men can and do deviate into sin. The whole point of constructing a polity was to guard against those who were no great respecters of justice, which, bluntly, was most of them; and we need hardly mention the Lockean menagerie, populated by wolves, which absolute monarchy would admit. Yet the text suggests that these specimens were deviating from norms they could well have met, 'whereby a Man so far becomes degenerate, and declares himself to quit the Principles of

---

[37] Laslett, I. vi. 54, p. 197.   [38] Ibid. II. viii. 111, p. 360.
[39] Ovid, *Metamorphoses*, I. lines 89–150. The phrase *amor sceleratus habendi* is at line 131.
[40] Laslett, II. vi. 58, p. 324.

Human Nature, and to be a noxious Creature'.[41] This is not the sort of Language one employs about people who are bound or even inclined towards evil by a force beyond their control. If these errors were in some significant sense unforced, what does this tell us about Locke's view of human nature?

Locke's educational works suggest that he felt able to discuss human nature without reference to the Fall. His confidence is apparent in the very mention of Adam in the *Directions concerning Education*, which he wrote for Edward Clarke and his family. 'Few of Adams children', he observed, 'are so happy as not to be borne with some byas in their natural temper.'[42] These biases were soon attributed not to the Fall but to nature, as the corresponding passage in *Some Thoughts concerning Education* makes clear. There we read that 'the Byass will always hang on that side, that Nature first placed it'.[43] Anyhow Locke's view that 'Seeds of Vice . . . must be carefully weeded out'[44] is hardly suggestive of the depth of evil which a *pronounced* degree of moral debility from the Fall implies: and if 'few of Adams children' had escaped bias then *some* must have done so, which is incompatible with the universality original sin must have. This was at some distance from Launcelot Andrewes's 'general corruption' that Adam had 'brought into the whole race of Mankind'.[45] Should we add that Locke mentioned the Fall in order to illustrate the compelling attraction of fruit?[46]

It seems hard to deny that if human capacities were impaired by the Fall it was to a degree hardly worth mentioning for Locke's purposes. Of course, it would be possible to admit any sort of damage which did not impinge upon his intentions. For instance, if we recollect Burnet's view that virtue was acquired by effort, and if we turn next to Locke's educational writings, we see that their views agree in this respect. Yet Locke did not explain the need for effort as a product of the Fall.

In short, the difference between Locke's earlier position on the effects

---

[41] Ibid. II. ii. 10, p. 291.

[42] John Locke, *Directions concerning Education*, ed. F. G. Kenyon (Oxford, 1933), sect. 70, p. 74.   [43] *Education*, sect. 102, p. 163.

[44] Ibid., sect. 100, p. 162. Cf. *Directions concerning Education*, sect. 36, p. 50 for parents corrupting nature. The idea that tendencies to sin derived not from Adam but from parental conduct was aired publicly by a friend of Locke's after *Directions concerning Education* was composed but before *Some Thoughts concerning Education* was published. See Philip van Limborch, *Theologia Christiana* (Amsterdam, 1686), III. iii. 4, p. 182, on the propensity to sin *cum si ab Adamo esset, in omnibus hominibus debet esse aequalis: jam autem admodum est inaequalis.*

[45] Launcelot Andrewes, *A Preparation to Prayer*, 5, in his *The Morall Law Expounded* (London, 1642).   [46] *Directions concerning Education*, sect. 18, p. 42.

of original sin and his later view is this: where before he was indefinite now he was silent. Silence, of course, is hard to explain, but an hypothesis is in order.

Locke needed to say little or nothing about original sin, for it hardly suited his treatment of representation. He had denied Adam's representative capacity and so debarred the use which Filmer could make of the first parent's role. But Eve, too, was a parent of mankind, as Locke conveniently remembered when assailing Filmer about his reading of the Fifth Commandment.[47] So for consistency's sake her representative capacity too had to go. What had Locke to deal with? The text runs: '*Unto the Woman he said, I will greatly multiply thy sorrow and thy conception; In sorrow thou shalt bring forth Children, and thy desire shall be to thy Husband, and he shall rule over thee*'. This passage was difficult to treat. If Locke denied the subjection of woman to man, he would assault a dominant prejudice of the day: if he denied female pain in childbirth he would belie facts which, if not central to a bachelor's life, were obvious to a medical practitioner. So instead he suggested that these examples of original sin could be eradicated. Women could opt not to be subordinate: and childbirth need not always be painful. For

there is here no more Law to oblige a Woman to such a Subjection, if the Circumstances either of her Condition or Contract with her Husband should exempt her from it, then there is, that she should bring forth her Children in Sorrow and Pain, if there could be found a Remedy for it, which is also a part of the same Curse upon her.[48]

Locke envisaged that the consequences of the Fall for woman could be eradicated, just as children could be educated into virtue: which is to say, they were not subject to insuperably pronounced difficulties.

If the moral consequences of original sin had become recessive in Locke, imputation was soon to be ruled out altogether. Before long Locke had assumed a position incompatible with any imputation of Adam's sin and punishment to mankind. That lies in his account of personal identity. The representative theory, in Lawson's words, reasoned that God regarded '*Adam*, and all his posterity as one person'. For Locke 'person' stood for 'a thinking intelligent Being, that . . . can consider it self as it self'. The latter operation was accomplished by the consciousness he found inseparable from thinking: 'for since consciousness always accompanies thinking, and 'tis that, that makes every one to be, what he calls *self*; and thereby distinguishes himself from all other thinking things, in

---

[47] Laslett, II. vi. 52, p. 321.   [48] Ibid. I. v. 47, p. 191.

this alone consists *personal Identity*'.[49] Plainly this is inconsistent with Adam and his posterity's being one person: a posterity as yet unborn could hardly have been conscious of anything at the Fall. As Locke himself remarked of the self, 'whatever past Actions it cannot reconcile or appropriate to that present *self* by consciousness, it can be no more concerned in, than if they had never been done'.[50] It is hard to see how this could be reconciled with an imputationist view of the Fall.

This, perhaps, is to anticipate. Locke's chapter 'Of Identity and Diversity' was written in 1693, when he was already thinking about Christianity. Let us see what he concluded about it.

IV

Consistency obliged Locke to write about Christianity in a way which agreed with his other doctrines. Those doctrines disregarded Adam's being mankind's representative and accordingly *The Reasonableness of Christianity* assumed quite a different position. If *Reasonableness* did not build on imputation, what had it to say about original sin? The major losses incurred by mankind at the Fall were said to be immortality and the Garden of Eden. This was original sin only in the narrow sense that it directs us to a sin committed in the original position of mankind. Adam suffered the loss of immortality and Eden as a punishment for his action. The rest of mankind suffered them as a consequence of their descent from him. The consequence displayed original sin in terms of a loss of immortality and Eden rather than a propensity towards evil on man's part.

How are we to understand the logic of Locke's position? Let us consider it as a series of answers to questions. The questions are found in a short piece entitled 'Peccatum originale', which dates from 1692, noted in Locke's 1661 Commonplace Book.[51] The paper is subtitled 'Queres concerning ye Imputation of Adam's Sin to his Posterity'. At the most general level the 'queres' divide into two and these correspond to disjunctive alternatives: either God 'reputes' mankind to have committed 'y^t Sin in

---

[49] *Essay*, II. xxvii. 9, p. 335.

[50] Ibid. II. xxvii. 26, p. 346. For a general account of the influence or otherwise of Locke's views in 18th-cent. England, see Christopher Fox, *Locke and the Scriblerians* (London, 1989).

[51] The questions will be found on pp. 294–5 of the Commonplace Book. The book is now in private ownership in France. A microfilm of it may be consulted in the Bodleian Library, microfilm no. 77.

Adam' or He 'only subjects them for ye Sake of y^t Sin comitted by him alone ye same Evills wch he incurred by comitting it'.

The former alternative, which assumes Adam was representative, was subjected to questions about 'how they can be said really to participate wth Adam in y^t Sin who did not concurr to it by any act of theirs, nor were in being when 'twas comitted?' If we answer the question affirmatively in the terms set, we are clearly in the world of Burns's 'Holy Willie':

> I, wha deserve most just damnation,
> For broken laws,
> Sax thousand years 'fore my creation,
> Thro' Adam's cause

so let us pass on to the second set of queries. Answering these goes some way to showing how the relevant parts of *Reasonableness* assumed their shape.

These queries enquire about three matters: (*a*) the evils which Adam incurred, (*b*) to which of these his posterity was subject, and (*c*) whether suffering these made it better to be or not to be. But, before answering them, let us turn to Locke's treatment of Adam's representative role.

Reasonableness proceeded by rejecting, as one of two undesirable extremes, the view that Adam was mankind's representative. Adam, Locke wrote, 'Millions had never heard of, and no one had authorized to transact for him, or be his Representative'. This criticism follows naturally from Locke's view that representation involves consent. It was a criticism which could hardly have been stronger: the Augustinian view as a whole Locke described as having 'shook the Foundations of all Religion'.[52] Such critical intensity imposes the task of providing an alternative, just as it suggests a keenness to perform it.

What would an alternative involve? There would be two requirements of a doctrine which should at once satisfy Locke's view of representation and be properly Christian. These requirements had to be made to function together. On the one hand, if Adam alone sinned then only he could be punished; on the other, was there any work for Christ to do in redeeming man? Locke was quite clear that '*God will render to every one . . . According to his deeds*' and, conformably, 'none are truly *punished*, but for their own deeds'.[53] His treatment of Adam demanded as much. So

---

[52] John Locke, *The Reasonableness of Christianity* (London, 1695), 1, cited from Locke's own copy, now in the Houghton Library of Harvard University. See also Locke on Romans 5: 12 ff. in *Paraphrase*, ii. 523 ff. for his treatment of Adam's fall.

[53] Locke, *The Reasonableness of Christianity*, 9 (order of quotations reversed).

the question arose, why did mankind, guilty of no aboriginal sin, require Christ? In observing how Locke answered the question, we should attend to the three questions to which he was alive.

What was Adam's punishment? Locke's supposed the immortality Adam had enjoyed depended on maintaining a state of perfect obedience to the laws of conduct God had set him. By sinning he therefore lost immortality. He was also turned out of Paradise and subject to the inconveniences of work. This, then, was his punishment.

How far were his descendants involved in his Fall? For them, it was not strictly a matter of punishment, but of suffering. There was no alteration by way of punishment in respect of their moral task. Locke supposed that the same standards applied to Adam and to his descendants; 'if any of the posterity of *Adam* were just,' he wrote, 'they shall not lose the reward of it, eternal life and bliss'.[54] Again, though the loss of Eden was a punishment for Adam it was merely suffering for his descendants. For Locke reasoned that no one was *entitled* to enjoy felicity: so 'they could not claim it as their Right, nor does he [God] injure them when he takes it from them'.[55] So there was suffering rather than punishment for the human race.

The suffering was in fact carefully specified to give a role to Christ. Whilst it was true that anyone who was perfectly righteous was entitled to immortality, it so happened that the standard of righteousness was set too high for anyone to meet out of their own resources. So, down to the coming of Christ, 'no one of *Adam's* issue had kept' the law of works.[56] It followed that they were liable to the same fate as Adam, namely a loss of immortality. One might suppose that this ran against the tenor of Locke's third 'quere', but he had an answer. It would certainly have been true that 'a state of extreme irremediable Torment is worse than no Being at all', but 'that such a temporary Life, as we now have, with all its Frailties and ordinary Miseries, is better than no Being, is evident, by the high value we put upon it our selves.'[57] Besides, there was a reason for this estimate of the law's difficulty. This supposition conveniently provided Christ's opportunity.

For He came to promulgate quite another law, the law of faith. Its terms prescribed the forgiveness of those who had endeavoured to keep the law of works, provided that they accepted this new dispensation. So it turned out that Christ had a role in containing the suffering of fallen man. Locke's two constructive needs were provided and his critical

---

[54] Ibid. 11.   [55] Ibid. 8.   [56] Ibid. 14.   [57] Ibid. 8–9.

criteria satisfied: 'And therefore though *all die in Adam*, yet none are truly *punished*, but for their own deeds.'[58]

This account of *The Reasonableness of Christianity* could be pursued further, but enough has been said about our theme. Adam was not mankind's representative in Locke's eyes, and original sin was specified in a restricted way. The Christian doctrine Locke developed was shaped by the implications of these facts.

This was the destination towards which Locke's political commitments pointed. Filmer's political theory had to include an explanation of the transmission of political power. It did so by invoking the motif found in Augustinian theology that Adam was the representative of mankind. Hence Locke found it necessary to discount that motif. The necessity lay in part with his attack on Filmer, which required principles of scriptural interpretation incompatible with the supposed biblical warrant of the motif. But Locke required too his own explanation of political power, which involved an entirely different view of representation and, additionally, of forfeiture and slavery. Besides representation, original sin too had to be interpreted carefully. When we turn to Locke's view of personal identity we find that imputation has been ruled out: and when we consider the view of Christianity he came to hold, we see that the rejection of imputation and the specificity of original sin have become explicit. Just as politics answered to Christianity, so Christianity in its turn was moulded by political theory.

[58] Ibid. 9.

9

John Locke and the Greek Intellectual Tradition: An Episode in Locke's Reception in South-East Europe

PASCHALIS M. KITROMILIDES

I

John Locke's first teaching appointment in 1661 at Christ Church, Oxford was to a lectureship in Greek.[1] Although the meticulous care with which he preserved his papers has not brought down to us any evidence that he ever attempted to compose anything in Greek or—like Hobbes—to translate from Greek sources, his intimate familiarity with the language of classical philosophy and literature is attested in many ways. It is first of all reflected in the standard practice of quoting from Greek authors in his writings such as the quotations from Aristotle in the *Essays on the Law of Nature*. It is also illustrated by the extensive allusions to Greek literary sources in the same text and in other works, including the *Two Treatises of Government*. A special dimension of Locke's Greek scholarship was his application of the terms *Φυσική*, *Πρακτική*, and *Σημειωτική* in designating the three branches of knowledge in his threefold typology of the sciences in the *Essay concerning Human Understanding*. Locke's sensitivity to the Greek language was not exhausted with these rather formal expressions. His surviving papers include one piece of evidence—unfortunately not in his own hand—which indicates that at least at some stage in his life he possessed an interest in the structure and diversity of Greek, its

For their comments on an earlier draft of this chapter I am indebted to John Rogers and to an anonymous reader for Oxford University Press. I also wish to thank George L. Huxley for his help and encouragement.

[1] Christ Church, Oxford, *Disbursement Book 1660–1661*, 126. John Locke as Lector Graecae Linguae was paid 13s. 4d. per term.

dialects, etymology, and lexical wealth.[2] The most significant and immediate evidence of the extent and depth of his knowledge of Greek, however,
comes from the annotations in the interleaved Greek Bibles in his library.
In these notes Locke's sense of the language comes together with his
profound religious piety to produce an occasionally surprising percep-
tiveness of the beauty of Greek.

In view of his deep appreciation of the Greek language it is somehow
ironic that despite the world-wide propagation of his works and their
appearance in languages as diverse and exotic, from the point of view of
his own society, as Hindi and Japanese, none of his texts was published
in Greek until quite recently. This little fact of cultural history tells us a
great deal about the character of the Greek intellectual tradition in the
centuries since Locke wrote, and it provides an occasion for considering
the broader issue of the reception of Locke's ideas in continental Europe
from a perspective that extends beyond the horizon of the European
north-west.

In this chapter accordingly I intend to do two things. First—and most
significantly—I would like to look at the reception of Locke's ideas in
Greek culture as a particular instance of the broader intellectual phenomenon of the dissemination of his thought in the Age of the Enlightenment. Secondly—and more briefly—I would like to look into one particular
aspect of this process of intellectual reception, which is graphically illustrated by the Greek evidence—the restricted audience of Locke's political thought on the European continent throughout the eighteenth century.

II

The conventional view of the reception of John Locke's ideas in European culture connects the spread of his philosophical, educational, and
political thought with the expansion and deepening of the movement of
the Enlightenment. Locke is justly considered the 'father of the Enlightenment', especially because of the contribution of the *Essay concerning
Human Understanding* to the emancipation of modern thought from the
Scholastic tutelage.[3] The transmission of Locke's writings, and the new

---

[2] Bodl. MS Locke f.33, fos. 1–6, 174 rev.–169 rev. on the dialects of ancient Greek
(Attic, Ionic, Aeolic, Boeotian) and fos. 29, 47ᵛ–55, 108 rev.–106 rev., 167 rev.–159 rev. on
the etymology of Greek words with examples from Xenophon, Homer, Musaeus, and the
Old Testament.

[3] This argument is set out by Paul Hazard, *The European Mind 1680–1715* (New York,
1953), first pub. as *La crise de la conscience européenne* (Paris, 1935). Characteristically this
work was translated into German with the more specific title *John Locke und sein Zeitalter*
(Hamburg, 1947).

conceptual frameworks they offered, from England to the Continent, and from the great conveyors of British thought, Holland and France, to the rest of continental Europe, is taken to register the steady growth of the Enlightenment in one society after another in the course of the eighteenth century. The Enlightenment meant English intellectual influence, and this was exerted to a significant degree through the medium of Locke's works. Already traceable in Pierre Bayle's interest in English Protestant authors in his *Dictionnaire historique et critique* as well as in the substantial reviews of English works that appeared in the cosmopolitan journals of the early Enlightenment in the tolerant environment of the Netherlands,[4] the initial curiosity about England and her intellectual life developed by the middle of the eighteenth century into a mixture of admiration and awe that directed an important part of continental culture toward what Paul Hazard characterized as 'the light from the North'.[5] From Voltaire and Montesquieu to Condorcet and Mounier in the revolutionary decade after 1789, down to Madame de Staël, the English model, English institutions, English ideas, and English values captivated the imagination and the hopes of liberal spirits throughout the Continent. Among authors writing in Greek, admiration for the English as 'the most punctilious and veracious and the foremost among European races for the attention it pays to modern inventions' was voiced in 1781 by Iosipos Moisiodax.[6] Furthermore, to love liberty and to engage in the cause of the lights, *les lumières*, essentially amounted to being intellectually oriented towards England. This attitude developed at the height of the Enlightenment into what has been described as 'Anglomania'.[7] It was within this symbolic environment that Locke's writings were canonized as the gospel of the Enlightenment. To remember Alfred Cobban: Locke's influence pervaded the eighteenth century 'with an almost scriptural authority'.[8]

It is time to modify this picture, to add more nuances to it. I do not wish to question the general conclusion of long years of research which has confirmed the centrality of Locke's place in Enlightenment culture. I do want to argue, however, that the reception of Locke's ideas in continental Europe was an embattled and complex process. Locke's philosophy was enthusiastically received in certain milieux, but it was met with scepticism and even hostility in others. Furthermore, his thought

---

[4] See Elisabeth Labrousse, *Bayle* (Oxford, 1983), 89.

[5] Cf. Hazard, *The European Mind*, 53–79.

[6] Iosipos Moisiodax, *Theoria tis Geographias* (Vienna, 1781), 162.

[7] Peter Gay, *The Enlightenment: An Interpretation*, i. *The Rise of Modern Paganism* (New York, 1968), 12 and 383.

[8] Alfred Cobban, *Edmund Burke and the Revolt against the Eighteenth Century* (London, 1960), 16.

was not accepted wholesale but selectively, with considerable degrees of modification imposed upon his central ideas. In addition, its propagation was not a unilinear and straightforward process: the widely held assumption that in Pierre Coste's and David Mazel's early French translations Locke's works became known to the rest of Europe thanks to the predominance of French as the language of the Enlightenment needs also to be revised. Close scrunity of the facts will reveal considerable regional variation and a remarkable complexity in the levels of transmission of Locke's works as well as in the channels through which his ideas were propagated.

A reconsideration of the conventional view about the structure of Enlightenment thought along the lines proposed above might allow a better grasp of the mechanisms whereby Locke's ideas were received on the Continent; consequently, such a reconsideration might yield a more substantive understanding of the modifications they brought to modes of cultural discourse and social thought. It is precisely by understanding the character and content of these modifications that we can hope to reach a fuller comprehension of the historicity of the Enlightenment as a movement of cultural change and social criticism, beyond the stereotypes of conventional intellectual history.

The way to proceed in this direction can only be by means of case-studies that allow detailed rereadings and reappraisals of the evidence. One such illustration of the propagation of Locke's ideas on the European continent I shall sketch in what follows in order to bring into focus some of the methodological issues I have outlined above, but also in order to assess the broader political implications of the ideological phenomena I will describe. The story I am going to narrate transposes us to the world of Greek culture in the eighteenth century.

The question may still be raised why the focus of such a re-examination should be on Greece, a culture on the distant periphery of European intellectual life in the eighteenth century. There is no doubt that before any revised conclusions could be proffered on the depth as well as the limits of the impact of Locke's ideas on continental thought, a serious re-examination of the evidence of Locke's reception in the main bearers of English influence on continental Europe, Holland and France, would be required. An examination of Greek culture, nevertheless, can provide a useful 'limiting case': First, its distance from the original source may illustrate well the extent of the radiation of Locke's ideas, which could be thus shown to have penetrated well beyond the conventional paths of mainstream Enlightenment culture. Secondly, the mechanisms of transmission and adaptation of Locke's ideas revealed by the particular case-study, may provide some sense, even through the rough detail of small facts of intellectual history, of the specific content of the dissemination of Western ideas in the pre-modern societies of the broader European periphery. From this point of view the study of the reception of Locke into Greek culture could be interpreted as an instance of the transformation of the Enlightenment, through various adaptations and modifications, into a common European inheritance. Indeed the investigation of the Greeks' reception of Locke possesses, I believe, an intrinsic interest of its own: it constitutes one of the earliest examples of the transfer of ideas emanating from the European north-west into non-Western contexts, which were thus exposed to the challenges of cultural change and intellectual modernization. The ways in which Locke's ideas reached this distant context are connected with the historical logic at the origins of that larger world-wide process.

III

The earliest instance of interest in Locke's work we can trace in Greek thought takes us back to the cosmopolitan universe of the early Enlightenment. Nicolaos Mavrocordatos, a member of the Phanariot aristocracy and Prince of Moldavia and Wallachia between 1709 and 1730, in his correspondence with Jean Le Clerc in the early 1720s expresses his interest in acquiring John Locke's *Traité de gouvernement civil*, among a number of works by other modern authors.[9] Mavrocordatos was the first Greek author who mentioned Hobbes by name[10] and appears well aware of the philosophy of Francis Bacon[11] and of the views of the French moralists of the seventeenth century.[12] His interest in Locke therefore came as a natural extension of this broader intellectual background. Nicolaos Mavrocordatos was an authentic citizen of the cosmopolitan 'republic of letters' of the early Enlightenment, as his exchanges with and praises by Le Clerc make clear.[13] This initial awareness of the importance of Locke's political theory, coming from the far south-eastern corner of Europe,

---

[9] The pertinent evidence comes from the papers of Jean Le Clerc at the University Library, Amsterdam. See Fonds Clericus, III F 16/4(f). For this information I am indebted to Jacques Bouchard of the University of Montreal.

[10] See Nicolas Mavrocordatos, *Les Losirs de Philothée*, ed. and trans. Jacques Bouchard (Athens, 1989), 164.　　　　　　　　　　　　　[11] Ibid. 126–7, 140, 172.

[12] Esp. La Rochefoucauld. See ibid. 120, 194–8.

[13] See Jacques Bouchard, 'Les relations épistolaires de Nicolas Mavrocordatos avec Jean Le Clerc et William Wake', *O Eranistis*, 11 (1974), 67–79.

illustrates well the role of the French Huguenot exiles in Holland as transmitters of British thought to continental European culture at large: Le Clerc's summaries of Locke's works and his biography of the man in his periodicals *Bibliothèque universelle* and *Bibliothèque choisie* were probably the immediate sources that stimulated Mavrocordatos's interest in Locke.

A second instance of interest in Locke's work in Greek thought during the first half of the eighteenth century can be found in another part of the Greek world, in the Venetian-held Ionian islands. During a visit to the island of Zante in 1744 the English traveller Alexander Drummond met several learned men, and among other things he recorded in his impressions the following observation: 'Locke and Clarke they admire.'[14] This interest, moreover, was combined with curiosity about experimental science but also about freemasonry.[15] Among Drummond's interlocutors was a Greek priest, Antonios Katiphoros, who had lived in Amsterdam and in Venice. If it was Katiphoros who expressed admiration for Locke, his image of the English philosopher had probably been formed during his residence in the Dutch capital of the 'republic of letters' sometime between 1740 and 1743. Drummond's travels coincided with the period when Locke's influence on the Continent after Coste's translations and the recession of Christian apologetic polemics against the religious implications of his philosophical empiricism was on the ascendant.[16] Voltaire's propaganda had already established English philosophy as the pinnacle of enlightened thought. Beyond France, where the resistance of Cartesianism to Locke's philosophy was still a force to be reckoned with, interest in Locke was rising in Italy. First in the Neapolitan Enlightenment around mid-century and later on in Venice during the last quarter of the eighteenth century, the appeal of Locke's ideas was keenly felt among liberal intellectuals.

I would like to suggest that it was through these two centres of cultural ferment in southern Europe that substantive contacts with Locke's texts themselves were eventually established by Greek thinkers in the course of the eighteenth century. One such contact emanated from the Neapolitan Enlightenment. In the early 1740s Eugenios Voulgaris, a young Greek scholar from the island of Corfu who sought higher education in Venice and Padua, became acquainted with, and was influenced to a degree that

---

[14] Alexander Drummond, *Travels through Different Cities of Germany, Italy, Greece and Several Parts of Asia* (London, 1754), 95.   [15] Ibid. 94–5.
[16] Cf. Jorn Schøsler, *La Bibliothèque raisonnée 1728–1753: Les réactions d' un périodique français à la philosophie de Locke au XVIIIe siècle* (Odense, 1985), 30–53.

has not yet been adequately appreciated, by the thought of the leading
light of the Neapolitan Enlightenment, Antonio Genovesi. In the pages of
Genovesi's treatise on *Metaphysics* Voulgaris made his first study in Locke's
epistemology.[17] This initial acquaintance with Locke through Genovesi's
interpretation bore rich fruit in Voulgaris's future intellectual career.[18]

After his studies in Italy Voulgaris returned to a remarkable teaching
career in the Greek east, assuming successively positions at leading schools
in Ioannina, Kozani, and Mount Athos. In all these places Voulgaris
taught modern as well as ancient philosophy, mathematics, and some
elements of modern science. Among the sources he translated and used
as manuals for his teaching were Genovesi's *Metaphysics*, the *Introduction
to Philosophy* of Newton's and Locke's Dutch disciple Gravesande, and
Locke's own *Essay concerning Human Understanding*. From the one surviving copy of Voulgaris's original manuscript we know that this translation was an abridgement of the *Essay* as far as chapter ix of Book III.[19]

---

[17] See *Genouisiou Stoicheia tis Metaphysikis*, trans. Eugenios Voulgaris (Vienna, 1806),
esp. 168–71 on the source of human ideas, and *passim*. This text was used by Voulgaris in
his courses at the schools of Ioannina, Mount Athos, and Constantinople. This is stated on
the title-page of the published version. Iosipos Moisiodax, who had been Voulgaris's pupil
on Athos in 1754–5, mentions that Voulgaris's translation was based on the first edn. of
Genovesi's *Elementa Metaphysicae* (Naples, 1743). See Moisiodax, *Apologia* (Vienna, 1780),
120. The textual evidence we possess in the pages of Voulgaris's translation of Genovesi
provides a firmer foundation for a new hypothesis concerning the initial channel through
which Voulgaris came in touch with Locke's philosophy. The earlier suggestion by A.
Anghelou ('Comment la pensée néo-hellénique a fait la connaissance de l'*Éssai* de John Locke',
L'Hellénisme Contemporain, 9 (1955), 231) that Voulgaris was first exposed to Locke's ideas
as a pupil of Katiphoros cannot be substantiated. It is based on a rather uncritical acceptance
of the testimony of nineteenth-century secondary sources, but it is denied by the biographical facts themselves. In the period up to 1742–3, when Voulgaris returned from Venice to
a teaching post in Ioannina, his movements never coincided with those of Katiphoros,
except perhaps for a brief period in 1739–40 when they both taught at the Flanginian College
in Venice. That was before Katiphoros's residence in Amsterdam where, it would be
reasonable to suppose, he became aware of Locke's ideas. The view that Voulgaris's initial
contact with Locke's ideas was through Katiphoros is repeated by practically all those who
have written on eighteenth-century Greek thought. Apparently no one has noticed the
extensive discussion of Locke in Voulgaris's translation of Genovesi's *Metaphysics*. This,
combined with Moisiodax's evidence and the statement by Voulgaris himself that he used
this text at Ioannina where he taught in the 1740s, should have drawn attention to Genovesi's
work as the source for the propagation of Locke's ideas to Italian-trained Greek scholars
around the middle of the eighteenth century. The importance of Locke's ideas in Genovesi's
'philosophical formation' has been signalled at great length by Paola Zambelli, *La formazione
filosofica di Antonio Genovesi* (Naples, 1972), 122–5, 308–19, 340–2, 581–91, 718–20.

[18] See G. P. Henderson, *The Revival of Greek Thought 1620–1830* (Edinburgh, 1970),
41–75.

[19] That Voulgaris had attempted a translation of Locke's *Essay* as far as the end of ch. ix
of book III has been recorded by Philipp Stahl, *Das gelehrte Russland* (Leipzig, 1828), 456.
The attribution to Voulgaris of MS Codex 1333 of the National Library of Greece, which

Voulgaris quotes two passages from this abridged translation in his monumental treatise on *Logic* which he published at Leipzig in 1766.[20] Thus this first Greek translation of the *Essay* must be dated before 1766 and after the early 1740s when Voulgaris returned to the east from Italy. The attribution of the manuscript, which survives in a later eighteenth- or early nineteenth-century copy in the National Library of Greece, to Voulgaris can be authenticated on the evidence of his own autograph list of his works, which includes an entry on the Greek translation of Locke's *Essay*.[21] Voulgaris's abridgement was based either on Pierre Coste's 1700 French translation of the *Essay* or, more likely in view of his accomplished scholarship in Latin, on one of the Latin translations of the complete original text of the *Essay*.[22] If this hypothesis is accepted, then Voulgaris's Greek abridgement represented a personal attempt at epitomizing Locke's text for readers of Greek. Voulgaris used his Greek version of the *Essay* as a text in the courses on modern philosophy he introduced in the school of Mount Athos in the 1750s.[23]

Voulgaris refers repeatedly to Locke in his *Logic* and he follows him to some extent in his discussion of the sources of human ideas.[24] Specifically he accepts the polemic against innate ideas and insists that the senses are the original source of simple ideas, which are later elaborated by the mind through reflection. Sensation and reflection, however, are not the only sources of human ideas according to Voulgaris: to these he adds revelation, which he accepts as the source of our ideas in matters of religious faith. Later on in his treatise on *Metaphysics*, which was prepared for publication forty years after the *Logic*, Voulgaris still refers extensively to Locke, but he assumes a more critical attitude toward his ontology.[25] His abridged Greek version of the *Essay*, however, was never published.

---

contains the Greek translation of this part of the *Essay*, was first proposed by I. and A. I. Sakkelion, *Katalogos ton Cheirographon tis Ethnikis Vivliothikis tis Ellados* (Athens, 1892), 242. The attribution has been confirmed through further research by A. Anghelou, 'Comment la pensée néo-hellénique a fait la connaissance de l'*Essai*', 234–5.

[20] Eugenios Voulgaris, *I Logiki* (Leipzig, 1766), 155–6, 173.

[21] See Stephen K. Batalden, 'Notes from a Leningrad Manuscript: Eugenios Voulgaris' Autograph List of his Own Works', *O Eranistis*, 13 (1976), 7–8.

[22] See H. O. Christophersen, *A Bibliographical Introduction to the Study of John Locke* (Oslo, 1930), 97 for a record of the main Latin versions of the *Essay* that might have been available to Voulgaris: these were the 1709 and 1731 Leipzig edns. and the 1729 Amsterdam edn.

[23] See Philipp Meyer, *Die Haupturkunden für die Geschichte des Athosklöster* (Leipzig, 1894), 76.

[24] Voulgaris, *I Logiki*, 139, 155, 159, 173. In his first reference to Locke Voulgaris states: 'the Englishman Locke's work concerning human understanding is admired and drummed into everybody because of its especial contribution to the uprightness of the mind' (p. 139).

[25] Eugenios Voulgaris, *Stoicheia tis Metaphysikis* (Venice, 1805), i. 11, 15, 26–7, 62, 127, 217, iii. 192, 224, 234.

IV

Eugenios Voulgaris, rightly described by another leading mind of the Greek Enlightenment, the classicist and political theorist Adamantios Korais, as the 'dean' of the Greek intellectual revival,[26] was the effective transmitter of Locke's philosophical ideas into Greek thought. The Hellenized version of Locke's name is ever-present on his authoritative pages, and from among his students at the Athonite Academy emerged two pedagogical theorists who introduced Locke's educational ideas into the thought of the Greek Enlightenment. These two authors were Iosipos Moisiodax and Gabriel Kallonas, both of whom had studied under Voulgaris in the school of Mount Athos in the early 1750s. Moisiodax was a remarkable cultural and social critic, one of the most passionate voices of the Enlightenment writing in the Greek language.[27] Among a number of other important works he published a *Pedagogy* or *Treaties on the Education of Children* in 1779, in which he relied extensively on Locke's *Some Thoughts concerning Education*, in order to articulate his own radical critique of the interconnection between education and social practices and values. Following standard contemporary practice, however, he nowhere acknowledged the source of his Greek adaptation of Locke's ideas.[28] Gabriel Kallonas, a clergyman and teacher in the Greek communities of central Europe, left at his death in 1795 another *Pedagogy*, which was published by his nephews in 1800. This work was largely a compilation of selections from Balthasar Graciàn's *El Criticòn* and Locke's *Some Thoughts concerning Education*. Like Moisiodax before him, Kallonas did not mention his sources in his book.[29] In these two works on educational theory, nevertheless, we essentially have a Greek equivalent to the work by Jean Pierre de Crousaz, *Traité de l'éducation des enfants*.[30] Crousaz's work, which did more than any other source in popularizing Locke's educational ideas in continental Europe, in all likelihood was the immediate source of the adaptations of Locke's educational ideas by Moisiodax and Kallonas.

[26] See *Mémoire sur l'état actuel de la civilisation dans la Grèce par Coray* (Paris, 1803), 16.
[27] For a general profile, see Paschalis M. Kitromilides, *The Enlightenment as Social Criticism: Iosipos Moisiodax and Greek Culture in the Eighteenth Century* (Princeton, NJ, 1992), esp. pp. 153–65 on Moisiodax's pedagogical views and his uses of Locke.
[28] Moisiodax's use of Locke's *Some Thoughts concerning Education* was first identified by Emmanuel Kriaras, 'I Paidagogia tou Moisiodakos kai i schesi tis me to paidagogiko syggramma tou Locke', *Byzantinish-Neugrichische Jahrbücher*, 17 (1943), 135–53.
[29] See Emmanuel Kriaras, 'Gavriel Kallonas, metaphrastis ergon tou Locke kai tou Graciàn', *Ellenika*, 13 (1954), 294–314.
[30] The work was first published in two volumes at The Hague in 1722. See Christophersen, *A Bibliographical Introduction to the Study of John Locke*, 126.

The gravitation of Greek thought to Locke's ideas had not produced by the last decade of the eighteenth century a printed Greek edition of any one of Locke's works, despite the many French and Italian editions that had accompanied the spread of the Enlightenment in continental Europe. This lacuna was filled as a result of the second direct contact of the Greek Enlightenment with Locke's work through Italian cultural channels. This time the contact was effected amidst the radicalization observable in Venetian culture in the last quarter of the eighteenth century. It was in this period that Giovanni Scola was propagating a radical reading of Locke's epistemology, primarily in the pages of the *Giornale enciclopedico*.[31] A telling indication of the upsurge of interest in Locke's philosophy was the appearance between 1785 and 1807 of five 'Venetian editions' of Francesco Soave's Italian translation of Wynne's abridgement of the *Essay*. In the decade between 1785 and 1794 three Venetian editions of the abridged text of the *Essay* made their appearance. This was the immediate background of the first and only—before 1990—Greek edition of any work by John Locke. A Greek version of Soave's Italian translation of Wynne's abridgement was published in Venice in 1796.[32] The Greek edition follows closely the previous Venetian editions of Soave. Although Soave's commentaries, notes, and appendices are omitted, the Greek translation follows faithfully the main body of the text. The respective tables of contents are identical and the Greek translator always uses Greek cognates of the Italian terms in rendering the work.

The Greek text appeared anonymously, but on the basis of a contemporary testimony the translator can be identified with Ioannis Litinos,[33] a lesser Greek scholar from the island of Zante, where Drummond half a century earlier had noticed awareness of, and even admiration for, Locke's work. We thus somehow come full circle—and this is almost the whole story. Not another of Locke's works was ever translated in Greek in the following centuries, and the 1796 edition seems to have had a limited readership. Another English traveller who toured Greece in 1809 and 1810 noted: 'A romaic translation of Locke's *Essay* may be found in Greece,

---

[31] See Franco Venturi, *Settecento Riformatore*, v-2. *La Repubblica di Venezia 1761–1797* (Turin, 1990), 238–9.

[32] The translation appeared under the title *Egcheiridion Metaphysiko-Dialektikon i Epitomi Akrivestati tou Deigmatos tou Kyriou Lockiou perivoitou Philosophou peri tis Anthropinis Dianoias* (Venice, 1796). Victor Cousin, *Philosophie de Locke* (Paris, 1861), 60, notes the Greek edn. as an indication of the wide dissemination of Locke's ideas on the Continent.

[33] See *Epistoli Apologitiki . . .* (Venice, 1802), 111. *Epistoli Apologitiki* was anonymously published as well, but it is attributed to Ioannis Donas.

but I never saw it.'[34] It seems that a decade and a half after its publication the translation was falling out of sight.

The obviously limited readership of the *Essay* in Greek society was indicative of the narrow social basis of the movement of the Enlightenment as a whole. In intellectual circles, however, Locke's philosophy held its own until the last phase of the Greek Enlightenment. Locke remained an important presence in the thought of the foremost philosophical mind in the Greek Enlightenment, Benjamin of Lesbos (Benjamin Lesvios), who published a major work on *Metaphysics* in 1820, just as the twilight of the Enlightenment seemed to invite the owl of Minerva to fly again in Greek culture.[35]

Lesvios was a remarkable philosopher. He conceived his intellectual role in Greek culture not simply as that of the transmitter of West European philosophical theories into a tradition dominated by neo-Aristotelianism until the end of the eighteenth century, but he attempted to develop also a critical perspective on what he gleaned from Western philosophy. Such had been his attitude towards Locke as well. The major themes in Locke that attracted his attention and found a place in his *Metaphysics* included the discussion of the sources of human knowledge in which he rejected innate ideas and adopted an empiricist posture that is clearly Lockean in inspiration. On the whole question of sense perception he even translates from the *Essay*, Book II, chapter viii.[36] He also stresses Locke's contribution in establishing the meaning of the term 'idea' in modern philosophy by noting that he, Locke, had made this a commonly accepted term in the 'republic of scholars'.[37] Lesvios identifies the concept of idea with that of quality and goes on to juxtapose to Locke's distinction of primary and secondary qualities his own distinction

---

[34] John C. Hobhouse, *A Journey through Albania and Other Provinces of Turkey in Europe and Asia, to Constantinople, during the years 1809 and 1810*, 2nd edn. (London, 1813), 573. The Greek edn. of the abridged *Essay* was also noted by two other British visitors to the Greek east at about the same time: William Martin Leake, *Researches in Greece* (London, 1814), 96, lists the translation among books in modern Greek of unknown authorship, while William Haygarth, *Greece: A Poem in Three Parts* (London, 1814), 286, attributes the translation to 'a Zantiot priest', which indicates that the authorship of the translation was known and discussed by contemporaries.

[35] See Veniamin Lesvios, *Stoicheia tis Metaphysikis* (Vienna, 1820). For a general appraisal of Lesvios's philosophical stature, see Henderson, *The Revival of Greek Thought*, 127–41, and for a systematic study of Lockean ideas in his works see Myrto Dragona-Monachou, 'Scholia stis anapohores ston Locke sta Stoicheia Metaphysikis tou Veniamin', *Proceedings of the Symposium Veniamin Lesvios* (Athens, 1985), 147–57. My analysis in the following paragraph draws on her important article.

[36] Lesvios, *Stoicheia tis Metaphysikis*, 31–33. [37] Ibid. 53.

between general and particular ideas. In his discussion of the will Benjamin translates Locke's definition from the chapter 'Of Power' (*Essay*, Book II, ch. xxi), but he believes that in his own devotion to the freedom of the will he had gone well beyond Locke and other European philosophers.[38]

In the same period Locke's epistemology and philosophy of language were echoed in the philosophical writings of another important Enlightenment figure, Daniel Philippides, a disciple of Moisiodax and thus indirectly a distant heir to Voulgaris. Philippides made contact with Locke's ideas through Condillac, whose *Logic* he translated in Greek.[39] In the years 1811–19, just on the eve of the Greek War of Independence, references to Locke were frequent in the pages of the leading Greek literary journal of the time, the *Learned Mercury*, which was published in Vienna and mirrored what was most lively in Greek intellectual life.[40]

The prestige in which Locke's philosophical work was held in Europe during the Enlightenment was recorded epigrammatically in a short survey of the history of philosophy by Constantine Koumas, a German-trained Greek educator. Koumas noted that Locke's 'psychological researches, his rules on Method and his work on education are things which cause eternal glory to the English philosopher. His philosophy received a great reception in England and France and to some extent in Germany as well.'[41] There could hardly be a more classic appraisal of the place of Locke in European culture. Coming as it did in a Greek source this evaluation reflected the extent to which Europe was developing a shared philosophical outlook as a result of the propagation of the Enlightenment, which brought together the major centres of the civilization of modernity with more remote and distant outposts of cultural life. The three elements of Locke's thought that were praised in particular by Koumas formed major themes in the shared mental world of enlightened Europe at the dawn of the nineteenth century.

V

Thus from Nicolaos Mavrocordatos to Constantine Koumas over exactly a century of intellectual change and cultural conflict, Greek thought was

---

[38] Ibid. 289 and 303–7.

[39] Étienne Bonnot de Condillac, trans. Daniel Philippides as *I Logiki i ai Protai Anaptyxeis tis Technis tou Stochazesthai . . . para tou Condillac* (Vienna, 1801).

[40] See e.g. *Ermis o Logios*, 1 (1811), 8, 115; 2 (1812), 280, 303; 8 (1818), 36, 192, 429, 644, etc.

[41] Constantinos Koumas, *Syndagma Philosophias* (Vienna, 1818), i. 21.

exposed to Locke's philosophical and educational ideas. What is strikingly absent from this story of intellectual transmission, despite
Mavrocordatos's original interest in the *Treatise of Civil Government*, is
Locke's political thought. Up to the Greek War of Independence contact
with Locke's ideas remained limited to his theories of knowledge and
language and to his views on education. The political thought of the
Greek Enlightenment remains stubbornly silent as far as Locke is concerned. Whereas the ideas of Montesquieu and Rousseau played a noteworthy role in the development of Greek and more generally Balkan
political radicalism at the time of the French Revolution,[42] Locke's views
on legitimate authority and his theory of resistance remained foreign to
Greek political thought. Although the *Second Treatise* had been Locke's
first work to be translated in French and it was reprinted nine times in
the course of the eighteenth century, and there had been as well an Italian
translation in 1773, it seems that it never attracted the attention of Greek
radicals. How else could we explain the curious fact that no Greek patriot
ever quoted Locke's argument in paragraph 192 of the *Second Treatise* in
favour of the right of 'the Grecian Christian descendants of the ancient
possessors of that country' justly to 'cast off the Turkish yoke which they
have so long groaned under'? Greek silence on precisely this point is
significant of the extent of ignorance about Locke's political thought in
the Greek intellectual tradition. When a theory of resistance was needed
in the 1790s it was readily found in French revolutionary documents.
There was a Lockean resonance in Rhigas Velestinlis's revolutionary
proclamation of 1796–7, when he urged his compatriots to take up arms
against their tyrants, to 'appeal to heaven' in view of the usurpation of
their legitimate rights.[43] The source of this, however, was in the French
revolutionary literature of the period; it represented only an indirect
contact with Locke, whose arguments in the *Second Treatise* constituted
an important source of all theories of resistance in the eighteenth century.
The one instance in which Locke's political ideas, especially his concepts
of the law of nature, natural rights, and property, appear to have been

---

[42] Cf. the survey of Balkan radicalism at the time of the French Revolution in Paschalis
M. Kitromilides, *I Galliki Epanastasi kai i Notioanatoliki Evropi* (Athens, 1990), 111–38.

[43] For the identification of this Lockean element in Rhigas's political thought, see P. M.
Kitromilides, 'Tradition, Enlightenment and Revolution: Ideological Change in Eighteenth
and Nineteenth Century Greece' (Ph.D. thesis, Harvard University, 1978), 363. Locke's
affirmation of the right of the 'Grecian Christians' to cast off their yoke nevertheless did
fulfil its ideological function in the arguments of British philhellenism during the early
nineteenth century. See Steven Schwartzberg, 'The Lion and the Phoenix', 1. 'British
Policy toward the Greek Question 1831–1832', *Middle Eastern Studies*, 24 (1988), 145.

incorporated into a Greek synthesis of moral philosophy was in the *Elements of Ethics* by Benjamin of Lesbos.[44] Characteristically, however, this work has remained unpublished to the present day.

Locke remained persistently absent from Greek political thought for the remainder of the nineteenth century. Although his successors in the British liberal tradition, Jeremy Bentham and John Stuart Mill, made transient but substantial appearances in the drama of Greek political thought during that century, Locke seems to have been completely unknown to Greek publicists and Greek political writers. In the proceedings of the National Assembly of 1862–4, which drafted the liberal Greek Constitution of 1864, despite wide-ranging references to European political writers from Machiavelli to Proudhon, including Adam Smith, Bentham, John Stuart Mill, and Macaulay, not one mention of Locke is to be found.[45] This is not surprising, however. The transient impact of British liberal thought on Greek political ideology in this period could transmit only the oblivion into which Locke had fallen in Victorian England. It might be relevant to remember that Macaulay, who enjoyed considerable prestige in Greece at the time,[46] refers to Locke only once and in passing in the *History of England*.[47]

The first instance in which the basic principles of Locke's political thought can be traced in Greek nineteenth-century literature does not come until the closing decade of the century. At that time—at last—a brief but remarkably rounded survey of Locke's political ideas, from his arguments on toleration to his theories of property and resistance, found its way into the general history of political philosophy published by Neocles Kazazis, Professor of Jurisprudence in the Faculty of Law at the University of Athens.[48] Presumably Kazazis also taught Locke in his courses on the 'Philosophy of Law and the State' at the university, but his teaching generated no particular interest that might have inspired a Greek translation of Locke's political writings.

---

[44] Two chapters of this text, dealing with 'natural rights' and 'natural obligations', have been published by A. Vakalopoulos, *Archeion Philosophias kai Theorias ton Epistimon*, 10 (1939), 471–82.

[45] See P. M. Kitromilides, 'European Political Thought in the Making of Greek Liberalism: The Second National Assembly of 1862–1864 and the Reception of John Stuart Mill's Ideas in Greece', *Parliaments, Estates and Representation*, 8, pt. 1 (June 1988), 11–21.

[46] Cf. e.g. the biographical profile by the historian Constantine Paparrigopoulos in *Pandora*, 1 (1850–1), 82–3.

[47] Thomas Babington Macaulay, *The History of England from the Accession of James II* (London, 1849), ii, 9.

[48] N. Kazazis, *Philosophia tou dikaiou kai tis politeias* (Athens, 1891), i. 255–7.

VI

It is time now to wind up this part of the story by returning to some of the methodological issues noted at the beginning of this investigation. The consideration of the Greek evidence is, I think, useful because it prompts us to reconsider three aspects of the reception of Locke's ideas in continental Europe. These concern the pattern of transmission, the media of transmission, and the selective reception of Locke's thought. As to the pattern of transmission, it must be recognized that Locke's reception was not an easy and triumphal process. The acceptance of his ideas encountered serious resistance on the Continent: in France from Cartesianism, in Germany from the philosophical tradition of Leibniz and Wolff, in Italy especially from the grip of Catholic theology on philosophical thought.[49] To this pattern of resistance to Locke must be added Greek neo-Aristotelianism, which, as the established philosophical doctrine in Greek schools in the eighteenth century, opposed, in many cases effectively, the introduction of modern philosophy until quite late in the century. An additional source of opposition in the Greek east was the spiritual influence of the Orthodox Church. Orthodox doctrine formed the outer limit of Voulgaris's initial acceptance of the basic principles of Locke's epistemology. Thus the pattern of the transmission of Locke's ideas was equally one of acclaim and resistance, which forced philosophical compromises in the continental version of Lockeanism.

When we turn to the media of transmission we will appreciate that despite the existence of full editions of Locke's original texts in the major European languages, the broad impact of his thought was to a larger degree due to the summaries, abridgements, and popularizations of his writings which circulated widely on the Continent rather than to the texts themselves. Locke's reception in Greek thought illustrates how Wynne's abridgement and Crousaz's popularizations had worked in promoting his philosophical and educational ideas in the distant environment of south-eastern Europe. Furthermore, it should be remarked that Italian cultural channels supplemented French ones as media of transmission. The Greek reception illustrates well the role of Italian culture as a conduit of Locke's ideas. We may thus talk of successive levels through which Locke's ideas were transmitted from the north-western cultural centre of Europe to the south-eastern periphery of the Continent.

[49] The critique of Locke by the representative of 'enlightened Catholicism' Lodovico Antonio Muratori is a case in point. See Alberto Vecchi, 'La critica del Muratori al Locke', *Divus Thomas*, 54 (1951), 213–22.

The most important aspect of the transmission of Locke's ideas on the Continent had to do with the selectivity that marked the reception of his thought. In this respect the Greek story is very similar to the German case of the reception of Locke's ideas: although Locke's epistemology and pedagogical theory and, in Germany, even his biblical scholarship did attract interest, his political thought was marked in both instances by almost 'universal insouciance'.[50] Here is one further example of this. In September 1798 a correspondent of the Leipzig literary journal *Allgemeiner litterarischer Anzeiger* was debating whether Locke's work on government had ever appeared in its entirety in either a French or a German edition, and admitted that he had only seen the Amsterdam French edition of 1691 but not the German edition of 1718.[51] So what is significant about the reception of Locke's ideas in central and south-eastern Europe appears to be a general silence about his politics. The silence, however, is eloquent: Locke is significant by his absence, as it were. This absence can be taken to illustrate the weakness at the source of the liberal tradition in the regions in question, and as such it can be connected with the explanation of a broad range of nineteenth- and twentieth-century forms of political expression.

VII

It must be noted, furthermore, that the eclipse of Locke's political thought in continental Europe during the eighteenth century parallels a similar phenomenon in the English-speaking world in the same period. Despite widely held assumptions of European cultural history, more recent research has shown that in both England and America interest in Locke's politics was rather limited[52] and tended to be confined to radical circles.[53] A similar conclusion has been drawn from a consideration of the case of Ireland as well: a rather surprising finding in view of the acclaim of Locke by Molyneux as a great political writer as early as 1698.[54] The pattern is

---

[50] Klaus Fischer, 'John Locke in the German Enlightenment: An Interpretation', *Journal of the History of Ideas*, 36 (1975), 441.

[51] *Allgemeiner litterarischer Anzeiger*, 3 (1798), col. 1464.

[52] John Dunn, 'The politics of Locke in England and America in the Eighteenth Century', in John Yolton (ed.), *John Locke: Problems and Perspectives* (Cambridge, 1969), 45–80.

[53] See esp. Caroline Robbins, *The Eighteenth Century Commonwealthman* (Cambridge, Mass., 1959), 234, 285, 306–8, 318, 325–6, 348, 383.

[54] Patrick Kelly, 'Perceptions of Locke in Eighteenth Century Ireland', *Proceedings of the Royal Irish Academy*, 89C/2 (1989), 17–35.

broadly similar in continental Europe. Despite the prestige of Locke's epistemological and educational ideas, his political views in the eighteenth century were somehow forced into the background. Although the conventional view saw the author of the *Two Treatises* as merely the ideological apologist of Whiggism,[55] genuine interest in and awareness of the import of his political thought could be traced only in the radical circles of the cosmopolitan world of the Enlightenment.[56]

The affinity of Locke's ideas with the radical expressions of the Enlightenment was grasped quite perceptively by some contemporaries. Thus the abbé de Brizard, in his memorial 'éloge' to the abbé de Mably in the Académie des Inscriptions et Belles Lettres, ranged Locke with Montesquieu, Beccaria, Rousseau, and the abbé de Mably among those who had restored to humanity its lost natural rights.[57] This would certainly appear rather strange company to Locke's twentieth-century socialist critics, such as Harold Laski and C. B. Macpherson.

The kind of radicalism which the abbé de Brizard had in mind when he aligned Locke with Mably and Rousseau was alien to the political tradition of central and south-eastern Europe, and this can explain the persistent silence about Locke's politics in those regions of the European Continent before 1789. When new forms of radical political thought and social criticism made their appearance under the impact of the French Revolution, Locke's presence had been pushed aside in European politics by the new dynamism of Jacobinism and its violent nationalist outgrowths. The future was to be shaped by them, not by the principles of Locke's inheritance, which emphasized toleration and the privacy of conscience. Furthermore, the general indifference to Locke in nineteenth-century England itself suggests why, during the age of the greatest prestige of British liberalism, in the rest of Europe there is such a curious forgetfulness about the political thought of its founder. The eclipse of interest in Locke in Britain and the condescension with which his thought was appraised whenever he was remembered in France (by Victor Cousin, for instance) explains why the cultural influences which emanated from London and Paris and shaped the intellectual life of the European periphery

---

[55] This was stated as early as 1717 in the work *Histoire du whiggisme et du torisme*, published in Leipzig by M. de Cize. See Paul Hazard, 'Note sur la connaissance de Locke en France', *Revue de Littérature Comparée*, 17 (1937), 705–6.

[56] See e.g. Margaret C. Jacob, *The Radical Enlightenment: Pantheists, Freemasons and Republicans* (London, 1981), 58, 84–6, 228, 236–7, and 'In the Aftermath of Revolution: Rousset de Missy, Freemasonry and Locke's *Two Treatises of Government*', *L'età dei Lumi: Studi storici sul settecento Europeo in onore di Franco Venturi* (Naples, 1985), i. 489–521.

[57] See *Œuvres complètes de l'abbé de Mably* (Toulouse, 1793), i. 36.

contained nothing that might rescue Locke from oblivion. Eighteenth-
and nineteenth-century Greek culture was a distant mirror of these intellectual developments. Essentially a cultural province of France in the
later nineteenth and in the early twentieth century, Greece was a rather
unfavourable place for Locke's ideas to generate any interest.

In this connection it might be appropriate to note one final instance of
the treatment of Locke by a major nineteenth-century Greek philosopher
whose work was the product of a confluence of some of the main currents
of continental philosophy. Petros Vraïlas-Armenis taught philosophy at
the Ionian Academy at Corfu in 1854–64 under the British protectorate
and later served as Greek Ambassador to London. His major philosophical text, *An Essay of First Ideas and Principles*,[58] reflects the profound
influence of continental philosophy. Descartes and Leibniz and Kant
loom large in his pages and, although he often remembered Bacon and
Hume when he wanted to criticize the failings of empiricism, British
philosophy for him was primarily represented by Thomas Reid. Locke
was relegated to a rather humiliating role: he was remembered infrequently
and then in order to be scorned for his empiricism, his neglect of first
principles, and his 'ridiculous observations' on the principle of identity.[59]
Locke's name is absent from Vraïlas's political philosophy,[60] but it re-
turns as a watchword for empiricist epistemology in a work on cognitive
psychology he drafted during his residence in London in the 1860s.[61] In
this practice Vraïlas-Armenis reflected the general attitude toward Locke
adopted by the philosophical schools that shaped his own general outlook,
Victor Cousin's eclecticism[62] and Italian Hegelianism.

Thus Locke's marginal presence in nineteenth-century Greek philosophy—in contrast to the prestige his name enjoyed during the previous
century—replicated a broader pattern marking European philosophy. From
this point of view the derivative nature of the philosophical tradition
taking shape in modern Greece provides useful evidence concerning the
way the topoi of European philosophy were established and transmitted
as the common ground of a shared philosophical culture. To the historian
of ideas who seeks to appraise the extent and character of intellectual

---

[58] Corfu, 1851.

[59] P. Vraïlas-Armenis, *Philosophika erga*, i, ed. E. Moutsopoulos and A. Dodou,
(Thessaloniki, 1969), 117, 122, 128, 148.   [60] Ibid. 453 ff.

[61] Appropriately entitled by the editors 'Opus Londinense'. See ibid. iii, ed. E.
Moutsopoulos and N. C. Banacou-Caragouni (Athens, 1976), 24, 37, 41.

[62] In his essay 'Of Logical Principles', Vraïlas-Armenis actually refers to Cousin's criticism of Locke. See ibid. iv, pt. 1, ed. E. Moutsopoulos and A. Glykophrydou Leontsini
(Athens, 1973), 83.

influences in a cross-cultural perspective, this could supply clues of some importance in recovering and interpreting a whole context of philosophical life. In this methodological sense what can be gleaned from the reception of Locke's ideas in a rather remote context, such as that of Greek thought, not only renders a better-integrated picture of the extent of his influence on European thought and education as a whole, but also provides hints for an understanding of the historicity of philosophical discourse. Let me then conclude with a final comment along this line of reasoning.

The conflicts of multiple forms of authoritarianism that dominated the political and intellectual life of twentieth-century Greece, and the predominance of German influences in the academic life of the country, can easily explain the marginal and incidental presence of Locke in the course of our waning century as well.[63] Since the publication of the Greek version of Wynne's abridgement of the *Essay*, no other text by Locke has ever made its appearance in Greek. It was against this background and in order partly to rectify some of its least attractive features that, at the tercentenary of the first edition of the *Two Treatises*, a translation of the *Second Treatise*[64] was published in Athens in the contemporary version of the language which Locke first taught at Christ Church in 1661.

---

[63] Cf. e.g. the treatment of Locke in such major sources of 20th-cent. Greek scholarship as Theophilos Voreas, *Eisagogi eis tin Philosophian* (Athens, 1935), 276, 309, and E. P. Papanoutsos, *Gnosiologia* (Athens, 1962), 144–6, 392–3.

[64] John Locke, *Defteri Pragmateia peri Kyverniseos*, trans. with intro. and commentary by P. M. Kitromilides (Athens, 1990).

John Locke and the Polish Enlightenment

JANINA ROSICKA

I. Locke and Lockeanism

John Locke was at the centre of inspiration of the English and French Enlightenment, and in Germany he rivalled Leibniz.[1] Although it might seem that it should be comparatively easy to study the influence of someone so illustrious, it is not in fact so. As the Polish historian of philosophy Władysław Tatarkiewicz pointed out: 'Although John Locke was not a genius he achieved more than genius.'[2] An insightful but not very clear formulation of the main problem facing a student of Locke is that there are two quite different images that we have of him. One shows him as the most influential person of the Enlightenment. The second gives a strange, incoherent picture of a compiler. How can a student examine the impact of someone who is not a genius but is in effect a genius? The most popular way—especially in countries which were the recipients of English and French Enlightenment ideas—is just by mentioning his name. In this way Locke's name has played the role of a convenient watchword whenever we refer to the Age of Reason. The set of popular judgements concerning human rights, toleration, and the senses as a source of cognition provides an acid test; anyone who upholds one item from this set is taken to be under the influence of Locke.

The tradition of the double image of Locke and of his name as the Enlightenment watchword started as early as the eighteenth century. At the root of it was the pragmatism of the Age of Reason, most manifest in questions of economics where the advantages of empiricism were most

---

[1] E. von Aster, *Historia filozofii* (Warsaw, 1969), 283.
[2] W. Tatarkiewicz, *Historia filozofii* (Warsaw, 1968), ii. 119.

apparent. This trend stimulated attitudes in which the appetite for knowledge was limited to photographing the world with the help of the senses and then to describing this picture by means of very simple language. And it was in this way that the *Essay concerning Human Understanding* was read. This naïve conception added an optimistic dimension to Locke's not very optimistic theory of knowledge. The minimization of epistemic problems generated specifically a vision of the world as a great supermarket in which the Encyclopedists attempted a stock-taking. This view, when contrasted with the 'splendid' seventeenth century and, in a later period, with the spirituality of Romanticism, had the result that the Enlightenment was regarded as dull and mundane.

The prosaic nature of the Enlightenment manifested itself in a preference for the material and the everyday, and an avoidance of metaphysics; it was expressed also in an enjoyment of simplicity which often had traits of coarseness; the pursuit of justice sometimes became an approval of despotism. Locke saw this danger, but men of the Age of Reason were optimists and they did not want to notice that. Locke was read carefully by a few, who then passed on his conclusions aphoristically. Perfunctory acquaintance with his books furthered his popularity. While neglecting Locke's irresolution, this 'Enlightenment reading' gave scholars the self-confidence they so much desired and this is why they created Lockeanism. In this way John Locke became a personified synthesis of the Enlightenment ideas not only for people of the eighteenth century but for later historians as well.

In John Dunn's telling phrase, Locke was a 'tragic thinker'.[3] But this tragic figure gave the Enlightenment an optimistic institution—Lockeanism—and we should think of Lockeanism as a creation independent of the man. It was essential equipment for eighteenth-century scholars, politicians, and men of letters, and for their eighteenth-century audience as well. Each of them could rattle off the set of Lockean ideas: the senses and the *tabula rasa*; property as a human right, and toleration. It was a common language and background for their activity. The *Essay* revealed the conditions of individual emancipation and of self-confidence; the *Two Treatises of Government* showed the conditions of man's emancipation and confidence within society. In this way the *Essay* and the *Two Treatises* generated a new logical, philosophical, and sociological entity which we may call Lockeanism. To this idea, the national context then added English, German, or Polish Lockeanisms.

---

[3] J. Dunn, *Locke* (Oxford, 1984).

The Enlightenment thinkers wanted to realize their Lockeanism and to materialize Locke's values of property, confidence, and toleration. They sought the measures to achieve their goal. This is why Lockeanism must be examined in the historical and sociological context of its contemporary society. The philosophical debates arose later. If we try to investigate only the narrow connections between the works of Locke and other authors, we shall find very few occasions to say, 'This is a distinct, plain, and conspicuous trace of Locke.' Rightly, we shall still be convinced that the impact of Locke on the eighteenth century was enormous, and it will appear to be a hopeless task to study that influence. Instead, then, we should divide the problem between the analysis, first, of the impact of Lockeanism and, second, of Locke's own works.

II. Locke and Lockeanism in Poland[4]

In the eighteenth century, although Poland and England were remote from each other, the political atmosphere was curiously similar. There was a marked resemblance between English and Polish political institutions: the two–chamber system, the existence of an opposition, self-government in towns, the role of jurisdiction. There was also similarity of political principles: conviction about the principal role of freedom in relation to the monarchy, and the personal and property rights of each citizen.[5] In spite of all its weaknesses, Polish republicanism gave more opportunity for Enlightenment ideas to flourish than the political systems of other European countries. In the rest of Europe the question was: Who ought to introduce liberalism in a non-liberal environment? In Poland the question was one of reducing Polish anarchy.

[4] The state of research on the Polish Enlightenment is unsatisfactory. Of the three periods of the Polish Enlightenment, the early Enlightenment (1730–64), the middle Enlightenment (1765–95, the latter date marking the third partition of Poland and loss of independence), and the third, classical period (1796–1830, the latter date marking the November Rising of the Russo-Polish War), only the second has been thoroughly analysed. Embracing the rise of the Enlightenment in Europe, the investigation has focused primarily on the national character of the Age of Reason and the relationship with Western thinkers, and the Polish Enlightenment has been pushed into the background. The French impact has been relatively well analysed, but the English influence still awaits study, especially in the area of the history of the social sciences. The English cultural impact on the Polish Press and *belles-lettres* is analysed by Zofia Sinko, especially the relationship between the Polish *Monitor* and the English *Spectator*. Personal contacts between Polish and English people are examined by Zofia Libiszowska. See her *Życie polskie w Londynie w XVIII wieku* ('Polish Life in London in the Eighteenth Century') (Warsaw, 1972).

[5] W. Konopczyński, 'Anglia a Polska w XVIII wieku', *Pamiętniki Biblioteki Kórnickiej* (1947), 93–129.

But in Enlightenment literature England became the paragon of a well-organized country and Poland was its antithesis. It was only when Poles started to ask questions about the differences between their country and England that we can say that Lockeanism had become assimilated into Polish culture. This took place in the last two decades of the eighteenth century, and culminated in Hugo Kołłątaj's book *The Letters of Anonym*. The time of Locke, the philosopher, did not come until the beginning of the nineteenth century. The first fifty years of the Polish Enlightenment from about 1730 to 1780 were a period of intensive education of Polish society. John Locke became its figurehead. A small number of people educated successive generations of students who were themselves looking for political reform during the last twenty years of the eighteenth century. So we can speak of three main periods in the acceptance of Lockeanism and Locke within the Polish Enlightenment: the initial 'educational' period when Locke was seen as a great teacher, then the next twenty years of Lockeanism—the time of great debate on property and freedom, and the last 'academic' period when Locke was recognized as a great philosopher by professional scholars, which gave him protection against Kant's followers.

III. The Educational Period

The Great Questions which appeared in the seventeenth century collided with the trivial reality of the Saxon period in Poland. Rural culture reigned supreme. Sarmatism—a culture characteristic only of Poland—controlled all. 'Golden freedom' and equality among the *szlachta*[6] were comfortable values which reinforced their self-admiration and were a useful myth uniting them. There was no felt need to create new ideas, behaviour, or activities. There was nobody able to show from outside what the *szlachta* were like. There were no merchant Whigs or 'glorious revolution', there was no powerful king. The *szlachta* had neither enemy nor opponent, and they had only one aspiration—to conserve the past. The torpor of Polish society seemed to be eternal, resistant to any change, a style of life on the margin of two cultures: the West and the East. At the

---

[6] I use the word *szlachta* to refer to that section of society known as the 'gentry' in Europe. However, in 18th-cent. Poland the word *szlachta* had a wider meaning, embracing both gentry and noblemen. This reflects Sarmatian approval of equality. The *szlachta* was not monolithic: it included 100 very rich families—magnates—but also landless people (*gołota*), who formed about 50 per cent of the *szlachta*. Another difference from the rest of Europe was the size of the *szlachta*, which comprised as much as 8 per cent of the population.

beginning of the eighteenth century. Poland was threatened by its neighbours, the future invaders, Prussia, Russia, and Austria. Economic circumstances deteriorated and there were more and more bankruptcies.
The *szlachta* had created a weak state with no future.

Reform began in the first thirty years of the eighteenth century. There
was a spirit of state reorganization and the reformers tried to reconcile
cameralism with republicanism. It came to nothing. The 1740s brought a
more efficient solution. The character of the rising generation began to be
moulded by means of the standard Enlightenment tool—a new pedagogy.
The first move for reform was made by Stanislas Leszczyński.[7] The next
came from his associate Stanislas Konarski,[8] the Piarist, who in 1740
founded the Collegium Nobilium in Warsaw. A careful reading of the
school prospectus[9] reveals that the shape of education prescribed was that
of John Locke. He is mentioned three times as the author of manuals of
instruction: *Some Thoughts concerning Education* and the *Essay*.[10] Konarski
evolved schemes that considered young pupils as rational creatures who
should be encouraged to develop their personality with the help of their
teachers. He drafted his prospectus consciously trying to put Locke's ideas
into practice, especially to provide time for physical exercise, as the health
of pupils affects their moral attitude. The main aim was Lockean too: the
purpose of education was to make men useful to the state, and such
usefulness was connected with self-reliance. In 1765 a patron of the
middle period of the Polish Enlightenment, King Stanislas Augustus
Poniatowski, founded the Knights' School (Szkoła Rycerska). The first
secular school was organized and then administered by the Englishman
John Lind.[11] Once again the school prospectus referred to John Locke's
precepts.[12]

---

[7] Stanisłas Leszczyński (1677–1766), King of Poland (1733), philosopher, moralist, and
political writer, Prince of Lorraine, founder of the Academy in Nancy (1751) and the
Knight's School in Luneville, author of *Œuvres du philosophie bienfaisant*, i–iv (1763); and of
the utopian *Entretien d'un Européen avec un insulaire du royaume de Dumocala* (1752).

[8] Stanislas Konarski (1700–73), educator, political writer, poet, Piarist, author of *De
Emendandis Eloquentiae Vitiis* (1741), *De Viro Honesto et Bono Cive* (1754). His famous work
O skutecznym rad sposobie (1760–3) was a severe criticism of the *szlachta*'s anarchy.

[9] The title of the prospectus was *Ordinationes Visitationis Apostolicae* (parts 1–5 1753–4).
This scheme received the Pope's breve in 1750.

[10] S. Konarski, *Pisma pedagogiczne* (Wrocław, 1959), 85 (twice) and 229.

[11] John Lind (1737–87), political writer. He was at the English Embassy in Constantinople in the capacity of chaplain. Then he went to Warsaw, where he dropped his clerical title
and became tutor to Prince Stanislas Poniatowski, a nephew of the king. As king, Stanislas
elevated him to governor of the Knights' School. In 1773, a year after the first partition of
Poland, he returned to England with a pension from the king. He is the author of *Letters
concerning the Present State of Poland* (1773).

[12] 'Ustawy królewskie', Biblioteka Czartoryskich, Cracow, MS 2808.

These schools were for a gentry élite, but in 1773 the Commission for National Education came into being. The institution was a sort of ministry of education. It was given the task of democratizing the Polish educational system, and again John Locke was the true author of its brief and of the main handbook for teachers written by Antoni Popławski, which plagiarized much of *Some Thoughts concerning Education*.[13] Also under Locke's influence was Grzegorz Piramowicz,[14] the outstanding Polish educationalist and author of *A Teacher's Duties*. In 1804 one of the members of the Commission for National Education wrote, with no exaggeration, that *Some Thoughts* was 'a guiding light of our century'.[15]

The Western system of education offered a range of possibilities. Teachers and those destined for the professions were catered for in the educational establishments; those wishing to pursue scientific interests had their scientific societies. The scholarly world maintained its tradition of intellectual contemplation but now took the new spirit of enterprise into account too. The majority took on enterprises on their own initiative, serving apprenticeships to merchants and entrepreneurs. Western enterprise was alien to Polish society with almost no townspeople. Only a scholar conscious of backwardness could accomplish the great task: to create a new society which in the West was the outcome of commerce, but the price of leadership in the modernization of Polish society was loss of independence. Polish scholars could not achieve the same degree of professionalism as their colleagues in England or France. They had to be both politicians and scholars at the same time. This was good for the popularization of Enlightenment ideas, but not so good for their professional level of specialization.

It was easier to obtain the *szlachta*'s approval to changes in pedagogy than to political reform. This relative easiness had the effect that the Enlightenment current identifying science with knowledge was particularly strong in Poland and was taken very seriously as a substitute for progress. The Enlightenment view was that science by itself made modernization possible. In this context the overcoming of underdevelopment meant the provision of elementary schools, the publication of handbooks, education of teachers. For Locke, science became an aid

[13] A. Popławski, *Przypisy do moralnej nauki na pierwszą i drugą klasę* (1778, Cracow; 2nd edn. 1785, Cracow; 3rd edn. 1787, Cracow; 4th edn. 1795, Vilnius).

[14] Grzegorz Piramowicz (1735–1801), educator, Jesuit, very active in the Commission for National Education. His book *Powinności nauczyciela* ('*A Teacher's Duties*') (1787) was very popular in the 18th and 19th cents. He was a co-author of *Elementarz dla szkół parafialnych* ('Elements for Parish Schools') (1785).

[15] J. Wybicki, *Rozmowy i podróże ojca* (Wrocław, 1804), i. 92.

towards the emancipation of those particular individuals who belonged to the Royal Society;[16] Polish thinkers used his pedagogical theory as an aid for the emancipation of all society. The weakness of this solution was its one-sidedness, that if we concentrate on education the rest would happen spontaneously.

The aim of the Polish Enlightenment upheaval was to achieve a change in mentality of the *szlachta*. Scholars thought of society as a large kindergarten full of idle children, some of them conspicuous for their restiveness. Moreover, these restive children voted in self-government and gave to themselves a right to decide about everything. This vision of society, common in the Enlightenment in the West and in the East, had its counterweight in absolutist monarchies. This was not so in Poland. There were two tasks: that of inculcating self-government and educating its voters; and to change naughty children into responsible citizens.

Who could do this? Scholars decided on John Locke. His book contained very simple advice, paid attention to man's physique and biology, and promised, instead of pains connected with upbringing, a healthy and reasonable society. From the point of view of the men of the Enlightenment this was the cheapest and, at the same time, the most effective investment. Locke acquired an authority never called in question. They abstracted from his *Thoughts concerning Education*, adapted it to Polish reality, and 'forgot' about his approval of private education. In the otherwise good translation of his book which appeared in 1781, the translator expunged all passages concerning private education. It was, in any case, in compliance with Locke's orders to protect children and young people from bad family influence. The 'educational theory' of self-acting growth was utopian, but it did bring one success. The generations educated in the Piarist and Commission schools were prepared for political reform. When they began their discussions they did not have a ready plan, but they created one. Once again, Locke became one of their chief advisers, but not Locke the educationalist.

IV. Lockeanism

Locke placed man at the centre of his interest and the starting-point of the whole world. In the chaos of conflicting arguments based on the

---

[16] This is a central thesis of J. W. Yolton's book *Locke and the Compass of Human Understanding: A Selective Commentary on the 'Essay'* (Cambridge, 1970).

Ancients' authority or that based upon the Bible, Locke invented his own vision. His pragmatic directions helped society to avoid religious and political fanaticism. He proposed a new social base founded on three secular values: property, confidence, toleration. Man has the right to his own person, his own work, and its fruits. He is a true human being when he has these three objects. Toleration becomes a condition of being the proprietor of one's own person, because it provides for the possibility of having one's own opinions. Those who have the space to be independent proprietors of themselves, exchanging the products of their work and thought, should, as a result, be full of confidence.

Since Polish society did not take part in the great Protestant discussion,[17] Polish scholars discussed questions of human nature in the political and economic sphere without analysing the religious and moral contexts. They tried to resolve the concrete Polish problem, but rarely thought about universal solutions. Poland was itself seen as a freak of nature. Investigations were limited to the economic, political, or educational arena. The result was that they produced only a one-dimensional solution which omitted both religion and philosophy. The hope that the activities of the Commission for National Education would call into being a modern state was never realized. Polish society continued to consist of the *szlachta* and serfs bound by patriarchal links. In the West the capitalistic market solved the question of social links. Polish economic crises, combined with an underdeveloped quasi-feudal market, could not do it.

When the first generation had been educated the question of the shape of society arose. So the public life of the 1780s was dominated by the problem of the correlation of mutual relations between enlightened, educated citizens and unenlightened, uneducated people. Polish scholars tried to analyse patterns of behaviour and differences between groups, and to explain the mechanism of division within society. The search for the solution to questions concerning human nature within a sociological framework initiated a great discussion comparable to that carried on during the Reformation. The problem of property became the essence of a discussion that lasted for years known as the 'peasant question'. Its main topics were the relation between the lord and the peasant, the shape of

[17] In general, as I have already mentioned, there were no discussions of religious questions in the 18th cent. However, I should mention a Polish trace in Locke's works, namely the Socinian thought which influenced Locke's religious opinions. But the Socinians (the Arians or the Polish Brothers) were rather an isolated group in Polish society. In the second half of 17th cent. they were accused of collaboration with Sweden—at that time the enemy of Poland—and were expelled from the country, so that their impact on Polish culture was minimal.

property, its historical traditions, and its origins. There were three quasi-parties: Sarmatian, Enlightenment, and Romantic.[18]

The success of the Enlightenment party consisted in the invention of a Polish equivalent of the English gentleman. This model was based on Lockeanism: man's aim is happiness and it can be reached only through wise upbringing. The Polish gentleman was open-minded; he took care of health and hygiene, believed in his own power, founded village schools, and was a clever propagator of the Enlightenment novelties. The object of the Enlightenment party's economic plan was to change serfdom into leasehold tenure.

The Lockean values came together in the Romantic model in unusual circumstances. As a pragmatist, Locke always stressed the importance of achieving advantage for both sides. The Romantics spoke about sacrifice: a lord should give his land to the peasants in the name of the country thus showing his nobility; nevertheless, a sacrifice remained a sacrifice. In the thinking of the men of the Enlightenment, confidence and toleration were the result of education. The romantics believed in landed property as the best educator. The absence of Western pragmatic cohesion in the Polish variant of Lockeanism bred contradictions and resulted in a loss of credibility. The men of the Enlightenment wanted to speak a pragmatic language, but they lacked the clinching argument. In the Romantic camp, property was the first object, but economic argument was replaced by an appeal to patriotism.

There was only one man, Hugo Kołłątaj,[19] who worked out a realistic plan for an evolutionary reconstruction of Polish society. Poland had to become a homeland of proprietors, where nobody could be the property of another man. Kołłątaj's 'soft revolution' expected payment from the *szlachta* for their privileges. They had to transform a serf into a lease-holder. In return for this Kołłątaj promised them 'frugality, work, and sweat'.[20]

Locke's triad, work, property, and freedom, was transformed in Kołłątaj's theory. He wanted to construct—out of a combination of work

---

[18] On the history of the 'peasant question', see my book *Polskie spory o własność: Narodziny nowożytnej myśli ekonomicznej na ziemiach polskich* ('Polish Disputes over Property: The Emergence of Modern Economic Thought in Poland') (Cracow, 1984).

[19] Hugo Kołłątaj (1750–1812), politician, writer, organizer of the education system, reformer, and rector of the Jagiellonian University, deputy chancellor of the Treasury (1791), historian, philosopher, known as the Polish Machiavelli. His chief works are *Listy Anonima* ('The Letters of Anonym') (Warsaw, 1788–9) and *Porządek fizyczno-moralny* ('Physical and Moral Order') (Warsaw, 1810).

[20] H. Kołłątaj, *Listy Anonima*, ed. B. Leśnodorski (Warsaw, 1954), i. 273.

and property—a kind of curb on the *szlachta*'s freedom. Work in Locke's and then in Smith's theory was the most important source of wealth and gave absolution to a proprietor, but in Kołłątaj's works *The Letters of Anonym* and *Physical and Moral Order* it was the citizen's duty. All Locke's conclusions concerning the analysis of property appeared in Kołłątaj's theory. Property is the law of nature and of reason, and an ethical command, and it is an instruction ensuring social order.[21]

Kołłątaj's state was a compromise between Polish anarchy and despotism. In fact, in his proposal the Sarmatic values such as freedom and autarky became the values of the state, when the scale of the Sarmatism was limited to a country neighbourhood. In Polish social circumstances the best solution was an acceptance of liberal principles and the building of an open society which could cure Poland of its provincialism. It was Kołłątaj's main goal.

Kołłątaj's system is a simplification of Lockean principles, following in Condillac's footsteps. His schema was manifested in his work *Physical and Moral Order*, which in many ways is a disappointment, coming from such an outstanding political writer. Nevertheless, it was probably the common fate of almost all Enlightenment thinkers. As Condillac became more Lockean than Locke himself, so Kołłątaj had started from Lockeanism and then brought in the logical consequences of the Aristotelian phrase 'nihil est in intellectu, quod non fuerit antea in sensu' to an end. Kołłątaj was not interested in the problem of the limits of knowledge; he was closer to d'Alembert's positivistic attitude. His guide to the European sciences was typical: it was the Enlightenment need for optimism.

In *Physical and Moral Order* Kołłątaj cited Locke twice and called him, together with Newton, Pascal, Cudworth, and Clark, one of 'the teachers of teachers'.[22] He knew *Some Thoughts concerning Education* and the *Essay*, but there is no clear evidence concerning the *Two Treatises*.

Kołłątaj's works show him involved in a national context. First of all he is a Pole and then a scholar. But he deserves the name of the Polish Locke. Thanks to his inspiration, Locke's *Essay* appeared in a Polish translation, and was dedicated to him.[23] Locke was his master when Kołłątaj

---

[21] Ibid. i. 294–5, 318; ii. 302; *Porządek fizyczno-moralny*, 558–74.

[22] H. Kołłątaj, *Porządek fizyczno-moralny*, 163–4.

[23] The translator, Andrzej Cyankiewicz (1740?–1803?), was a poet, lecturer at the Jagiellonian University, and Catholic priest. The *Essay* appeared in 1784 in Cracow, the translation probably having been commissional by Hugo Kołłątaj. It was a detached and rather literal translation of selected parts of the *Essay*. The *Letter to the Reader* and some unimportant fragments of the *First* and the *Third Books* were omitted. The *Second* and the

wrote 'Legislation cannot pass over human rights in silence; society cannot make a sacrifice of people to people.'[24]

V. Academic Period

In the first quarter of the nineteenth century the time finally came for Polish scholars to absorb Locke's theory. The Warsaw Scientific Society was founded in 1800 and it was then that Polish scientists started to practise science for its own sake. They began to read the *Essay* line by line. Locke's philosophy was taken as providing basic arguments against Kant.[25] Jan Śniadecki[26] was a conspicuous admirer of Locke and critic of Kant. The Piarists' Patrycy Przeczytański and Anioł Dowgird were Lockeans as well.[27] Apart from Anioł Dowgird, who understood to some extent the relationship between Locke and Kant, scholars saw Kant as opposed to Locke. The anti-Kantian lobby showed the importance of the impact of Lockeanism. The superficial consequences of this reception of Locke's philosophy were clearly visible: the solemn approach to Locke and the perfunctory studies of Kant, as with Locke in the eighteenth century. But there were emotional differences in the approach to Locke and Kant as individuals. Throughout the Polish Enlightenment Locke was perceived in a friendly way, as an attractive and wise person possessing scholarly and moral authority. In no way can we say this about Kant.

VI. Locke and the Polish Audience

The first time the name of Locke appeared in the Polish Press was in 1766 in the *Monitor*, the Polish journal modelled on the English *Spectator*

Fourth Books were translated almost complete. It is likely that Kołłątaj was responsible for this appropriate selection.

[24] H. Kołłątaj, *Do prześwietnej deputacji*, in *Listy Anonima*, ii. 167.

[25] See W. Wąsik, 'Antykantyzm oświeceniowy', in *Historia filozofii polskiej* (Warsaw, 1958), i. 364–77; S. Harasek, *Kant w Polsce przed rokiem 1830* (Cracow, 1916).

[26] Jan Śniadecki (1756–1830), mathematician, astronomer, philosopher, rector of Vilnius University (1807–15). His chief publications were *O Koperniku* ('About Copernicus') (1803), *Żywot literacki Hugona Kołłątaja* ('The Literary Life of Hugo Kołłątaj') (1814), and *Filozofia umysłu ludzkiego* (The Philosophy of Human Mind') (1822).

[27] Patrycy Przeczytański (1750–1817), the author of *Logika czyli sztuka rozumowania* ('Logic; or, The Art of Reasoning') (Vilnius, 1816); Anioł Dowgird (1776–1835), the author of *Wykład przyrodzonych myślenia prawideł* ('Lecture on Natural Rules of Thinking') (Vilnius, 1828).

but less lively than its original. In it we meet the name of Locke seven times in all,[28] where he is seen as a philosopher of clarity and an educator.[29] In the 1779 issue of the *Monitor* he is reckoned together with Christian Wolff among the philosophers whom we need to study as distinct from Jean-Jacques Rousseau, Diderot, and Condillac, whose 'heretical books' are full of 'the deists' errors'.[30] In the 1770s in the *Monitor* there are many references to Locke's pedagogic ideas but none to the contents of the *Two Treatises*. For the *Monitor* it was Montesquieu who constituted the authority in political matters. In another, more popular Enlightenment journal, *Pleasant and Useful Amusements*, Locke is quoted five times.[31] The author of the paper 'On Liberal Sciences under Louis XIV' devoted three admiring pages to him.[32] But we cannot find much information on Locke's philosophy. The writer censures Plato, who is for him a perfect example of obscure philosophy. Locke is presented as the patron of simplicity and clarity because he did not have the awful habit of writing about fire and numbers as Plato did. On another occasion his statement about the importance of touch serves as a crucial argument in the *Speech against the Custom of Swaddling Babies*.[33] The best periodical, *Political and Historical Diary*, recommends Locke among other philosophers.[34] A curious detail is the correct orthography of his name. It happens for the first time in a Polish journal. But it seems that it was only by chance because the names of the remaining philosophers are more or less distorted. The second mention of Locke, as Master of the Mint (the author mistook Locke for Newton), can be found in a paper concerning the conditions of the life of scientists in England.[35] In another journal, *Pole Patriot*, a critic reviews a Polish novel using as a criterion the pedagogic instructions given by the 'immortal Locke'.[36]

At the beginning of the 1780s two translations of works by Locke were

[28] *Monitor* (1766), 175, 208, (1772), 110, 745, (1773), 656, (1779), 259, 574. The *Monitor* was printed as a few pages twice a week with continuous page-numbering over the whole year.

[29] Ibid. (1772), 745–6.   [30] Ibid. (1779), 574.

[31] *Zabawy Przyjemne i Pożyteczne z Różnych Autorów Zebrane*, 5 (1772), 277, 279; 7 (1772), 141; 9 (1775), 197; 11 (1776), 47.

[32] Anon., 'O naukach wyzwolonych w Europie za czasów Ludwika xiv', ibid. 5 (1772), 277–9.   [33] Ibid. 7 (1772), 141.

[34] *Pamiętnik Historyczny i Polityczny Przypadków, Ustaw, Osób, Miejsc i Pism Wiek Nasz Szczególniej Interesujących*, 1 (1783), 7.

[35] Ibid., 1 (1787), 34. Locke was a member of the Board of Trade, not the Mint. Newton was Warden and then Master of the Mint.

[36] Anon., 'Uwagi Polaka Patrioty nad Zdarzyńskimi temi czasy z druku wyszłym', *Polak-Patriota*, 2 (1785), 545.

published: *Some Thoughts*, whose Polish title was *Książka o edukacji dzieci J. Locke'a* ('The Book about Child Education by J. Locke'),[37] appeared in 1781, and the *Essay*, whose Polish title was *Logika czyli myśli z Lokka o rozumie ludzkim wyjęte* ('Logic or Thoughts about Human Reason from Lokk'),[38] was printed in 1784. These books were handbooks recommended by the Commission for National Education and they did not bring any response from the Press. I have found only one piece of information about the second one. A Catholic priest wrote 'for fun' in his letter to a Polish scientist in 1786 that a Polish bishop had ordered a confiscation of twenty copies of the *Logic* as a 'heretical book',[39] but it was rather a singular occurrence.

The 1780s were characterized by a contrast: a strong presence of Locke's works and yet few mentions of him in the Press. The change in approach meant that his name lost novelty value, but we have to interpret this as the act of his assimilation into Polish culture. Journalists started to write about a 'naked' or 'blank' tablet without citing a source. In the 1780s there was full acceptance of Locke's pedagogical theory as a norm.

VII. Conclusions

Statements like 'There are no people that are good by themselves' and 'There are no innate ideas' cleansed the intellectual atmosphere of the eighteenth century of the traps of scholastic thinking. As Isaac Newton deprived Cartesian space of the whirls of nebulous matter, so John Locke liberated the moral discussion at the turn of the seventeenth century from the tendency to classify man's passions, which had been changing moralizers into book-keepers filling both sides of the account, and hoping thereby that the accurate balance could give a possibility of gaining knowledge of who man is. The formation of intellectual empty space created the opportunity to reveal the power that made the true man. This power was property. Education and freedom became for proprietors a condition of welfare for both individuals and states.

First of all the Enlightenment trusted in the possibilities of education. Polish fascination with this trend was not exceptional in Europe, though

---

[37] In 1795 the Piarist Edmund Truskolawski translated this work from the French edn. by Coste. The second translation, by Jan Znosko, appeared in 1801. It was not as good as the first. The third and most recent edn., translated by F. Wnorowski, appeared in 1959.

[38] Andrzej Cyankiewicz was the translator. It is impossible to show which French edn. was the basis of this translation. The second translation, by W. M. Kozłowski, was edited in 1915 and 1921. The third and last one appeared in 1955, translated by B. Gawęcki.

[39] Archive of Jagiellonian University, MS 274.

in contemporary domestic conditions it was a great advance, an acceptance of one of the elements of Locke's theory. They started by educating
the proprietors. Then it became obvious that there were uneducated
peasants. What a hard life for the educated in an uneducated environment! But it was impossible to educate non-proprietors. It was then that
Polish disputes over property began. They gave to Polish Lockeanism a
strange feature: the patriarchalism and softening of its utilitarian economic base. In Locke's state both the rulers and the ruled were similar,
they possessed the same rights. In Poland there was a great gulf between
a gentleman and a peasant. This society without a middle class could not
assimilate Lockeanism in its 'clean' liberal form as in England or France.
The clarity and cohesion of Western Lockeanism were washed away in
Poland. Lockeanism did not become an object of worship. In England
and France it turned into the religion of the mercantile class, in America
even of the plebeian one. In Poland the gentry were a cult object. The full
acceptance of Lockeanism demanded a sacrifice of the uniqueness and
monopoly of landed property. It required not a Sarmatian but a society of
angels to make such a change.

Even if that happened, who could be the businessmen? The attraction
of Lockeanism consisted in economic prosperity as a result of citizens'
efforts. The social gulf could not be filled with words only. The nascent
idea of creativity and industrial production could be linked together only
by the businessman. It was very difficult to show the place of the activities of businessmen in the quasi-feudal society. Economic success was
dubious. On the one hand it was limited by the Sarmatian negation of
success and, on the other, Polish patriotism required sacrifice for the
country. Educated by the Piarists and the Commission schools the *szlachta*
was entering the economic empty space.

The Lockean values of property, confidence, and toleration were the
values of merchants as well, who wanted to gain profit under safe circumstances, where confidence and toleration coexisted with economic transactions and where their fortunes were well protected. Machiavelli and
Hobbes believed that only the power of a strong sovereign could control
this new society. Locke offered economic values instead of the Leviathan.
Free individuals obtained their individuality through a free market.
Lockeanism became the foundation of all activities. With its simplicity
and intelligibility people felt at home. Lockeanism supplied the Enlightenment with the 'civil canopy'.[40] That civil canopy made possible a soft

---

[40] A paraphrase of Peter Berger, who spoke about the Reformation canopy for capitalistic
economy.

landing on the secular land and gave some kind of nobility to the prosaic economic sphere of life.

Lockeanism brought to Poland a perspective, but it was a perspective in a country with no merchants, no roads, no money, a few magnates' workshops, and a multitude of the *szlachta* and peasants. As a tool of censure Lockeanism proved correct, but as a tool for creating future prospects it was imperfect. Only one man, Hugo Kołłątaj, gave the realistic recipe for the new open society and showed the way towards the gentle revolution, but he had only partial support. The Polish Locke was the Locke who had read the Physiocrats, the German cameralists, and Adam Smith. He believed in political economy and wanted to infect Polish society with his faith. For him the foundation of morality was the satisfaction of biological needs. Few people thought in this way. For the majority, religion and morality were an integral whole, and cupidity was against morality and the gentry's code. A conflict between the spiritual values of feudalism and the economic inclination of the new age was interpreted on the religious plane as a conflict between the Catholic Church and the deists' 'reasoners'.

In the West Lockeanism became a self-sufficient ideology and the motive force of modernizing society. The *Second Treatise* was a guide for the middle class. The *Letters of Anonym* and bolder pronouncements of the 'peasant question' remained the testimonies showing the most enterprising Poles' aspirations. The Western dispute between spiritual and economic values took place in the realm of myth and symbol, and simultaneously in the realm of the real social institution—the market. In Poland it remained only in booklets. The market was too weak to enter into this conflict.

What did the Polish Enlightenment owe to John Locke? We must answer that it owed a very great deal. *Some Thoughts concerning Education* became the main oracle in pedagogical matters in Poland. In the West, the social changes together with the sciences cleared a way for Enlightenment ideas; in Poland, inversely, the new education prepared people for the social changes and new sciences. The acceptance of Locke's precept by the Commission had the effect that this institution, on its surface like similar institutions in Enlightenment monarchies, avoided their myopia and made use of all the trumps of self-government.

The Polish reception of Lockeanism had visible national features. It was a kind of gentry's debate, where everybody felt qualified to speak, where emotions were softened by the Lockean arguments. By the close of the Enlightenment an enlightened Pole knew the handbook of logic written by John Locke or at least he had heard of it. Perhaps his parents had read it, but his tutors had certainly held *Some Thoughts* in their hands. Probably this Pole was a gentleman, so he was greatly affected by the 'peasant question' and either he was both an editor and an author himself, or he was reading all the news on the issue and thus he knew all the nuances of the theory of human rights. His son was probably studying at the University of Vilnius and had heard Jan Sniadecki there saying, 'To try to improve John Locke . . . is an illness of mind worthy of lament.'[41]

[41] Cited by Harasek, *Kant w Polsce przed rokiem 1830*, 24.

Select Bibliography

Manuscript Material

The major collection of Locke manuscripts is the Lovelace Collection in the Bodleian Library. The standard work on this is P. Long, *A Summary Catalogue of the Lovelace Collection of the Papers of John Locke in the Bodleian Library* (Oxford, 1959). The Bodleian Library also contains other substantial Locke material which it acquired after 1959. There are also important Locke manuscript holdings in the British Library, the Pierpont Morgan Library, and the Huntington Library.

Books

The following is a select list of books relevant to Locke published since 1980.

AARSLEFF, HANS, *From Locke to Saussure: Essays on the Study of Language and Intellectual History* (London, 1982).

ALEXANDER, PETER, *Ideas, Qualities and Corpuscles* (Cambridge, 1985).

ASHCRAFT, RICHARD, *Revolutionary Politics and Locke's 'Two Treatises of Government'* (Princeton, NJ, 1986).

—— *Locke's 'Two Treatises of Government'* (London, 1987).

AYERS, MICHAEL, *Locke*, 2 vols. (London, 1991).

BILL, E. G. W., *Education at Christ Church Oxford 1660–1800* (Oxford, 1988).

BUCKLE, STEPHEN, *Natural Law and the Theory of Property: Grotius to Hume* (Oxford, 1991).

COLMAN, J., *John Locke's Moral Philosophy* (Edinburgh, 1983).

COOK, HAROLD J., *The Decline of the Old Medical Regime in Stuart England* (Ithaca, NY, 1986).

DUNN, JOHN, *Locke* (Oxford, 1984).

FRANK, ROBERT, *Harvey and the Oxford Physiologists* (Berkeley, Calif., 1980).

HARRIS, JOHN, *The Mind of John Locke* (Cambridge, 1994).

HORTON, JOHN, and MENDUS, SUSAN (eds.), *John Locke: 'A Letter Concerning Toleration' in Focus* (London, 1991).

HUNTER, MICHAEL, *Science and Society in Restoration England* (Cambridge, 1981).

—— and WOOTTON, DAVID (eds.), *Atheism from the Reformation to the Enlightenment* (Oxford, 1992).

HUTCHISON, ROSS, *Locke in France 1688–1734* (Oxford, 1991).

JOLLEY, NICHOLAS, *Leibniz and Locke: A Study of the 'New Essays on Human Understanding'* (Oxford, 1984).

KROLL, RICHARD W. F., *The Material Word: Literate Culture in the Restoration and Early Eighteenth Century* (Baltimore, 1991).

—— ASHCRAFT, RICHARD, and ZAGORIN, PEREZ (eds.), *Philosophy, Science, and Religion in England 1640–1700* (Cambridge, 1992).

LEVINE, JOSEPH, *The Battle of the Books: History and Literature in the Augustine Age* (Ithaca, NY, 1991).

MEHTA, UDAY SINGH, *The Anxiety of Freedom: Imagination and Individuality in Locke's Political Thought* (Ithaca, NY, 1992).

MONTUORI, MARIO, *John Locke on Toleration and the Unity of God* (Amsterdam, 1983).

POPKIN, RICHARD H., *The Third Force in Seventeenth-Century Thought* (Leiden, 1992).

—— and ARJO VANDERJAGT (eds.), *Scepticism and Irreligion in the Seventeenth and Eighteenth Centuries* (Leiden, 1993).

PUSTER, ROLF W., *Britische Gassendi-Rezeption am Beispiel John Lockes* (Stuttgart, 1991).

SCHOULS, PETER A., *Reasoned Freedom: John Locke and Enlightenment* (Ithaca, NY, 1992).

SHAPIRO, B., *Probability and Certainty in Seventeenth-Century England* (Princeton, NJ, 1983).

SIMMONS, A. JOHN, *The Lockean Theory of Rights* (Princeton, NJ, 1992).

SPELLMAN, W. M., *John Locke and the Problem of Depravity* (Oxford, 1988).

TULLY, JAMES, *A Discourse on Property: John Locke and his Adversaries* (Cambridge, 1980).

—— *An Approach to Political Philosophy: Locke in Contexts* (Cambridge, 1993).

VIENNE, JEAN-MICHEL, *Expérience et raison: Les fondements de la morale selon Locke* (Paris, 1991).

WOOD, NEAL, *The Politics of Locke's Philosophy: A Social Study of 'An Essay concerning Human Understanding'* (Berkeley, Calif., 1983).

—— *Locke and Agrarian Capitalism* (Berkeley, Calif., 1984).

WOOLHOUSE, R. S., *Locke* (Brighton, 1983).

YOLTON, JEAN S., *A Locke Miscellany* (Bristol, 1990).

—— *Thinking Matter: Materialism in Eighteenth-Century Britain* (Minneapolis, 1983).

YOLTON, JOHN W., *Perceptual Acquaintance from Descartes to Reid* (Minneapolis, 1984).

—— *Locke: An Introduction* (Oxford, 1985).

—— *Locke and French Materialism* (Oxford, 1991).

—— *A Locke Dictionary* (Oxford, 1993).

Index of Names